D0149500

SOLE SURVIVOR

SOLE SURVIVOR

Children Who Murder

Their Families

ELLIOTT LEYTON

SEAL BOOKS

McCLELLAND–BANTAM, INC.

TORONTO

SOLE SURVIVOR

A SEAL BOOK / NOVEMBER 1990

CANADIAN CATALOGING IN PUBLICATION DATA

Leyton, Elliott, 1939–
Sole survivor : children who murder their families

ISBN 0-7704-2408-2

1. Juvenile homicide.   2. Family violence.
I. Title.

HV9067.H6L4 1990   364.1'523'083   C90-094298-3

PRINTED IN CANADA

COVER PRINTED IN U.S.A.

FFG   0 9 8 7 6 5 4 3 2 1

FOR MY BELOVED SONS
A. Marco Leyton
Jack Sean Leyton

AND MY ADORED GRANDSON
Mark Sean Leyton

This is the second of two volumes on multiple murder. My earlier book, *Hunting Humans: The Rise of the Modern Multiple Murderer,* struggled to comprehend the motivation of those who murder strangers. *Sole Survivor* is an interpretation of those who murder their intimates, that is, massacre their natal families.

The two books are otherwise separate and distinct, and can be read independently and in any order.

ELLIOTT LEYTON

JANUARY 1990

Corte Petriana,   *St. Thomas,*   *Lancer,*

Venezia   *New Foundland*   *Saskatchewan*

CONTENTS

SOLE SURVIVOR

The Annihilation of Families

Solon fixed no penalty for parricide because he thought
no one would commit it.

—ATHENIAN HOMICIDE LAW

Any murder is a statistically rare event in the modern world. Everywhere, homicide's death toll is dwarfed by industrial disease, warfare, and revolution. The young annihilator of families is rarer still. Yet he appears in all nations in all recent decades, and his autopsy uncovers some of the major diseases of the middle-class family—disorders that lead him to shoot, burn, knife, beat, bomb, crush, poison, smother, or otherwise orchestrate the deaths of his parents and siblings (and sometimes grandparents, uncles, and aunts). Having violated our most sacred taboo, the killers further confound us by professing no comprehensible motive, although some claim to be insane.[1]

Most often the killer appears to be quite sane—though his acts are tinged with madness—as in August 1988 in Tokyo, when a fourteen-year-old schoolboy stabbed to death his parents and his grandmother. In Japan, the London *Observer* reported, "what has shocked the public more, it seems, than the crime's careful premeditation, its sickening violence and the boy's complete lack of repentance, has been the family background: a model of urban Japanese hard-working, education-obsessed, upper-middle-class prosperity."

In the boy's statement to the police, his confessed motives seemed little more than childish spite. He told police that his mother had provoked his homicidal temper tantrum because she "never took care of me herself. She always let grandmother look after me. She never showed any affection for me." He also considered his father a poor parent, one who worked late through the week in the approved Japanese executive manner, and then golfed on Sundays with his colleagues. Often, the killer complained, his father "came home drunk and vented his anger on me." When he entered junior high school, his parents increased their pressure on him to perform well in the intensely competitive Japanese school system: "They became a nagging pain. They pushed me to study so that I could get into a prestigious high school. I didn't like studying at all. My mother always told me that she had high expectations of me. My father was never at home. He doesn't know anything about me, but he believed what my mother told him and scolded me. My father had always exerted an overwhelming superiority. I needed a knife to shut him down." All this might appear to possess a certain inhuman logic were it not for the fact that he also murdered his grandmother, who loved and pampered him, showered him with presents, and consistently took his side in family arguments: "My grandmother was the only person who loved me," he told police. His grandfather survived only because he was away on a business trip on the night of the murders.[2]

The events leading up to the murders seemed unexceptional. As the only child of Hirosuke Sawanoi, aged forty-four, president of a thriving building supplies company, and his wife Asako, aged forty, the boy had naturally been enrolled in one of the most demanding schools. When he failed three subjects, his mother not unreasonably cancelled his allowance. It was then, some three months before the murders, that he began to mention to his school friends his idea of killing his parents. They thought he was joking, despite the fact that he offered one friend $212 to help him with the killings. On the night of their deaths, his parents had both scolded him for his poor marks. An upset stomach kept him awake in bed until three-thirty A.M., when he went to his parents' bedroom to ask for some medicine; his mother angrily ordered him back to bed. An hour later, he reentered his parents' bedroom and struck his mother on the head with a baseball bat, then stabbed his father with a knife thirty-seven times in the chest. As his mother struggled to reach the telephone to call for help, he stabbed her seventy-two times. When his grandmother, the beloved Fumi, shouted to ask what was happening, he ran to her side and stabbed her fifty-six times before strangling her.

Displaying the remarkable posthomicidal indifference so characteristic of these family annihilators, the boy then shampooed his hair and watched a videotape of his favorite singer, Yoko Minamino. Then he collected all the money in the house and sat in his father's car in the driveway, before telephoning his friends to tell them of the murders. Because several of his friends would not believe his story, he showed them the bodies. One of the boys told their teacher, who alerted the police. They found him in a nearby park, carrying the bloodstained knife and $1,480 in cash. According to the journalist Peter McGill, the boy "has since shown calm and unhesitating cooperation with his police interrogators." The Japanese press thoughtfully assessed the case, finding both son and parents the victims of Japanese society, with its work-obsessed and largely absent fathers. An editorial in the *Yomiuri Shimbun* noted that "among the standards set by parents for 'good' children is the distorted emphasis on the results of their school tests." One result of the "fiercely competitive examination race to get into more prestigious schools" is that the system "does not allow for failures." This is undoubtedly true; but why should this one boy have protested against the system in this homicidal manner when so many others have chosen to endure it?[3]

If some of these family killers give no indication of anything resembling insanity, others provide too much evidence, and appear to manufacture the appropriate delusions for the benefit of the police and the courts. On January 18, 1983, at approximately five A.M. in Coquitlam, British Columbia, twenty-two-year-old Bruce Blackman shot and beat to death his parents, his brother, two sisters, and a brother-in-law, one of whom is reported to have knelt on the lawn begging for his life. Blackman admitted being the killer, but acted quickly to ensure that the police "understood" his diminished capacity. "Believe me, I'm insane," he insisted to the arresting officers. After his arrest, he told one of his first psychiatric interviewers, "I don't think I killed them. I think I liberated them. I hope I did." Later, he developed this argument still further, drawing heavily on themes from the well-publicized Son of Sam serial killings in New York, with imagery of baying dogs and malevolent spirits. "In December [the month before the murders] the voices were getting stronger and stronger," he told his interviewers.

It started when I was watching *The Magic Christian* starring Peter Sellers and Ringo Starr. I was getting messages from the TV shows. There was a man's voice, dogs barking, a woman's voice. And the music. I would hear these things in the music. It was as if it was being programmed into me. It was very powerful December 3. I was totally possessed. Most of all I heard the voice of the woman. She had come to get me. The white woman with eyes of fire. An all-white woman, totally white with eyes of fire. She said I was God, and the Devil and the Antichrist. I was also

Zeus, because my name was Bruce. I was a "reebl" because I drank beer and the opposite of beer is "reeb," which makes it "reebl." I cannot cry since December 3, I have no feeling.[4]

Blackman's father had been an engineer with the Vancouver Fire Department, and his mother a clerk at a Vancouver newspaper; they had only recently moved into their handsome and expensive home. Blackman himself, a part-time garbage collector, had quit work a few days before the murders. We know little about any tensions that might have been within the family; but father and son had often hunted together as friends, and former neighbours were astonished at the killings. One told a newspaper reporter that the Blackmans "just seemed like any other family and seemed quite close. I just can't get over it myself." Another insisted that "they were just a very nice family." Neither the courts nor the press questioned Blackman's "insane" version of the events, and he was found not guilty by reason of insanity. To clinch this verdict, he had told them that he had been possessed by spirits and that he had killed his family to save them from a "big bang," which he supposed was soon to end the world. "I loved my family very much. I never killed them. The thing that was with me did. I don't think I murdered, I think I delivered [them to the family of God]."[5]

In any given family annihilation, a curious social process emerges in which the courts, police, press, and public embark together on a shared search for meaning. Typically, they struggle to construct an explanation of the tragedy that can make sense in terms of conventional understanding: thus the Sawanoi family died because of the intolerable pressures of the Japanese school system and the Blackmans died because of Bruce Blackman's insanity. But the matter is infinitely more complicated than that, and it is only through an examination of a wide variety of cases that we can begin to construct a general explanation.

VARIATIONS ON FAMILY ANNIHILATIONS

Dad, I'm really sorry that I did this because I don't know if you really love Mary and me. You didn't come to her [grammar school] graduation, that was a big thing to her, so now I'm not even going to graduate.... I wish all the kids would join the revolution and start killing off their parents.

—LETTER FROM A 15-YEAR-OLD BOY WHO HAD STRANGLED HIS SISTER, MARY[6]

Can anything be shared in the disparate experiences of a Japanese schoolboy and a part-time garbage collector in British Columbia that might lead
us towards an understanding of this troubling phenomenon? How can we
hope to gain access to the private internal tensions of a family when such
knowledge is routinely denied to most friends and neighbours? The
human being is an extraordinarily complex creature, full of evasions and
creative rationalizations, and it should not surprise us that the motives
underlying familial annihilations appear to be many and varied. Each
human family is a unique machine that malfunctions in its own way, and
families can create a rich variety of homicidal motives. As we shall see,
these range from a desperate attempt to end child abuse (Dresbach), to
part of a calculated plan to fulfil some absurd adolescent fantasy (Bamber
and Andrews), to the consequence of a morbid set of tormenting delusions (Burton).

A family annihilation is both a singular social event and one illustration of a worldwide pattern. Its singularity stems from the distinctive
combination of personalities, stresses, and conflicts that lead to the tragedy. Its generality stems from the common historical, sociological, and
economic pressures brought to bear on a family incubating this disease. In
the few following illustrations examined in summary form, we shall focus
on the *diversity* that makes each family annihilation a special case.[7]

''GREED AND ARROGANCE'': JEREMY BAMBER

The Bambers lived the sweet life of the southern English landed gentry—in
a soft and gentle climate amidst the unsurpassed beauty of the verdant
Essex countryside. Jeremy's wealthy parents, Nevill and June, dwelt in
their rambling eighteenth-century mansion on the several hundred acres
of White House Farm; and both assumed the social responsibilities of the
country squire—Nevill a justice of the peace and a magistrate, June active
in village church affairs.

We can never know the true quality of their family life, since they are
all dead and cannot defend themselves. There were, however, curious
comments from neighbours and relatives that suggested that all might not
have been as it appeared to be. Indeed, there were several hints that the
Bambers, with their adopted children Jeremy and Sheila, may have
maintained a sterile emotional atmosphere—but we can only speculate.
Still, it was odd that after Nevill's murder, a neighbour, meaning to laud

him for his generosity, should damn him with faint praise: "He was a real gentleman. He did a lot for the village. Every Christmas he took his men for a drink."[8]

Similarly, Jeremy's sister Sheila's documented history of mental illness and drug abuse suggests an unhappy life. Moreover, her parents' attitude towards her in her final years seems remarkably indifferent. A former London model, Sheila was described by the head of her model agency as "financially and emotionally alone." After the murders, the agency head told *The Times* that Sheila had worked with her only four or five times before leaving the agency in April of 1981, then added, "It's strange, but only on Monday I received an application for her from a domestic agency. She was obviously applying for some kind of 'daily' work. I was terribly sad to receive the application for that kind of work. . . . It suggests she had not worked too much since." It also suggests, of course, that her parents were unwilling to help this troubled and divorced mother of two sons, or to spare her the social and physical ordeal of domestic work. Jeremy's word is less reliable; it is worth recording, however, that he claimed his parents considered their daughter to be a poor mother of her six-year-old twin sons, but that rather than offering to take them in, "the question of their being fostered had been raised" on several occasions.[9]

Then there was the puritanical religious streak in June Bamber that cannot have failed to reverberate through this family. Sheila's psychiatrist, Dr. Hugh Ferguson, told the court of Sheila's fixation with evil: Sheila's concept of evil, *The Times* recorded, "had emanated from her adoptive mother. 'At the age of 17 her mother found her in a rather sexually provoking incident and called her the devil's child. This concept of the devil's child had lingered to some extent,' " the psychiatrist commented. When Sheila was admitted to his hospital in August of 1983, "she said she had to have some kind of exorcism and that if there was no hope of that she would want to die," Dr. Ferguson told the jury. "She wanted to be in touch with God and she wanted to be by Jesus's side, but she was very demented and incoherent." Still, the psychiatrist "did not regard her as actively seeking to die, or as suicidal." In a similar vein, when Jeremy's girlfriend began to overnight with him, the mother strongly disapproved and called the young woman a harlot. As Julie Mugford told the court, "Mrs. Bamber told me she couldn't understand how my mother could allow it to go on. She said she thought our relationship was just a sexual one and she thought I was just a loose woman and a harlot. I was upset and offended and told her we were very good friends."[10]

Jeremy's relations with his parents were so stormy that five months before the massacre, he had blurted out, "Uncle Bobby, I could easily kill my parents." Addressing the jury, his uncle recalled the conversation and his own response to it: "The important thing is that he said he could 'easily' kill his parents. I was deeply shocked and said, 'Don't be so stupid, boy' before I walked away." Jeremy was remembered as especially hating his mother. His girlfriend's mother, *The Times* noted, "claimed that Jeremy had told her that his mother would allow no opinions in the household," and that this oppression caused Jeremy's sister, Sheila, to behave "like a frightened rabbit." Jeremy also "resented her for sending him away to boarding school," Mrs. Mugford explained. "He couldn't understand why she had adopted him only to send him away. He said she never showed him any affection." Jeremy also "allegedly spoke of his mother as a religious maniac, and blamed her for making his stepsister mad."[11]

Jeremy naturally denied at the trial that he had ever hated his parents. "He told the jury that he had a 'loving' relationship with his parents," *The Times* recorded, "though he added that there had been a lack of under-standing between himself and his mother. Sometimes it had not been easy to cope with his mother's interest in religion." In any case, the family's relationships were by no means as uniformly hostile as the prosecution sometimes made it out to be: this was made clear when a warm and loving letter from Mrs. Bamber to her family—intended to be opened only after her death—was read out to the court. According to witnesses, it provoked a tear from Jeremy—one of his rare displays of emotion. However authentic this emotion may have been, Jeremy hinted at his own guilt in a fashion strikingly reminiscent of American serial killer Ted Bundy who during one of his many trials had made the remarkable statement to the media that "more than ever, I am convinced of my own innocence." When the prosecutor barked at Jeremy, "You are not telling the truth, are you?" Jeremy merely replied, "That is what you have got to try and establish."[12]

Prior to the murders, his girlfriend testified, Jeremy first considered a plan in which he would tranquilize his parents, then shoot them and set fire to the house. His second plan was still to shoot his parents, but now make it appear to police that his mentally disturbed sister had committed the crime. He reassured his girlfriend, *The Times* summarized, "that he had found a way to get in and out of the house without a trace, leaving through a kitchen window which would appear to have then been shut from the inside due to the design of the catch." Testing his ability to kill, he captured several rats on the family farm, apparently by tranquilizing their bait, and calmly rehearsed the murders. His girlfriend told the court that he was heartened by his performance with the rats and "decided to go ahead with them [the murders] after testing his willpower by strangling" the rats "with his bare hands." On the morning before the murders, he telephoned his girlfriend and told her that he "had been thinking of the murders and decided it would be tonight or never. She told him not to be so stupid," *The Times* reported.[13]

We cannot know the precise details of the murders, since Jeremy has not confessed, but we do know that he fired his .22-calibre Anschutz semiautomatic rifle twenty-five times into the bodies of his adopted parents, his sister, and her twin sons. The silenced rifle killed the twins in their beds as they slept. However, according to the Home Office pathologist, Jeremy fought violently with his powerful father after the first four shots failed to disable him: Nevill Bamber suffered two black eyes and extensive bruising of his face with the rifle butt before Jeremy finished him with four shots to the head. "In my opinion," said the pathologist, Nevill "was no longer struggling when the four shots to his head were fired, but with all the other wounds he obviously was. These were fired while he had been immobilized." Jeremy shot his mother seven times, wounding her in the neck, right arm, right knee, and chest as she thrashed to avoid the shots; he then shot her twice in the head.[14]

The manner in which he murdered his sister, Sheila, was one of the major errors that ultimately led to his arrest and conviction. The pathologist noted that "unlike the other two adult murder victims, there was nothing to suggest that Sheila had tried to fight off her attacker." He appears to have shot her once through the neck, then placed the rifle across her chest to suggest that she had killed the family and then shot herself. Having tried this, however, he realized that the rifle was too long—with the bulky silencer attached to the end of the barrel—for her to have shot herself. He therefore removed the silencer, placed it in the family's gun cabinet, and shot her once more through the neck. He left the family Bible by her side and the rifle across her chest before returning to his own home.[15]

He apparently changed his clothing and cleaned himself thoroughly before contacting the police to say that he had been speaking to his father on the telephone about farming matters when his father had suddenly shouted, "Please come over, your sister has gone crazy and has got a gun."

After a cautious siege, the police entered the farmhouse. They did not notice that Sheila had apparently shot herself twice in the neck, nor did they find the missing silencer (that would be left to a knowledgeable relative). They were not struck by the fact that Sheila's hands were clean of oil and her fingernails unbroken despite having supposedly assaulted her father and firing twenty-five shots, reloading several times. Indeed, with little rumination they were convinced by Jeremy's careful orchestration of the evidence that Sheila had been the killer, and they virtually closed the investigation.[16]

Hours after the murders, Jeremy chuckled and remarked to his girlfriend, "I should have been an actor." Only an hour after the police had told him of the murder of his entire family, *The Times* observed, Jeremy "announced he was starving and cooked himself a breakfast of fried bacon, toast and coffee." The police noted at the time that "he appeared calm and even jovial later on." The morning after the killings, Jeremy bought copies of several national newspapers, in order to read their accounts of the killings. His girlfriend marvelled when Jeremy expressed the hope that "the news would report what he said that day and show 'his best side.' " The very day that the killings were discovered, the police noted that Jeremy had authorized them to remove from the farmhouse, and destroy, any of the damaged or bloodstained objects. Two days later, according to police, Jeremy "asked if police could give the [precise] sequence in which his family died because according to legal advice he had received, this could affect his parents' wills." He then removed from the farmhouse the family silver, china, paintings, and guns, "but said it was to raise money to pay death duties." For the family funerals, he treated himself to an expensive designer suit for £198 [about $400] and an extravagant tie priced at £30 [about $60]. The night after the funerals he and his girlfriend got drunk on champagne and cocktails. A few days later, in anticipation of his forthcoming half-million-pound inheritance, he began to spend money in expensive restaurants and hotels in England and Holland.[17]

Julie Mugford became increasingly disturbed by her boyfriend in the days following the funerals. The prosecutor told the court that, "as days passed her loyalty became more strained and at one point in a restaurant he said he had no feelings about the killings, and agreed there must be something wrong with him." Mugford was also discomfited by his spending sprees: "I commented that in public Jeremy looked far too happy. I said I was feeling guilt for both of us and wanted him to know what it was like. He said that he was doing everyone a favour and there was nothing to feel guilty about." Ultimately, she went to the police and reported their conversations.[18]

Jeremy was charged with all five murders on September 9, 1985, and went to trial in October of the following year. At the trial, the judge instructed the jury: if Sheila was the murderer, the slim model would have had to savagely beat her six-foot four-inch father, then shoot him and the other family members "before detaching the silencer from the murder weapon, hide it in her father's gun cupboard, return upstairs, wash herself and kill herself all in 22 minutes," *The Times* reported. On the other hand, Jeremy "had ample time after the killings to get home, clean himself and make himself presentable before alerting the police." To reach a reasonable conclusion, the judge told the jury, they would have to consider three issues, any one of which would determine the guilty party. Did they believe Jeremy or his girlfriend, who said he had plotted to commit the "perfect murder"? Were they certain that Sheila did not kill her family and then commit suicide? Finally, did Jeremy really receive the telephone call from his father in which his father had supposedly claimed Sheila had "gone berserk with a gun"?[19]

The jury found Jeremy's case not credible. Mr. Justice Drake, in handing down five life sentences, told Jeremy, "Your conduct in planning and carrying out the killing of five members of your family was evil almost beyond belief. It shows that you, young man though you are, have a warped, callous and evil mind concealed beneath an outwardly present-able and civilized manner." The judge thought Jeremy killed his family "partly out of greed because, although you were well off for your age, you were impatient for more money and possessions. But I believe you also killed out of an arrogance in your character which made you resent any form of parental restriction or criticism of your behaviour. I believe that you wanted at once to be the master of your own life as well as to enjoy the inheritance which would have come to you in any event in the fullness of time." In determining the length of the sentence, the judge found "it difficult to foresee whether it will ever be safe to release into the community someone who can plan and kill five members of their family and shoot two little boys asleep in their beds."[20]

Despite the evidence revealed at the trail and the thoughtful remarks of the judge, without knowing more about the nature of the family we are left with an imperfect understanding of the motivation for these murders. On this matter, Jeremy, still protesting his innocence, helps us not at all. British writer Ken Smith interviewed Jeremy in prison, and published the results of these encounters in his book *Inside Time*. Since the trial, Jeremy had launched several unsuccessful appeals and planned still another. In prison he maintained the hope that his girlfriend would retract her damning statements about him, which he claims were concocted out of spite. He professed to have lost all respect for the conservative values of free enterprise and law and order that he claimed to have once so deeply loved, and to have grown embittered by the system's false imprisonment of him. Yet he lived in hope of some dramatic new evidence that might release him: "I have to hope," he told Smith. "I have to hang on to something. And if the appeal goes down I still have to have something to hope for. Perhaps a miracle ... Who knows. Who knows what will happen? Where there was a bad man might turn out to be a rose."[21]

KILLING FOR ADVENTURE: LOWELL LEE ANDREWS

On Thursday, November 27, 1958, three-hundred-pound University of Kansas biology major Lowell Lee Andrews, described by one Kansas newspaper as "the nicest boy in Wolcott," made the final decision to kill his family. His ostensible motive was to eliminate at one stroke all obstacles to his inheritance of the family farm. His fantasy was that he would sell the farm, and use the funds to finance a new career as a gangster playboy. Despite his adventurous pretensions, however, his mentality was still mired in lower-middle-class frugality; he made a fatal error in asking the bread delivery man not to leave the family's usual order for the weekend (this would be used against him in court to prove his premeditation). After the family consumed a hearty Thanksgiving dinner, Lowell walked to his bedroom to finish reading *The Brothers Karamazov* and to load his .22-calibre rifle and revolver. Those tasks completed, he shaved and put on his best suit.

Truman Capote's masterpiece, *In Cold Blood,* records that Lowell then walked into the living room where his family was gathered around the television set and opened fire. He first shot his sister, Jennie Lee, in the head and killed her instantly; then he fired three shots at his mother and two at his father. When his wounded mother lurched toward him, opening her mouth as if to speak, Lowell told her to "shut up" and shot her three more times. The father was writhing in agony on the kitchen floor; Lowell, Capote records, emptied his revolver into his father's body, then reloaded and emptied it again, hitting him with a total of seventeen bullets. As Lowell later described the shooting to the authorities, he "didn't feel anything about it. The time came, and I was doing what I had to do. That's all there was to it."[22]

He then ransacked the house, trying to leave the impression that there had been a burglary: he opened drawers and scattered their contents, and removed the screen from his bedroom window. He then drove the forty miles to his university town, threw his weapons into the Kansas River, and tried to arrange an alibi. He told his landlady that the snowstorm that was currently raging had made the roads so slippery that it had taken him two hours to make the trip from Wolcott; then he went to a film, making sure that the usher noticed him. After the film, he returned to his home in Wolcott and walked through the house, stepping over his father's body to get milk from the refrigerator for the family dog. He telephoned police and said, "My name is Lowell Lee Andrews. I live at 6040 Wolcott Drive, and I want to report a robbery."[23]

The first police officers to reach the scene were taken aback by Lowell's nonchalance as he casually patted the dog and gestured in the direction of his family's corpses, telling them to "look in there." This typical indifference displayed by family annihilators is often interpreted by observers as a certain sign of mental disorder; but it may well be that it is nothing more than the calm satisfaction of someone who has eliminated obstacles that meant nothing to him. In any case, when the coroner asked Lowell what funeral arrangements he wished to make for his family, he dismissed the enquiry with the remark, "I don't care what you do with them." He continued to insist to the police that he had returned home late to discover the robbery and the killings.[24]

Late that night, the police wisely called in the Andrews family's clergyman and left the interrogation to him. As Lowell later described his encounter with Rev. Virto Dameron in a letter to a friend,

> Mr. Dameron said, "Now, Lee, I've known you all your life. Since you were just a little tadpole. And I knew your daddy all his life, we grew up together, we were childhood friends. And that's why I'm here—not just because I'm your minister, but because I feel like you're a member of my own family. And because you need a friend that you can talk to and trust, and I feel terrible about this terrible event, and I'm every bit as

anxious as you are to see the guilty party caught and punished."
He wanted to know was I thirsty, and I was, so he got me a
Coke, and after that he's going on about the Thanksgiving
vacation and how do I like school, when all of a sudden he says,
"Now, Lee, there seems to be some doubt among the people here
regarding your innocence. I'm sure you'd be willing to take a lie
detector and convince these men of your innocence so they can
get busy and catch the guilty party." Then he said, "Lee, you
didn't do this terrible thing, did you? If you did, now is the time
to purge your soul." The next thing was, I thought what difference does it make, and I told him the truth, most everything
about it. He kept wagging his head and rolling his eyes and
rubbing his hands together, and he said it was a terrible thing,
and I would have to answer to the almighty, have to purge my
soul by telling the officers what I'd told him, and would I?

Lowell did.[25]

The renowned Menninger psychiatric clinic examined Lowell and
concluded that he fully understood the nature of his acts, and that he did
not suffer from delusions, false perceptions, or hallucinations. "But," said
Dr. Joseph Satten, "Lowell Lee Andrews felt no emotions whatsoever. He
considered himself the only important only significant person in the
world. And in his own seclusive world it seemed to him just as right to
kill his mother as to kill an animal or a fly." Ultimately, the clinic's staff
concluded that Lowell suffered from schizophrenia and was therefore
unfit to stand trial, but the court refused to accept this interpretation and
Andrews was sentenced to death. Displaying once again the behavior that
is so characteristic of family annihilators, Lowell at no time expressed
remorse for the killings. Indeed, he seemed quite happy with the entire
course of events, occupying himself while awaiting execution in prison
with reading Robert Frost, Walt Whitman, Emily Dickinson, and Ogden
Nash; preparing a scrapbook of favourite food pictures cut out from
magazines; and correcting the grammar of his unlettered fellow inhabi-
tants of death row: "Don't say *dis*interested. When what you mean is
*un*interested," he told one killer.[26]

Another inmate remembered saying to him, "The trouble with you,
Andy, you've got no respect for human life. Including your own." Lowell
agreed with him, and added, "And I'll tell you something else. If ever I
do get out of here alive, I mean over the walls and clear out—well, maybe

nobody will know where Andy went, but they'll sure as hell know where Andy's been." Inmate Richard Hickock told Capote,

> I really liked Andy. He was a nut—not a real nut, like they kept hollering; but, you know, just goofy. He was always talking about breaking out of here and making his living as a hired gun. He liked to imagine himself roaming around Chicago or Los Angeles with a machine gun inside a violin case. Cooling guys. Said he'd charge a thousand bucks per stiff. But for someone his age he was the smartest person I ever come across. A human library. When that boy read a book it stayed read. Course he didn't know a dumb-darn thing about *life* ... I saw every side of life there is—things that would make a dog vomit. But *Andy*. He didn't know one dumb-darn-darn thing except what he'd read in books. He was innocent as a little child, some kid with a box of Cracker Jack.[27]

Lowell was hanged on November 30, 1962, his fantasy adventure unfulfilled. An inmate told Capote of Lowell's last hours:

> Right before they hanged him, he sat down and ate two fried chickens. And that last afternoon he was smoking cigars and drinking Coke and writing poetry. When they came to get him, and we said our goodbye, I said, "I'll be seeing you soon, Andy. 'Cause I'm sure we're going to the same place. So scout around and see if you can't find a cool shady spot for us down there." He laughed, and said he didn't believe in heaven or hell, just dust unto dust. And he said an aunt and uncle had been to see him and told him they had a coffin waiting to carry him to some little cemetery in north Missouri. The same place where the three he disposed of were buried. They planned to put Andy right alongside them. He said when they told him that he could hardly keep a straight face ... We joked on like that till it was time to go, and just as he was going he handed me a piece of paper with a poem on it. I don't know if he wrote it. Or copied it out of a book.

It was a stanza from Gray's "Elegy Written in a Country Churchyard," and its last line added a lurid touch of melodrama to Lowell's customary good-humored cynicism: "The paths of glory lead but to the grave."[28]

KILLING TO ESCAPE ABUSE: WAYNE DRESBACH

On January 7, 1961, in the affluent community of Franklin Manor on the shores of Chesapeake Bay, gentle, even-tempered fifteen-year-old Wayne Dresbach shot to death his adopted parents. When police apprehended him a few hours later, he was sitting in a car with some friends, drinking soda pop and chewing bubble gum. State Trooper Grzesiak was struck by the absence of emotion on Wayne's face or in his voice when he asked Wayne, "What have you been doing this morning?" "I shot my parents," Wayne told him. During Wayne's initial interrogation, Police Lieutenants Vick and Smith were equally surprised at Wayne's apparent indifference: "He was calm and unemotional" through the confession, said Vick, and "as we got down to the immediate investigation he talked very straight-forward and was very unemotional."[29]
Police records quoted Wayne's confession.

"I got up this morning about 9:00 A.M., went to the bathroom to get a drink of water and then I went to the office and got a .22-caliber automatic rifle and went back through the catwalk to my room. Then I went downstairs when I heard them moving around downstairs. I went to the living room and stood behind the television so that I would not be seen easily and waited for my father to come out of the bedroom. I waited for about two or three minutes and my father came out of the bedroom and started towards the kitchen; as he got about five feet from the kitchen door I shot him in the back. I'm not sure how many times but I think I shot him about four times. He hollered, 'Shirley,' and my mother came out of the bedroom. I moved out to the middle of the living [room] and while she was standing about at the foot of the steps I shot her about three times. I think the bullets hit her in the front chest and shoulder. She, Mother, ran back in the bedroom downstairs."

Police queries probing for premeditation elicited the reply from Wayne that, "I had planned it before but I never did it, then last night I made up my mind that I was going to do it." When asked why he had shot them, he could offer only the unsatisfactory explanation "that they were yelling at me."[30]

Wayne's parents were described in the local press as "socially and politically prominent." Harold Dresbach, aged forty-seven, was from a poor farming family, but had graduated from a minor law school and gone into private practice. He had twice run unsuccessfully for election to the Maryland General Assembly. His wife, Shirley, aged forty-six, was from a prominent family: her uncle had been governor of Kansas and gone on to serve as secretary of war in Roosevelt's prewar administration. The Dresbachs' social circle expressed "shock," "disbelief," and "amazement" that such a tragedy could have occurred. One neighbour described Wayne as "a cheerful, happy kid, a real outgoing boy who seemed never at a loss for something to talk about."[31]

Nevertheless, as the family biographer Mewshaw observed, "there were nagging suggestions that things weren't altogether right at home." One neighbour told Mewshaw that the Dresbachs "drank a lot. And Dresbach, he beat the boys. [His wife] Shirley told me she was afraid he'd hurt them someday. Really hurt them." Another neighbour concurred: "He beat her almost as often as he did the boys. I saw the bruises. I think Shirley was a good mother. Anyway, she wanted to be. But what could she do against him?" When Mewshaw asked the neighbour how often Wayne was beaten, he was told, "All the time. He got the worst of it. Who knows why? I guess there's just no saying why parents like one kid more than the other. They probably couldn't tell you themselves. Me, though, I liked Wayne."[32]

The stresses at home began to reveal themselves in what a colleague of Dresbach referred to as Wayne's "wanderlust": Wayne frequently ran away from home, and he failed ninth grade despite his solid average intelligence. Wayne's school counsellor remembered Wayne complaining that he was unhappy at home, and that his parents had taken him to a psychiatrist. A few months before the murders, Wayne was arrested for stealing guns from his father: Mewshaw notes that his parents "declared him incorrigible, charged him with larceny, and left him in jail for several days." Although the criminal charges were eventually dropped, the Dresbachs took Wayne to the County Mental Health Clinic where he was examined by Dr. Elizabeth Winiarz. She continued to see Wayne until the week before the killings, but did not feel that he showed any violent tendencies. "He could get excited and act on impulse," Winiarz said, but he remained passive with his parents. Indeed, Winiarz told reporters that on their last visit, "he and his mother were in a good humor," and they had "talked about how wonderful Christmas had been."[33]

The Dresbachs' curious rigidity and their intense concern with status were first publicly manifested when they pressured Wayne to enroll in a college preparatory course, despite the fact that he was dyslexic and had previously failed both the seventh and ninth grades. They would not allow him to transfer back to a general high school program that would have been more appropriate to his abilities, and Mewshaw recorded that when Wayne "flunked every subject from gym to algebra, his father had beaten him with a garrison belt. The brass buckle cut through his shirt, drawing blood from his shoulders and back. After that, the real punishment began. Laying on a heavy load of domestic chores and remedial schoolwork, Mr. Dresbach ordered him to stay indoors all summer." Dresbach humiliated Wayne still further by frequently comparing him unfavorably to his younger brother, Lee, who was an accomplished and popular athlete. At the time, Wayne confided in one woman neighbour that if he was a few minutes late for his evening curfew, he was beaten: once, he said, his father had attacked him with such ferocity that both his eyes were blackened and his mouth bloodied. Wayne told another neighbour that he hated his father and wished him dead. "You don't mean that," she remembered telling him. "Yes I do. If you knew him, you'd understand. He's always yelling at me, always beating me and punishing me. There are other things, too. Things I can't tell you." Another neighbour recalled Shirley Dresbach's protests of her husband's harsh regime: "I've talked to him," Shirley told her, "I've tried to reason with him. I've tried everything. Sometimes I get so tired, I just don't want to go on. But what can I do? I've tried to commit suicide. Several times."[34]

Dresbach's need to dominate his wife and sons seemed quite extraordinary. He tried to control every aspect of his sons' lives, choosing for them everything from their friends to their clothing to their school curriculum, and denying them any independence of action. The son of a stockman, he appeared both to resent and envy his wife's loftier social origins. If in private he claimed his retribution by beating her, in public he sneered at her for her failed suicide attempts and called her "the worst piece of ass I ever had." His personal pornography collection emphasized photographs of women in oral and vaginal intercourse with animals. Still, Wayne usually remained passive with his father: he once tried to fight back and a lucky punch to the throat left his father gasping for breath. Wayne was exuberant, but a few days later his father beat him badly and left him feeling "just like a cork floating on the water. So useless. He always made me feel useless, worthless."[35]

After the killings, Wayne's attempt to explain himself to the many examining psychiatrists appeared to lack all logic. "I went to a basketball game," Wayne told them. "My bus came home slower than the team bus which my brother was on. I got home about an hour later than my brother. I told them what happened but they didn't believe me. They got mad and started fussing and I went to bed. I got up the next morning, went to the office, got the .22 and when my father came out, I shot him and when Mother came out I shot her." The distinguished psychiatrist Dr. Manfred S. Guttmacher interviewed Wayne and thoughtfully concluded that Wayne's frequent running away from home "resulted from an unconscious fear of his own powerful and hostile impulses and was an instinctive effort on his part to prevent the very type of tragedy that did occur." Guttmacher understood that Wayne's "hatred of his adopting father was so intense that violence toward him is not surprising in retrospect," but he found it "impossible to reach any rational explanation for the killing of his mother. This has a preservative quality—when he had once started shooting he could not control his destructive urges." Another examining psychiatrist, Dr. Leonard H. Ainsworth, concluded with no little insight that Wayne "views authority figures, both male and female, as remote, rather forbidding people who lack warmth and spontaneity. This view of authority figures is characteristic of children who have suffered an early severe maternal deprivation experience. Such a deprivation experience very frequently leaves the child emotionally and intellectually impaired. A distinctly diminished impulse-control system also appears as a part of this syndrome." If this diagnosis seems too hard on the passive and suicidal Shirley Dresbach and too kind to Harold Dresbach, it also leaves us wondering how so many parentally deprived young persons are able to control their homicidal impulses. Moreover, what traumatic stress left Harold Dresbach with such a need to control through cruelty and humiliation? In any case, since the murders occurred in 1961—long before the reality of child abuse was understood by the public or the courts—Wayne was sentenced to life imprisonment despite the acute and sympathetic intervention of the psychiatrists.* Paroled more than a decade after his arrest, he now drives a truck.[36]

---

* For a richly detailed discussion of this case, see Michael Mewshaw's *Life for Death*.

KILLING TO ESCAPE MORBID ANXIETY: GARY BURTON*

A third variation is the development in the emerging killer of such high levels of morbid anxiety that he or she begins to fear a forthcoming expulsion from the family. Still, although this is often the stated motive, it raises far more questions than it answers. What, for example, is responsible for instilling in the killer such high levels of anxiety? Why should a matter as easily resolved as living arrangements provoke such fantastic retribution? Gary Burton's case does not answer these questions, but his rich and revealing confession edges us closer to an understanding of the phenomenon.

Like so many family annihilators, Burton was raised in a house that symbolized the lofty social aspirations and pretensions of the owners—in this case a gingerbread bungalow that would prove beyond the reach of his father's modest income as a uniformed customs inspector for Canada Customs. When mortgage interest rates suddenly doubled in the 1980s, the parents' natural anxiety about keeping their home metamorphosed in their troubled son's mind into imminent catastrophe.

In high school, Burton was exceptional both for his musical gifts and for his fine academic record. At university in the early 1970s, he quickly joined the drug culture of the time: as journalist Gerald Porter later wrote, the university's student centre was then "like a Warehouse for the Wired." Gary "quickly became involved in a whole smorgasbord of drugs—speed, acid, organic mescaline, mushrooms, coke and 'lots and lots of dope.'" He became both a fixture in the student centre and a well-known university character, but his behavior grew increasingly bizarre. "More than anything," Porter wrote, "it was the Stare that made Gary different. It was the Stare that would give young women in the English department 'the creeps' and would sometimes send cold shivers even through people who knew him. Gary would squint up his eyes and stare ... with his whole face—and not AT you, but INTO you. To the more cynical and experienced of the Thompson Student Centre crowd, Gary tended to be lumped into that ever diminishing sub-species of the Centre: the Bad Acid Casualty," most of whom had either graduated to the mental hospital or to a new life in British Columbia.[37]

---

* A better-known example of this syndrome is James Ruppert, who murdered eleven members of his family on Easter Sunday, 1975. However, as Jack Levin and James Fox emphasize in *Mass Murder*, it is not clear if he killed because he believed he was about to be evicted from the family home, whether he simply wished to inherit the familial estate, or if there was an unknown motive.

Although the question was avoided at the trial, other students were aware of Burton's occasional explosions of violence. "Booze made him quite hostile," Porter wrote, "so much so in fact that he sometimes became afraid of himself. He'd take on people twice his size or destroy bar-rooms. He had a tendency to go berserk when tanked. And with drugs, he tended to binge ... take one drug for a week or a month on end. 'Most people sort of gradually got out of it,' one old-timer observed. 'But Gary, he sort of remained in the haze.' " There were other problems too that were not brought out at the trial, especially his difficulty with women. "He would come on very strong and took every friendly gesture from a woman to be a romantic overture." In his last year at university he proposed marriage to four women, and seemed fiercely to resent their rejection. When he turned to one young woman he hardly knew and said, "You're a very good cook, will you marry me?" the woman was struck by his lingering resentment: "He would phone her up at 6:00 A.M. 'What are you doing?' he asked once, and when she said 'sleeping,' he replied 'Sure,' referring to the presence of her boyfriend in the house." As another insightful fellow student saw it, Gary "sees in every woman the woman he can't have."[38]

On Wednesday, March 3, 1982, Burton lunched at the university. His friend, Peter Slade, later told the court that Burton "gave no indication of anything abnormal," and that "he was in a fairly good mood." Their conversation revolved around their attempt to form a new band. When asked in court to describe his friend's personality, Slade testified, "I suppose that for many people Gary would not be considered the norm or the usual in a lot of ways. He was subject to mood changes, quite often he would be very depressed, sometimes about things which were not pressing but major, other times about things that were really irrelevant." Slade sensed that Burton

seemed to be searching for something, searching for a value, a meaning if you will, for his everyday goings-on. He could change very abruptly. He would be very, very down one minute perhaps, and you might say something, or he might see somebody, which would cause him to soar, but five minutes later he might be down in the dumps again. He was usually pretty quiet, in some senses almost quieter than most people would be—frequently stopping and staring off into space and thinking his own thoughts, and it always seemed as though there was a line that nobody but Gary was going beyond.

When asked if he thought Burton was aggressive, Slade said that "he would be subject to violence only under provocation or under great agitation."[39]

Slade thought Burton's relationship with his parents was both solid and conventional: "he and his father were avid sportsmen and liked to fish and hunt" together. "As far as I ever observed, his relationship with his parents was quite good. They were supporters of Gary, he was trying to get himself ahead, get a good university education, and put himself in a good successful position." Slade insisted that Burton "seemed to get along in a favourable way with his parents. I never witnessed any fights or arguments amongst them: all discussions or interaction that I witnessed were of a very positive nature, very friendly and caring nature."[40]

Nevertheless, Gary appeared to be subject to high levels of anxiety. "The weather could have a far more depressing or heightening effect on Gary," Slade testified. "There were a number of things that bothered Gary about lighting and fluorescent lights—it made his eyes pain [and] he believed there was radiation emitted by fluorescent lights. On one occasion he said something to the effect that there might be a life form of some variety that could exist in a fluorescent light." At that time, Gary seemed intensely concerned about his parents' finances; and not without cause, for in that year of extreme inflation, his father's salary was less than $23,000. Slade remembered that

> several weeks before the death of his parents, Gary was very, very depressed one day, and when I asked him what was the matter, he was worrying about the ability of his parents to be able to meet their payments, to meet their mortgage payments, pay the bills, and so on. He was afraid that they were going to be short of money, or that they weren't going to be able to manage to meet expenses—that perhaps they wouldn't be able to pay the mortgage and the family would end up out on the street, losing their home. It was on that topic that he was consistently worrying, consistently kept mentioning his anxiety. He was afraid that the three of them were going to be in a position where they wouldn't have the house, they'd have to move into an apartment, wouldn't be able to afford to have their own house anymore, the family home. He was quite bothered by it.[41]

Burton returned to his home after lunch. Within minutes he argued with his mother, and then impulsively shot her in the head with a shotgun. He waited for his father to return from work and shot him in the head as he entered the house. Removing his father's wallet, he stepped over the body to take cold chicken from the refrigerator. He spent the night in his bedroom, under a framed poem entitled "Self-Esteem and You." By morning he had constructed a dubious alibi, and he crossed the street to speak to a neighbour. As the neighbour recalled in court, Burton had said,

> "I want to use your telephone, I want to phone a friend, it's an emergency." I asked if there was anything I could do to help, and he said, "No, somebody broke into our house yesterday and shot my mother and father." I didn't believe it, and I said, "Gary, no, that's not true. Then I think I'll go over with you." He said, "No, you better not, because you wouldn't like what you see. My mother is in the kitchen and my father is in the living room." I said, "Gary, we're going to have to phone the police," and he said, "But Mr. Evans, they may blame me." I said, "Gary, we're going to have to phone anyway." He said he was afraid "they" were going to get him, the people that shot his mother and father.[42]

Burton appeared to be "calm" when police arrived. "He didn't speak in the police car unless he was spoken to," one of the investigating officers testified. "Most of the time he was staring out the windshield, like he was daydreaming, thinking about something. And every once in a while he'd put his hands up to his face and put his head down between his legs. Then he'd lean forward and look over at the house. There was no expression on his face, he was just staring off. His face was white." At the police station, when one officer asked him, "Do you want to tell us what *really* happened? It was at this point that he broke down, became emotional, and tears came to his eyes. He asked, 'What's going to happen to me?' and I said, 'You'll probably be sent to the mental hospital for treatment.' " When Burton admitted that he had stolen his father's wallet from his pocket, a senior officer "made the decision to arrest Gary Burton. I placed my hand on his shoulder and told him he would be charged in the deaths of his parents." Before making his first statement to the police, Gary asked, "What help is for me if I admit killing my father and my mother? I've been too long outside society. I'll never be able to speak to my family again." When an officer asked him what had really happened, Burton replied, "You won't understand. How can you if I don't understand?"[43]

At nine A.M. he gave a verbal statement to the police, which one officer transcribed by hand.

Memorial University Radio* closing down, felt it was end of the world, went home, felt he was going to be thrown out, had argument with mother over classes and things—"she was in the kitchen—I felt I had to defend the house, that everybody was after me, I went to the bedroom and loaded my gun, a 12-gauge single-shot Winchester, there were two of them actually. I can't believe it. It's like I turned into an animal, worse than an animal, animals don't kill their parents. My mother went for the phone to call the police. I shot her right in the head. I tore it [the telephone] off the wall. I waited for my father to come. I had to kill him or anybody else came I would kill them too. I had nowhere to go, I was failing university. My father came home, pounded on the front door, on the back door, the windows—I had the curtains over. Then he broke down the door and I shot him. That's not like me, I'm not a killer. I think I went in my room, [but first] I took my father's wallet from his pocket. When I first went to a psychiatrist I could never understand why my mother wanted me to go. This morning I got up and hid the guns. I lay on the bed all night but I didn't sleep. I went across the street after and called the police. At the time I said somebody else had done it, I didn't know who. I know why I did it. I thought they were going to put me out on the street and let me freeze. I really don't know, it was just automatic, like a machine."[44]

If Burton seemed troubled and distracted during his arrest and confession, he behaved quite differently once he was inside the mental hospital. Forensic psychiatrist Dr. Douglas Paulse testified that Burton was elated and strangely relieved. "I went into the ward and Gary Burton shouted, 'Hi, Dr. Paulse, I'm Gary,' and I greeted him." Paulse cautioned Burton that their conversation could be used against him in court, but "I was not entirely sure that he was particularly concerned about that at the time because he was in a state of *euphoria,* M'Lord, and after about five minutes he left and he said, 'Now I don't want to talk about anything, I'm going over to have lunch.' " Burton was at first reluctant to discuss the murders "because he believed that I was working for the police," but

* The student-managed and -operated radio station, in which Burton spent much of his time.

within two weeks he had given Dr. Paulse "a very logical, sequential account of things."[45]

Paulse searched for thought disorders and delusional thinking but found Burton's account "a very logical flow of conversation. Any question that I put to him I got a very pointed answer, and if he continued with the narrative, it was logical—one thought flowed into another, very sequential. He knew precisely what was going on." On the day of the killings, Paulse testified, Gary ate the lunch his mother had prepared for him:

> His mother stood behind him and berated him for not doing well at university. She told him that he was a daydreamer, that he was not getting very far in university. He said, "I then went into my room, came out and shot her. After I shot her, I suddenly got cold, and upset, and I became extremely anxious. I then wondered what was going to happen to me. I knew my father was to come home from work ... I shot him in the head ... I then tried to drag my father into the kitchen, but he was too heavy. I could only drag him a few inches." He then told me that he went into his bedroom to lie on his bed, and he had the radio playing, and he again stated that he was lonely, frightened, and cold. I asked him to tell me how he and his parents got along, and he said that they were constantly after him because he wasn't doing as well as they expected at the university. He said that there was a coldness about his mother and father. He said, "I don't know that there is any love in that house. I wondered if they ever had sex together."

When the psychiatrist asked Burton how he had felt in the months prior to the killings, "he told me that there were times when he was tremendously troubled; he felt that life was hopeless, that his parents were against him. He felt that he was getting smaller, he felt lonely, smaller in their eyes ... and he felt that they would some time in the future abandon him and he didn't know what would happen to them. He was very troubled at that time."[46]

Dr. Paulse was "surprised" that he was unable to detect "any of the elements of schizophrenia" during his interviews with Burton. However, rather than concluding from this that a serious mental illness was absent, he assumed that the weeks of "treatment" at the hospital must have put the disease into remission. Ultimately, he reasoned that despite the logic and rationality evident at every stage of the killings, only a mentally ill person would commit such an act: therefore, Gary must be mentally ill.

> Certainly he was able to form the intent, he was able to appreciate the nature and consequence of the act. He knew it was a gun he had in his hand, he knew that he had loaded it, and he knew that he pulled the trigger, and he appreciated that he had directed the gun at his mother. Following that, he had set up a train of maneuver that he thought would get him off the hook. Everything was so logical that there was no way I could be convinced that he was not in a position to appreciate all the events of that particular day. He told me that he knew it was wrong, he had the ability to distinguish right from wrong.

The psychiatrist admitted that he found himself "stuck" for an explanation for the killings; but since "nobody in his right mind would do that ... that's not normal behaviour ... it doesn't fit into the acceptable notions of what your average individual, or your reasonable person, would expect of any individual," the answer must lie in a hidden illness. He concluded that while Burton was only "minimally psychotic" on the day of the murders, he was nonetheless a paranoid schizophrenic, whose disorder "vascillates—there are times when he's well, then he gets sick, then he gets well, then he gets sick."[47]

His tentative psychiatric opinion was confirmed by Dr. Clive Mellor, a specialist in schizophrenia whose adult daughter was a roommate of Gary's surviving sister. Dr. Mellor told the court that although Gary "presented an appearance of normality," often speaking quite "sensibly and apparently quite rationally," his "delusions" soon became apparent.

> Burton told me that in fact he had a belief that the world was coming to an end, extensive climatic changes were going to take place in the world, and that people would likely perish unless they were living ... he presumed the safest place for them to live would be at the North Pole, in some sort of subterranean house. Apart from that, he also complained of difficulty in breathing, he felt that his chest was made tight at times, he felt that his heart was expanding in his chest, and he believed that these feelings that he had in his body were due to the effects of radar, or some type of radio waves, and that he was being used by some agency as a form of navigation beacon. He found this rather perplexing

because he felt that any navigational point should be fixed, and as he was moving around, he couldn't understand why these particular rays were being played on him which were affecting his body in this particular way.[48]

On the basis of these easily fabricated symptoms, Dr. Mellor reached a diagnosis of paranoid schizophrenia. "When I raised with him the subject of his parents' deaths, he said it was unimportant, it had no relevance as far as he was concerned because he couldn't have had anything to do with it because he had no emotions about it." Dr. Mellor concluded that while Burton might have understood that he was killing his parents, his delusions would have compelled him to think that "there was probably no other course open to him in order to save his life and save his own existence." The world was seen as in a state of "dissolution, where everybody is going to die within a short period of time [and] that life in itself in this particular world has become meaningless." Despite the contradictory evidence, the court judged Burton insane. Within four years of treatment, his recovery was considered so remarkable that he was given free access to the telephone and a day's freedom each week to wander through the city and its environs.[49]

A MIDDLE CLASS FORM OF MURDER

Having examined some of the distinctive characteristics of family annihilations, we can now search for what they share in common. It is a curious fact that despite our contemporary heightened awareness of the many forms of emotional, physical, and sexual abuse that actually take place within families, we have done so little to explore this ultimate manifestation of family violence. Indeed, we hardly have a name for it. The ancient Greeks, so fascinated with murder, coined all the words we still use: parricide for the murder of a parent; matricide and patricide for the murder of a mother or father; filicide for the murder of a child; and fratricide signifying the killing of a brother or sister. In the absence of alternatives for the modern killer who aims to exterminate his or her entire family, the ugly and newly minted word *familicide* will have to do.

The social origins of these killers, these familicides, are almost as startling as the actual murders. Sociologists have long made it clear that most homicides are acts of the poor, the disenfranchised, and the oppressed:* the rich and privileged have alternative means of redress, and other ways of acquiring prestige or substance. We might thus expect familicides to come from such humble backgrounds as well, and to be driven to their acts by intolerable poverty and humiliation. If the low quality of international statistical data makes categorical statements impossible, our analysis of all available cases shows clearly that familicide is most likely to occur in ambitious, even prosperous, families. Indeed, if we know the social class of someone who kills an entire family, we can predict with no little precision which family he is most likely to destroy: if he is working class, he will, perhaps in the course of a burglary or a dispute with his girlfriend's parents, kill someone else's family. Should he be middle class, however, he is most likely to *kill his own.*

Thus this book necessarily becomes a journey into the soul of the modern middle-class family, and a detailed explication of its torment. In order to comprehend a familial crucible so malformed that it unconsciously programs its child to destroy it, it will be necessary to integrate insights† from psychology and social psychology, sociology, history, and anthropology, bringing them all to bear on what George Eliot long ago recognized as "those minute processes which prepare human misery and joy, those invisible thoroughfares which are the first lurking places of anguish, mania, and crime, that delicate poise and transition which determines the growth of happy or unhappy consciousness."

Where in our civilization can we find an understanding of familicide? Traditional psychiatry commonly offers an interpretation that assumes the killer suffers from a specific mental disease, which somehow causes the murders. Actual diagnoses may vary, but their essence is not all that far from the folk belief that "something came over him" or left the victim with an uncontrollable impulse to kill. Unfortunately, there are problems with such an answer, not the least of which is that such a position conflicts with the observation that mental patients in general, and schizophrenics in particular, are less likely to be homicidal than the normal population.[50] Why then should their disease cause a murder? Moreover, why should the victims of a certain mental disease act out their misery in a homicidal fashion in one nation, while in another society

---

* See, for example, Palmer (1972), 40.
† In the stultifying intellectual climate created by the academic disciplines in this century, disciplines have become political empires as much as intellectual achievements. For a devastating critique of the manner in which they have divided all human experience into "bits" (such as economy, or psychology, or sociology) and made no attempt to reconstruct what has been so artificially disassembled, see Eric Wolf's masterful *Europe and the People Without History.*

they may pass their lives in an institution or harmlessly roam their village's streets?

An additional problem is that if the murders are the result of a mental illness, why do so few of the killers display any of the objective symptoms of insanity (other than the killings)? Indeed, delusions and hallucinations, disorders of thought and affect, are relatively rare among our cases (and often appear with a self-serving, even bogus, cast); and the diagnosis of mental disease is often based not on objective symptoms, but on the crime itself! Thus in the attempt to explain such unthinkable behaviour, the murders themselves become the prime diagnostic criterion—that is, anyone who would commit such an act *must* be insane. For example, when the psychiatrist in the Burton case failed to find the expected symptoms of schizophrenia in the killer's psyche and behaviour, he fell back on the assumptions that "that's not normal behaviour," "nobody in his right mind would do that," and "it doesn't fit into the acceptable notions of what your average individual, or your reasonable person, would expect of any individual." Obviously he is correct in saying that familicide is both statistically and morally abnormal, but there are any number of alternative and equally plausible explanations. Such logic is impeccably circular, and can be reduced to two linked statements: (1) Anyone who could commit such an act must be insane, (2) Therefore, he is insane. Tragically, there is plenty of evidence that people who are quite sane can commit such acts. Indeed, in the cases that follow we will encounter motivations that are chillingly mundane—removing obstacles to a career, silencing a source of harassment, or reclaiming a stolen identity.

If psychiatric explanations suffer occasional lapses of logic, they are important interpretive attempts nonetheless, and provide us with rich data. No such praise can be accorded the pseudobiology dispensed by some branches of medicine and psychology. These dispense to the public glossier versions of their own folk beliefs, one focusing on the alleged "bad blood" of the killer, the other on the unremarkable fact that "he was hit on the head." The underlying assumption is that anyone who could commit such an act must be the victim of some biological disorder, whether it be genetic flaw or head trauma. This tradition produces a circularity similar to what we have already criticized. Its propositions are as follows: (1) Anyone who could commit such an act must have a biological abnormality, (2) This killer was hit on the head as a child, or has crinkly toes, (3) Therefore, in a way as yet to be determined, the abnormality caused the murders. Once again, this theory uses the crime itself as the major diagnostic criterion, and ignores the reality that few can have reached adulthood without enduring a blow to the head or displaying some minor physical abnormality. More important, this tradition typically ignores the most fundamental of scientific requirements—that of isolating and describing a mechanism that could transmute a blow to the head or a malformed chromosome into a homicidal impulse.[51]

A third explanatory tradition now comes from a variety of political, sociological, journalistic, and even police, sources. It codifies the common assumption that the killer must have been physically abused as a child. It is true that the personal histories of murderers are riddled with instances of child abuse, but the majority of our familicides were not subject to such anguish. Moreover, why should most abused children harm no one, while others kill their own families or unrelated individuals? There has recently been an avalanche of revelations of child abuse from persons incarcerated in the criminal justice system. While many of these stories are undoubtedly true, many can be seen as self-serving tales by persons wishing to justify their behaviour in order to receive more lenient punishment or to be confined to a mental institution rather than a prison.* Some modern authorities state confidently that child "abuse has to be regarded as the number one cause of sons and daughters killing their parents," but it must be understood that killers in each generation turn to the fashionable themes in their culture for mitigation of their crimes. In previous eras it may have been evil spirits possessing the soul of the killer,† but now it is more likely to be unverifiable charges of child abuse. The problem, however, is more complex and subtle than this.[52]

None of this is to deny the possibility that some familicides may have had psychological problems, or experienced child abuse, or suffered from some biological abnormality. Nevertheless, a balanced explanation must probe beyond fashionable assumptions. We shall show that if at one level there is great diversity of motive and cause, there are also regularities that occur in all our cases. Briefly, the killings tend to occur in niches in the social structure (especially the aspiring middle classes) in which parents may become heavily dependent on their children for their own social

---

* If we may raise matters that are usually left unsaid, it is obviously to the advantage of a prisoner to be housed in a facility that provides him with access to heterosexual sex, to drugs (in the form of "medication"), and to the opportunity for an early release once he or she has mastered the appropriate linguistic and behavioural repertoire (that is, "been rehabilitated"). No one in his right mind would prefer the horrors of the world's prison systems.

† In the radicalized 1960s some black intellectuals were even able to justify to a sympathetic audience the rape of white women by black men as a natural response to centuries of oppression. See, for example, Eldridge Cleaver's *Soul on Ice*.

needs. So intense may this reversed dependence become that the parents begin, often quite unconsciously, to obliterate the identity, to deny the *autonomy*, of their developing child so that the child may be used as the vehicle for their own aspirations. If such a family restricts the options of the child to the point where there appears to be no escape from the parental regime, and if the familial culture encodes violence and duplicity as part of the acceptable behavioural repertoire (validating violence as an appropriate solution to a variety of personal problems), then a potential familicidal milieu has been created. Here, the child may form the impression that the only escape from his or her obliteration is through the annihilation of the family. In what follows, we examine four cases in great detail, delving into the rich information provided by social historians and journalists to elicit both the singularities of each case and the qualities they all share.

CAVEAT

A warning should be issued here. To be a parent is to be a failure. Each child-rearing success is almost inevitably accompanied by a corresponding omission. If thoughtless parents duplicate the errors of their own parents (as when the children of child abusers abuse their own children in turn), sensitive parents, determined to avoid such mistakes, tend to neglect whatever was positive in their own childhoods. Thus the person who was loved but impoverished is ever inclined obsessively to ensure that his children do not endure poverty—even if in the rush for economic success they may leave their children alone and unloved.

Moreover, a book of this nature initiates a kind of social hypochondria. Just as the young medical student, immersed in her book of symptoms, finds herself prey to all its manifestations—suddenly and simultaneously afflicted with diabetes, leprosy, and angina pectoris—so each parent will find echoes in this book of her parenting style. The successful rearing of children is the most difficult single task that modern humans can undertake. There was a simpler time when the food quest alone consumed all the parents' time and energy, and when there were no contradictory and ever-changing theories of child-rearing to befuddle the prospective parent. One of the dubious benefits of modern life is that it gives most parents the time to contemplate the magnitude of their failure.

We live in a social structure and economy that by historical standards offer dizzying social mobility, and we are often quite unprepared for the social and economic roles we will come to occupy. Everywhere, experts compete for the right to advise us on the correct way to raise children. This book will be a monstrous failure if it merely claims one more experthood, or functions to lacerate parental guilt. Its object is to point to some of the more powerfully deforming forces in the modern family, in order to provide a deepened understanding of what enables a young person to contemplate the unthinkable.

CHAPTER TWO

The New Millionaires
Steven Wayne Benson*

A millionaire by the time I'm 30!

—STEVEN BENSON[1]

The murders captured the world's imagination from the instant the bombs exploded on July 9, 1985, until Steven was sentenced to life imprisonment on September 2, 1986. The case undoubtedly fascinated the public because it appeared to support the conventional wisdom on a variety of themes including the degeneracy of the aristocracy, the price of drugs and sexual immorality, the corrupting quality of wealth, and the unbridled greed of spoiled youth. Yet a closer examination of the family denies all these propositions. The family was nouveau riche, not truly aristocratic (not of the Benson and Hedges families as they sometimes allowed people to think, but other, unrelated Bensons whose tobacco wealth was barely half a century old). More perplexing was the revelation that the founder of the family's fortune had struggled to avoid conflict between his descendants by passing vast sums to them long before his death, thereby ensuring their financial independence.

The killer, the founder's grandson, Steven, has told us nothing: he sat as a mute during his trial, and did not testify in his own defence. We are forced to reconstruct his brief homicidal career from the memories of friends, relatives, employees, and police investigators. We shall see that although his brother and sister were subjected to far more intense paren-

* The evidence for this chapter is drawn from *The New York Times,* from Mary Walton's *For Love of Money;* from the Benson family's authorized biography, *Blood Relations,* by John Greenya; and from Christopher P. Andersen's *The Serpent's Tooth.* The books are richly detailed and should be read by anyone interested in the case.

tal interference in their lives, it was Steven—the colourless unloved one—who felt free to murder.

THE KILLINGS

> I am Steven Wayne Benson's grandfather. A substantial
> sum of money will be available to Steven on my death
> . . . and I am afraid for my own safety if Steven were
> free.
>
> —HARRY HITCHCOCK[2]

Early in his life Steven had demonstrated a special aptitude for electronics: by the time he was ten, according to his mother, he had constructed his first Heathkit radio and was able to take apart and reassemble a television set. A high-school classmate remembered Steven carrying copper tubes and wires near the family home, then hearing three explosions: "I set off some bombs on the tennis court," Steven explained to him. Another classmate recalled discovering a box of Steven's, which contained batteries, wire, and alligator clips: "I guess you'd call them bombs," he concluded. Years later, attending the funeral of Steven's mother and brother, an employee asked Steven if he knew how to build a bomb: "Yes," he told her, "I have made bombs. It was when I was younger. I exploded them."[3]

On Friday, July 5, 1985, he visited a construction supply firm a few hundred yards from his own offices and purchased two 4-inch pipe end caps. Steven asked that the receipt be made out to Delray Construction, a fictitious company, and signed for the purchase in an illegible scrawl. However, he was careless in resting his palms on the paper he signed, and he left behind a set of clear palm prints. It is not known where he obtained all the other necessary materials for the construction of two 27-pound pipe bombs, but he was familiar with wire, batteries, and switches, and gunpowder is readily available at sporting goods stores. On Monday, July 8, he purchased the last of the materials; wearing a simple disguise—a baseball cap he had borrowed from one of his employees, and wire-rimmed spectacles—he bought two galvanized metal pipes, one foot in length and four inches in diameter.[4]

On July 8 it became possible and desirable for him to arrange a social event that would bring together the targeted family members. That afternoon, he telephoned his sister and expressed a desire to accompany her as she looked at property the following day. He also suggested that their brother should accompany them on this expedition, although he did not say why he thought their brother was required. That evening, when friends dropped by his home to visit, they found him unusually distant, even abrupt. Normally, he would have talked animatedly with his friends, but this evening he merely stared at the television and hardly spoke. At eleven P.M., an unusually early hour for him, he went to bed.[5]

He raised familial eyebrows the following morning by arriving at his mother's home at the agreed time of seven-thirty—for he was notoriously tardy. He parked his van in front of the house, then walked to the rear of the van where, his sister later remembered, he appeared to be adjusting something. As he entered the house and saw his sister and his mother's lawyer preparing instant coffee, he found his opportunity to plant the bombs. "You don't want to drink that instant stuff," he told them. "I'm going out to get coffee, and since you're on a diet, I'll get you some Danish." He was gone with the family's Suburban for an hour and a half, during which time he completed the final assembly of the bombs and placed them in the wagon. When he returned, he warded off complaints about the time he had taken for his errand with the excuse that he had bumped into a construction worker he knew, and chatted with him. Later, after the killings, he would not be able to name this construction worker.[6]

He asked his sister to awaken their young brother, Scotty, and asked his mother if she was ready to go. This was the first his mother had heard that her son expected her to accompany him on the outing, and she said that she had made other arrangements for the morning. Nevertheless, Steven prevailed. Just as they were leaving, a servant reminded his mother that she had an appointment that morning with a swimming-pool designer, but Steven deflected that by hastily sketching the proposed pool and providing a list of the types of tiles and designs that would be required. "If you have any problems," he told the servant, "tell them to go down to see the Rutenberg model. That's pretty much what we want to do."[7]

He herded his family towards the Suburban: in its centre console was one 27-pound pipe bomb, and under its back seat was another similar bomb. Family custom usually dictated that Steven did the driving, but this morning he placed his brother Scott in the driver's seat and his mother in the front passenger seat. He moved into the right rear seat behind his mother, leaving only the left rear seat for his sister. When his mother asked for the car keys, Steven, rather than simply passing them over the front seat to Scott, left the car and walked around to the driver's seat, giving his sister a helpful little boost into the vehicle and trying to close the door behind her. Her life would be saved by the Suburban's malfunctioning air conditioner, which made her insist that the door be left ajar until they drove off—allowing some of the force of the blast to be released through the open door instead of being contained within the closed vehicle. Steven passed the keys through the open window to Scott, then said he had forgotten something in the house and would return in a moment. Seconds later, as Scott moved in his seat to start the vehicle, as Carol Lynn moved to pick up a cooling drink she had rested on the floor, the first bomb exploded.[8]

As Carol Lynn later told police, "Suddenly, it was like there was this big orange thing all around me, and holding me down, and my reaction was that I was being *electrocuted* ... And I called out, 'I'm being electrocuted. Somebody please help me, I'm being electrocuted!' " The explosion, which came from the bomb in the centre console, immediately killed Scott and Margaret, tearing off Margaret's lower left arm and stripping the flesh from her face. As Carol Lynn tumbled from the burning vehicle, she saw Steven "staring straight ahead" at the Suburban as if he were a mere onlooker. "I couldn't understand why he wasn't coming over to help me ... I think I called for him to help me, but he turned around and he ran back into the house." Seconds later, the bomb under the back seat exploded. Steven shouted to his mother's lawyer to "call an ambulance."[9]

Steven appeared to be frantic a few moments later when neighbours and police began to arrive. Witnesses remembered that he told each new arrival that "I was only three feet from the car," and called repeatedly for his wife, Debra. Moreover, he appeared to be anxious as each new face arrived in the house: "Who's that? Who's that?" he asked in a highly agitated voice. Scott's girlfriend, Kim, saw Steven sitting on the front steps, moaning and rocking back and forth. Police soon became suspicious of Steven's performance; and he was arrested when they discovered his palm prints on the supply company's receipts for pipes and end caps. He was charged with the murder of his mother and brother, and the attempted murder of his sister.[10]

SOCIAL HISTORY OF THE FAMILY

> If rough seas make good captains, then I qualify as an
> admiral.
>
> —HARRY HITCHCOCK[11]

THE FOUNDER: HARRY HITCHCOCK

The reconstruction of an event as catastrophic as the simultaneous murder of a mother and brother and the terrible disfiguring of a sister often entails surprises. In the Benson case, we might expect to find a tyrant tycoon who bullied and humiliated his children and grandchildren until one of them could bear it no more and retaliated in kind. Yet there is not the slightest evidence of any such abuse. Harry Hitchcock, a poor boy from Baltimore, was the unlikely founder of the dynasty. In 1909, when Harry was twelve years old, he was forced to leave school to help support his family, since his mother was dead and his blind father—who ran a sixty-seat nickelodeon—was in financial trouble. Competition from the rising film industry ultimately closed the nickelodeon, and his father returned to an earlier career, singing in nightclubs as "Baltimore's blind singer professor Walter T. Hitchcock." Harry took a position in a mail-order-shopping house and remained there until the First World War. Deferred from service during the war, he worked as a paymaster at the military's Camp Meade. After the war he joined Bethlehem Steel's payroll department, working as a bookkeeper for $25 a week. In 1919, he married Charlotte Brown and made the career change that would radically alter the family's social and economic trajectory: he took a job with a tobacco company he thought might provide an opportunity for advancement.[12]

Years later, after the murders, Hitchcock talked about his decision to enter the risky arena of sales. "It was the best decision I ever made," he told the family biographer Greenya, "from a financial standpoint, but it was one that would take a great toll on my family." With increasing frequency, and for longer periods, he was on the road. "It was a quirk of fate that I got into the tobacco business because I never used it and I wasn't a salesman. I was driven not by the lust for money or the power that money can bring, but solely by a fear of failure." Yet he told his biographer that he regretted those years: "I neglected my family. My job became not only the most important thing in my life, but my whole life. The only vacations I ever took were short ones, and if I was home I was always on the telephone, talking business." Despite his ignorance of the product, he sold a great deal of it to the hundreds of small cigar factories in the area: "I would make it clear to customers that the little I knew about tobacco did not extend beyond what was on the tags, and my naivete convinced customers that I was genuine. I sold myself rather than the tobacco."[13]

In 1927, Hitchcock became president of Lancaster Leaf and received 25 percent of the stock. The firm and its new president prospered, but Harry and Charlotte Hitchcock did not flaunt their new wealth; indeed, they seemed indifferent to it. They did not live in the best neighbourhood, for example, because Charlotte did not drive and their old house was on a public bus line. Nor did they make an attempt, when they left Baltimore for Lancaster, Pennsylvania, to struggle for a niche in the old city's complex social heirarchy. "I was never really conscious of being wealthy. My wife insisted on doing her own housework, and the only car I had was a company car. People in Lancaster were surprised when the newspaper disclosed that Lancaster Tobacco Company was such a prosperous company and that I owned part of it. I didn't live rich."[14]

When his wife complained of the time he spent at his work, Hitchcock turned his energies to fundamentalist religion. His testimony at revivals and services emphasized, he later recalled, how

> with a consuming determination to get ahead, I became too busy for Jesus Christ. I gave up my Sunday School class, the official board and all of my church activities, and finally church attendance. On those Sundays when I was home, I was either talking business on the phone or asleep with exhaustion. Then I was made Vice-president and with the increased earnings bought the big house, a Fleetwood Cadillac, mink coats, and diamonds. But my wife, in tears of loneliness, neglect and frustration, said, "This isn't what we want—we were happier when you made fifty dollars a week."

When they moved from Baltimore to Lancaster in 1949, Harry built a great garden around his home, planted fifty thousand tulip bulbs each spring, and opened the grounds to hordes of visitors. Walton reports that people who knew Charlotte during those years "described her as a salty old woman who spoke her mind." Nor, Walton wrote, did Charlotte "conceal her resentment of her husband's increasingly fervent Christianity and the publicity his garden received."[15]

All this was twenty years after he had turned a significant portion of the company's stock over to his wife and daughters. "I don't want to go into dollar amounts," he told Greenya, "but when the company was set up I let my daughters have some of the stock. At the time I gave it to them it had relatively little value. The value of it developed later." By the 1960s, Lancaster Leaf had grown into the world's largest cigar and chewing tobacco trading company: Harry, his wife, and two daughters were each independently wealthy. He had ensured that they would be, he said, "because I didn't want them to have to wait until I died to enjoy whatever benefits came from my activities."[16]

After the murders, he blamed that decision for the familial nightmare. "What do I have now? Years ago, I gave my money away to my children in the expectation that it would make their lives easier, so that they could enjoy it while they were still young. Yet this is what happened. Every night I could go to bed praying that I will wake up in the morning and find that it was just a very bad dream, a nightmare." He might have been expected to know that his daughters would not share his generosity and wisdom, since he had never taken the time to instruct them in these virtues. He might have guessed that such wealth carries with it great power, which may be used either for liberation or enslavement; but no one had instructed him regarding wealth's awesome potential. In this special sense, modern society's greatest strengths—the possibility of social mobility and the relative freedom from rigid rules and prescriptions—are among its greater weaknesses. The absence of a clear social curriculum in which specific expectations must be learned leaves too much room for manipulation, anxiety, and exploitation.[17]

THE INHERITOR: MARGARET HITCHCOCK BENSON

I'm free. Now I'm free.

—MARGARET BENSON[18]

Margaret Benson's empty and tragic career embodies and validates the feminist critique of the traditional family. A woman who possessed both the intellectual gifts and the personal resources to pursue an independent career as a biologist, she was nonetheless a product of her time. The mentality of her era insisted that she treat her career as a mere prenuptial adventure, not a source of lifelong identity and fulfillment. Therefore once she had found an appropriate mate, she opted for the role dictated by the wealthy merchant class of the time—wife and mother, submerging her spirit and identity in that of her husband. In doing so, and especially in embracing the role of mother—for which she seemed to have neither aptitude nor interest—she experienced a kind of imprisonment in the narrow role of *grande dame*. Thus ensnared, she was never given the opportunity to develop a balanced sense of proportion, or even to discern the rough shape of reality. When her dominant husband died and her children were grown, three decades of party-giving and home improvements left her utterly unprepared for the new role of presiding over a vast inheritance.

The elder of Harry Hitchcock's two daughters, Margaret was a competent student at Eastern High School in Baltimore who went on to major in biology at Goucher College. She spent the summer of 1942 working at Woods Hole Oceanographic Institute's laboratory in marine biology, adding to the institute's algae collection; in her final year at college, the biology department recommended her for special honors. No narrow academic, she studied piano at the Peabody Institute, dance at the Fetzer School, and acting with the Ramsay Street Players. During her final year at Goucher, Wellesley University offered her a scholarship and a place in their graduate studies program. But Margaret was an unassertive and proper young woman; she refused the scholarship and the meaningful career it might have entailed, for she had met Edward (Benny) Benson. On the surface he seemed an inappropriate match, for he was of undistinguished social origins (the son of a railroad employee), and was himself working in a department store. Still, he was ambitious, and his dashing good looks and confident, if distant, manner seem to have overridden their disparate social backgrounds. They married during the war, when he was stationed in Texas as a pilot in the U.S. Army Air Corps. Their first child, Carol Lynn, was born in 1944.[19]

After the war, Margaret's father brought Benny into Lancaster Leaf, and the young family moved to class-conscious Lancaster, Pennsylvania. Benny worked hard and rose rapidly in the corporation, soon earning a very large salary, which they began to spend with nouveau riche recklessness. Relatives and friends emphasize that within the family Benny was the dominant force: "Margaret never got a chance to blossom under Benny," a friend and colleague later commented. Margaret's role was entirely appropriate to her social class and her time; subordinate to her husband, shorn of her own career, saddled with children she may not have wanted, her task was to oversee the material plant (the homes, furnishings, automobiles, and clothes) while guiding the aspiring young family up the social ladder. But Lancaster is a city with a long-established tradition of wealth and old families: in such a snobbish milieu, the ostentatious Bensons could never be fully accepted. The upper limits of the elite gatherings were always closed to them, as were some clubs and social institutions. Thus the Junior League never opened its doors to Margaret, and the highest-ranking elite families snubbed them. As one Lancaster dowager later told Walton, "I never knew the Bensons, and no one I knew knew them." In a spirit of defiance Margaret organized her own club, which sponsored formal dances through the year; she held bridge parties for the Women's Symphony Association and tea parties for the hospital auxiliary, modelled evening gowns at the Horse Show, and was chairperson of the Red Cross auxiliary. Nevertheless, just as Margaret had been snubbed by the Junior League, her daughter was not asked to become a debutante—an exclusion that permanently ostracized Carol Lynn from the elite assemblies.[20]

During those Lancaster years, Margaret cultivated what would become a lifelong passion for altering her homes; as their income grew, so did their home. A swimming pool was converted into a lily pond with a Japanese garden when she decided to build a much larger pool; a new wing with a greenhouse was added to the home. Her taste was always a shade vulgar, thought her peers, and her fourteen-karat gold fixtures in the bathrooms seemed to prepare her for her later years in Florida, when she would seriously prepare plans to move a lake to enhance the view from her home. In any case, it should not be surprising that a woman whose assigned roles were social aspirations and home furnishings might, after a lifetime of shouldering these responsibilities, become obsessed with them and much exaggerate their importance. Increasingly, their social isolation made them select their friends among those who worked for them.[21]

When Benny died, she was heard to cry, "I'm free. Now I'm free." But the exultation was short-lived, and her world began to spin apart. This woman who had never written a cheque in her life, and who had always depended on her husband to supervise the practicalities of life and ensure that spending was appropriate to the family's income, was now responsible for matters she had never been taught to understand. These new burdens seemed to fill her with anxiety and dread, which transformed themselves into an intense possessiveness over her children (the only social relationships she could easily control). Her friends now were always employees or business contacts, one of whom—her son Scott's tennis coach—later remembered: "That was the way Margaret started operating as soon as Benny died. Before that, Benny would kind of handle things, and Scott was pretty independent, kind of his own man. But when Margaret took over the purse strings, well she dominated practically the whole thing. Scott was really on the leash. But that was a *complete change of personality* for Margaret. She was using the money to control him."[22]

Margaret and Benny had purchased a half-million dollar retirement home in Naples, Florida, a city with a less rigid social hierarchy than Lancaster's, where her nouveau riche style might be less discordant. But even here, the elite grew uncomfortable. When Benny was dying, Margaret ordered an $85,000 mausoleum for the family plot, insisting that its vestibule be built several feet wider than normal to give it a more impressive appearance. Behind their new home were their three luxury pleasure boats, one with a $100,000 security system, and in front were some of their cars—a blue Cadillac Seville, a Cadillac El Dorado, a Chevrolet Suburban, a white Ford van, a black Jaguar, a Lincoln Continental and, as Walton wryly notes, a "couple of Datsun 280Zs, or maybe it was three. People lost count."[23]

Still, her new home was less grand than the one she had left behind in Pennsylvania. To remedy this, she purchased a new and larger lot, and commissioned architects to design a home that would be her ultimate personal expression—a twenty-eight-thousand square foot building with many luxuries, including a sunken tennis court and a swimming pool. However, the city's architectural committee, which reviewed all proposed building plans, rejected the proposal on the official grounds that the enormous house would be too large for its lot. Privately, Walton notes, "they thought it was tasteless, with all those turrets and walks." Moreover, she seems to have become a compulsive buyer, filling her kitchen with electric gadgets she never used, haunting auctions to buy in bulk, and once purchasing six antique chandeliers, sight unseen, from a friend.[24]

Indeed, Margaret spent so much that even with a $10,000,000 estate, she was spending far more than she earned. At the end of 1984, her accountant stepped in to tell her that she had spent $1,500,000 in the first eleven months of the year, cutting deeply into her capital. In the future, he told her, she could spend no more than $500,000 each year. This news seems to have unhinged her: she understood that she had to economize but her training left her with no sense of economic reality, and her response to the anxiety so engendered was an absurd miserliness in some areas to counter her extravagance in others. Thus after buying a $30,000 speedboat and a $15,000 wristwatch for her son, she would count every potato chip or cookie her maid served in a bowl, or engage in an endless dispute with a cable television company over a $30 charge. She would purchase a pair of $50,000 Lotus sports cars, but haggle with Scott's tennis coach over the price of tennis lessons. With a $10,000,000 estate, she was fearful that she would become destitute and be placed in a nursing home. Financial ruin beckoned, she thought, and she moaned to her daughter, inaccurately, "I don't even have a house to live in anymore." Her anxiety also expressed itself in compulsive list-keeping: she became obsessed with her accounts, rising long before dawn to pore over her sales receipts, computerizing her extravagance in stupefying detail and itemizing every expenditure, no matter how trivial. Despite her computerized accounting, bills went unpaid, employee contributions were not submitted to the government, and she had to ask for an extension for payment of her income taxes. Amidst this great wealth, she rebuked a secretary for making fifteen-cent calls to information and she began to hoard food.[25]

Despite these grandiose expenditures and plans, or perhaps because of them, she was rejected by Naples's elites just as she had been by Lancaster's. Mary Walton argues with great acuity that the Naples architectural committee's rejection of Margaret's proposed enormous home was a symptom of a much deeper problem: "Margaret hadn't fit into Port Royal very well." She had formed a close friendship with only one couple, and she "had not become active in any of Naples' civic causes, beyond giving a few dollars to the local Episcopal Church—literally, a few." With decades of social rejection behind her, her husband was dead and her closest friend was her interior decorator. The primary focus of her emotional life shifted more and more to her troublesome children. The only way she knew to control them, to reward or punish them, was through her money; increasingly, the meaning in her life seemed to come from dominating every aspect of her children's lives.[26]

THE RIVALS: CAROL LYNN, STEVEN, AND SCOTT

I don't see any reason for [Carol Lynn] to be married.

—EDWARD (BENNY) BENSON[27]

Margaret had children, her friends thought, because it was the thing to do; and they thought her performance as mother was erratic and half-hearted. Her husband was little help since (like her father) he travelled frequently, and when he was at home he preferred not to deal with the children's emotional problems. Margaret floundered almost unassisted through motherhood, and if her children ran out of control, as they so often did, she would exasperatedly ask her friends, "How come your children behave and mine don't behave?" From the beginning, Margaret and Benny used their wealth to control their children. They lavished gifts upon them, so much so that it took all of Christmas Day just to unwrap the presents. In high school, Steven wore a leather coat and drove a Mercedes, while Carol Lynn's mink coat matched her Ford convertible. But even in their childhood, family friends report, they knew the gifts were conditional, theirs only under constant threat of dispossession.[28]

This parental stratagem might have worked if the price the parents demanded had been mere loyalty, or successful performance in the out-side world. But Margaret and Benny expected much more than that: "The parents owned the houses and the cars. And their children," Walton comments. Indeed, the essence of the parental effort appeared to be a sustained demand for the obliteration of any independent act or identity. Thus the generosity was purposeful, consciously or otherwise. The children understood early that the only way for them to enjoy the family wealth was through the earnest cultivation of their parents' goodwill. The only element of risk in their lives lay in the increasing conflict between them.[29]

CAROL LYNN

First they stole her son. Impregnated during a brief affair at college, her pregnancy was lived out in secret, since public knowledge would shame the family. Scott was born on Christmas Day of 1963, when Carol Lynn was 19. Scott's natural father remembered the relations between Carol Lynn and her parents at the time: "They were a pretty domineering family, and they used their wealth as leverage with their kids—'If you don't do this, then I won't give you. . . .' " The relationship between Carol Lynn and her lover withered on its own, requiring no parental intervention. But "after Scott was born," Carol Lynn later recalled,

> everyone kept at me, telling me I could not keep him. My father promised me that they would take care of Scotty while I was finishing school, and then when I was out of school and could get a job, I would get him back and raise him myself, as my son. One day, my parents showed up at Goucher [college] and, without telling me where we were going or why, took me to a little town somewhere in Maryland. I can recall a long hallway and an old man, a justice of the peace or something, and there was a paper they wanted me to sign. I didn't want to sign it. But my father insisted, told me it was better this way, that I could have him back when I got out of school. But I still didn't want to sign it. That would be like having part of me torn away. I only signed because I believed my father.

One year later, when Carol Lynn had finished college, she asked for the return of her child. Her father refused, telling her that while they had had every intention of honouring their promise, they now found themselves unable to give up Scott. "I can recall it as clearly as if it were yesterday," Carol Lynn told Greenya. "My father said to me, 'I'm sorry, but it would hurt your mother too much.' "[30]

Then they stole her career. Like her mother before her, Carol Lynn had made a spirited attempt to carve out an independent career, graduating in economics from Goucher College, and enrolling in Southern Methodist University's law school in Dallas, Texas. The career in law was stopped by a brief marriage, but her subsequent attempts to establish a career appear to have been systematically circumscribed by the family. In 1982, for example, Carol Lynn registered at Boston University for a Master's degree in communications. Her mother accompanied her to Boston, ostensibly to help set her up in proper housing; but the assistance soon deteriorated into wild arguments that seemed orchestrated by Margaret—over what kind of housing was appropriate, and under what terms Margaret would pay for it. Margaret reminded Carol Lynn that she had rejected a graduate scholarship in order to marry Benny, and that her daughter should be seeking a "Mrs., not a Master's." Indeed, Margaret's attitude towards the career aspirations of her daughter was encapsulated in an anecdote later recounted by Carol Lynn: "I called my mother to tell her about the new position I had at the television station—head of production. I was *so* excited and proud. When I'd finished, she said, 'That's nice dear. Now tell me about the important things. How's your love life?' "[31]

Then they stole her husband. As a young woman at law school in Dallas, she had met and married the blond water-skier, Tom Kendall. But her parents were jealous gods and the marriage was doomed. When the young couple—over Benny's protests—moved to California to find employment, Benny soon appeared on their doorstep with an offer of a lucrative position at Lancaster Leaf. The couple returned to Lancaster, where Benny had purchased a home to his taste for them. Upon the birth of his grandson, Benny said, "I don't see any reason for the two of them to be married," and began a terrorist campaign to break up the marriage. Benny struggled to invalidate each of his son-in-law's decisions. He expressed outrage when Kendall bought Carol Lynn a Pontiac instead of the family's approved Chevrolet or Oldsmobile. When Carol Lynn chose to push the baby carriage to her parents' home because she wanted the exercise, while Kendall brought the car so that they could later leave the home for another engagement, Benny screamed at him, "What the hell's the matter with you? Has chivalry disappeared? You ought to be pushing the carriage and her driving the car!" Kendall was instructed to stop his weekend hunting and fishing trips, and to spend his weekends at the Benson holiday home. Ultimately, the relationship ended by force. In August of 1969, Benny asked his son-in-law to go to the store and when Kendall arrived, two men approached him and said, menacingly, "Ed doesn't want you around anymore. Why don't you leave before you get hurt?" Kendall remembers demanding that Carol Lynn choose between him and her parents, and telling her, "If you go up there this weekend, and you don't stay here and help me straighten things out, I'm not going to be here when you get back." Capitulating to her parents, she left for their cottage. They never saw each other again.[32]

A few years later, they stole her lover. On holiday in Montreal, she met a Canadian businessman named Don, who moved to Lancaster to live with her. The parents quickly disciplined him. When Don mentioned to a Benson family friend that he thought Margaret and Benny spoiled young Scott, the remark was passed on to the Bensons. The minor indiscretion was transformed into an explosive issue. Greenya reports that Don "was summoned to the Benson home and told, in no uncertain terms, to mind his own business." Unaccustomed to this kind of humiliation, he left

Carol Lynn. "When Don left me," she later said, "my life hit rock bottom. It took me several *years* to get over it, but it did have a positive effect, because it forced me to sit down and evaluate my life. But losing Don was a devastating blow at the time, and, to a great extent, I have my parents to blame for that loss." Still, the loss was not enough to provoke a break with the family.[33]

Having stolen her son, her career, her husband, and her lover, the lonely widow Margaret took pains to ensure that Carol Lynn understood her subservience. To underscore this, strange public rituals would sometimes be staged. Family friends recall an elaborate formal dinner that Carol Lynn cooked and prepared: mysteriously, Carol Lynn ate in the kitchen like a servant, and did not join the party. She admitted later that this was no unusual incident, but a long-established practice: even in the Lancaster years, it was Carol Lynn who was expected to do the laundry and cook the meals, tasks that might well have been shared among the family, or assigned to the family's servants. Despite these depredations upon her, it was not Carol Lynn who killed. Unlike Steven, she felt loved: "My mother and I were very close, and we didn't have anybody else except each other. You know, you stick by your family."[34]

SCOTT

> Now Scotty, don't do that.
>
> —MARGARET BENSON[35]

First they stole his mother. Then they stole his sense of social and biological self by blurring all distinctions between himself, his mother/ sister, his brother/uncle, and his parents/grandparents. As if in recompense, but in fact to bind him close to them, they indulged him most of all. In doing so, they produced a much-loved, self-absorbed devotée of all manner of intoxicants and fast cars who lived in a fantasy world—the central fiction of which was the belief that he had the drive and natural talent to become a national tennis star. His character was expressed most clearly in high school when, after ingesting alcohol and antidepressants, he swerved his car into the oncoming lane, striking and severely injuring a motorcyclist: high school friends remembered that he expressed concern not for the victim, but whether police would discover he had been drinking. Later, and despite the finest tennis coaches money could buy, his game was so erratic that mediocre women players might beat him in practice, and sudden illnesses would prevent him from competing in major tournaments. His insightful coach recalled asking Scott to practice three hundred serves. After fifty, Scott left the court, claiming he had done the three hundred. His coach sensed that Scott had not so much lied as convinced himself.[36]

Then they stole his lovers and his child. Piloting his $50,000 red Lotus (for which his mother Margaret kept the keys), bullying the skipper and crew of the family's yacht, finding it hard to live on his $7,000 monthly allowance, he brought his 14-year-old girlfriend, Tracy, to live with him at home. When Tracy became pregnant, she encouraged Scott to tell Margaret. "I'm afraid," Tracy remembered Scott replying. "What's the worst thing she can do?" Tracy asked. "Cut me out of her will." When Tracy asked, "Do you want money, or do you want me and the baby?" Scott insisted that "I want both." Temporarily emboldened, he confronted his mother: "I don't give a damn if you cut me out of the will," he is reported to have told her, "I'm going to be with her." According to Walton, Margaret vowed that if she could not stop them from seeing each other, she would disinherit him, cut off his present family income, and have his dog put to sleep. At this triple threat to his lover, income, and dog, Scott apparently burst into tears and said, "Why won't mother let two people be together who want to be together?" Still, Tracy quickly grasped that Scott had already made his decision: "I'm going to keep seeing you," he promised her, "but we have to keep it a secret." Tracy took the bus to her grandmother's. The Bensons refused to contribute to the support of the grandchild, for their lawyer advised that to do so would involve the acceptance of a long-term liability. They questioned whether the child's father was Scott. Tracy considered a lawsuit, in response to which Scott and his lawyer submitted a letter acknowledging his mother's superior wisdom: "She [Margaret], not being blinded by the forces of sexuality, very quickly perceived the true character of Tracy Mullins and was much opposed to my seeing her."[37]

Scott's family would have stolen his second live-in lover, Kim Beegle, but he and Margaret were both dead before it could happen. Margaret corrected Kim's grammar, patronized her for her humble social origins, and blamed her for Scott's many failings—not the least of which was his gargantuan appetite for nitrous oxide, an entire tank of which he kept in his bedroom. Kim remembered Margaret complaining that she was a bad influence on Scott. "How am I a bad influence?" Kim asked. "Because you let him do that [sniff nitrous oxide]." "I don't want him doing it any more than you do," Kim remembered replying, "it scares me." Margaret is then reported to have ordered Kim out of her house. But when Kim went to the bedroom to pack her things, Scott threw her against the wall and told her, "You're not going anywhere." "I can't take this," Kim responded. "You're doing this stuff and she's blaming it on me. It's not fair to me, you know." Scott is reported to have cried to his mother, "Look what you did, Mother. You're making her leave. Now she's upset with me. She'll never talk to me again. You ruin everything. Everything I ever do, you ruin it." He locked himself in his bedroom. Kim remembered hearing through the door the sound of Scott inhaling nitrous oxide.[38]

Protesting his impotence in adolescent fashion, Scott fought with everyone in the family. When his mother/sister Carol Lynn joined him and his grandmother/mother Margaret in Florida for Thanksgiving, Carol Lynn was outraged that while the television set in Scott's room had a remote control, hers did not. It came to blows between Scott and Carol Lynn, with Margaret timidly interjecting, "Now Scott. Don't do that." In a similar incident, Margaret's secretary remembered hearing a woman screaming; running into the room, she found Scott slapping a naked Carol Lynn and pulling her hair (fresh from her shower, Carol Lynn's towel had fallen off during their struggle).[39]

Then they committed him to a mental institution. Margaret had protested to Scott that his dog had soiled her carpet, and this complaint provoked a fierce argument that Margaret taped. The next time the tape was heard was in court during Steven's trial for murder, when the defence was desperately scrambling to find plausible alternatives to Steven as the killer. "Leave my dog alone," Scott had shouted at Margaret. "Can you understand that? He is an attack dog, Mother. An attack dog. And I can have him kill you anytime I want. If you ever do that again, I will have him kill you. I will have him tear you to pieces. Tear you to pieces, Mother. . . . Just because it's your house, it doesn't mean you do what you want with my dog. Can you understand that? Huh? Do you? Do you?" Margaret ordered a servant to call the police, and spoke into a tape recorder, "If you could only hear what you sound like talking to me." When the police arrived, Scott was speaking on the telephone. One officer told Scott to get off the telephone, and a servant remembers Scott replying with adolescent bravado, "Who the hell are you, coming into my house, telling me to get off my phone?" His tone changed once he was grabbed and handcuffed. Kim remembered him pleading, "Oh Mother,

please look what they're doing to me. Oh help me, Mother, please."
Mother was on the telephone, telling someone she was committing Scott
to an insane asylum, Kim later told Walton. Scott was taken to Naples
Community Hospital, where he was diagnosed as having organic brain
syndrome, brought on by the excessive inhalation of nitrous oxide. He
was released in a matter of days.[40]

STEVEN

Curiously, the killer Steven was the child who in many respects was
harassed the least. He was always given the most independence, and until
the bombings his rebellion was the most subtle and submerged. Steven
was the only child allowed to keep a spouse, partly because he was least
loved, but a more important reason was that his assigned role within the
family was to replace his father and grandfather as the family businessman. If he was given considerable rein with the family's resources, he was
nevertheless frequently disciplined and brought to submission. As one of
Steven's few childhood friends recalled, "It was carrot and stick from day
one, and it permeated Steven's entire relationship with his parents. Everything was always in Daddy's name. The threat was always there that if
Steven didn't behave the way his parents wanted, he would be cut off. I'm
not sure anyone can survive positively in that atmosphere." From earliest
childhood, Steven's tactic was never to rebel or confront: he was always
the obedient little boy who never showed anger or fought back but merely
withdrew into silence, appearing to capitulate.[41]

Indeed, Steven could only assert himself through his mates. He
selected his wives for their "anti-establishment" personalities and ceased
to love them the moment they stopped rebelling on his behalf against his
family. His first wife, Nancy, at first fought her new parents-in-law, who
bought and furnished their home and demanded that she participate in
all Benson family activities. Nancy was uncomfortable on the family's
skiing weekends, for there were constant quarrels over issues as trivial as
who could have which cereal in an assorted cereal pack. Scenes would
also be staged to remind Nancy of her subservient status, as when she
commented on how tired Peggy, the Belgian maid, appeared, and asked
her, "Are you feeling all right, Peggy?" Margaret at once demanded that
Nancy accompany her to a private room, and exploded, "How *dare* you
imply that Peggy is overworked! You are never, *never* to talk to my
servants again like that, is that clear?" Similarly, when Margaret de-

manded that Nancy destroy her pet cats because Scott was allergic to them, and Nancy suggested a compromise in which she would put the cats outdoors when Scott was visiting, Margaret retorted, "You get rid of the cats, or we get rid of the house." Before that house had been purchased, when Nancy had expressed a dislike of its contemporary design, Margaret had snapped, "You don't like this house? This beautiful, *expensive* house? Maybe you've forgotten who's paying for it, Nancy dear."[42]

Nancy ultimately succumbed to the demands of her parents-in-law that she quit her career and devote herself exclusively to the process of becoming "a Benson woman." "Steven Benson just isn't used to a wife who works," Benny told her one day. "I think it would be better for the marriage if you stayed home." Nancy resigned her teaching position, set aside her graduate studies, and allowed the Bensons to remake her in their own image. They bleached her auburn hair blond to match their shade, taught her how to dress "correctly," which games to play, and the socially appropriate charities to support. She made these sacrifices to please her husband, but since he told her nothing of his inner self, she could not have known that his true desire was that she continue to rebel against his parents on his behalf. Disenchanted, he began to have affairs with "disreputable" women, giving his insightful wife the strong impression that he did it to buck the establishment.[43]

They were soon divorced. Steven had found a tougher woman, Debra, who would rebel against the Bensons as his proxy. She did not yield to the Bensons' attempts to control them, and the subsequent bickering and quarrels resulted in Debra virtually severing relations with her mother-in-law. Her children rarely saw their grandmother and were allowed to do so only under rigid conditions that were specified by Debra. Margaret was forbidden to call the home under any circumstances and, the family biographer Andersen records "Debra enforced the rule with gusto, slamming the receiver down the instant she heard Margaret's voice." Understanding little, the family was mystified that Steven made no attempt to heal the breach between his mother and his wife.[44]

THE EVOLUTION OF A FAMILICIDE

I've never known what happiness is.

—STEVEN BENSON[45]

Founder Harry Hitchcock and each of his direct descendants tried at some time in their lives to avoid the stultifying effects of great wealth and make themselves independent people. Driven by his fear of failure, Harry accumulated wealth yet affected an indifference to it through his religion and his gardening. His daughter Margaret made a spirited attempt to be a biologist, but the narrow attitudes of the time decreed that she devote herself to interior decorating and social climbing: her failure at both must have intensified her dependence on her husband and children, for without them she had nothing. Her daughter Carol Lynn also struggled for independence, securing a degree in economics and enrolling in law school, but her possessive father drove away her lovers, and the familial teat offered milk too rich to be spurned. Even the playboy Scotty—whose possessive mother drove away his lovers over his weak objections—dreamed of becoming a tennis professional. Had he lived, he might very well have become the coach at a minor tennis club. The aspiring family produced men and women of some character and then devoured them. Yet it was Steven's failure that was the most spectacular, for he aimed the highest and achieved the least. If he seemed to fail at *everything*, the reasons for it are clear: as a former colleague commented, Steven "inherited his grandfather's ambition, his father's somber mien, and talent from no one."[46]

   A search for Steven's character must surely begin with his father's powerful, possessive, and identity-crushing love for Carol Lynn, and his mother's strangely similar love for Scott. In his earliest years, Steven seems to have been the younger son forever in the shadow of his much-loved elder sister. Suddenly, at the age of thirteen, he was dispossessed by a lie! His sister's love child, Scott, was brought into the house and adopted as his pampered younger brother. With exquisite insensitivity, Margaret felt Steven was old enough to understand and be unthreatened by such a drastic alteration in the family. Family reports make it clear that she told him the whole truth—that the child was Carol Lynn's but that no one must know the secret. Ever the obedient and unprotesting little boy, Steven could only protest his condition through the presentation of migraine headaches and minor infections. The little boy who had learned to conceal his anger dutifully went to Junior Cotillion each week in his white gloves and formal outfits, learning the arcane dances of his parents' social circle. Overweight, with thick glasses, withdrawn and diffident, he was ridiculed and rejected by his classmates. The only independent talent he demonstrated was his flair for electronics.[47]

In high school, like many other insecure young people, he developed a flamboyant and self-indulgent style, driving to school in his new Mercedes sports car, a gift for his sixteenth birthday. At seventeen, he wanted a Ferrari instead, and when his father refused to make the purchase, Steven tested the parental love by threatening, "I'll wreck it, and then you'll have to buy me a new one." When his father replied, "What if I don't?" Steven countered with, "I'll have the insurance." Yet his suppressed anger was always visible, as was his self-absorbed insecurity. He lost one of his few girlfriends in high school when he expressed delight that her beloved horse had been killed in a fire: "Good," she remembers him saying, "now that he's dead, you'll have more time for me." On a date, he demonstrated his grasp of electronics and explosives: at Steven's request, the girl carried the dry cells, wires, tubing, alligator clips, and firecrackers; Steven tossed the explosives on a police car and detonated them by remote control the instant they touched the cruiser.[48]

The obedient child—who his mother thought old enough to know secret and hurtful things—became the ostentatious and self-centered adolescent who grew into a quiet, even repressed, young man. Even his laughter was a "restrained, businessman's laugh, like his father's," his first wife later recalled. "He was always on the serious side." His grandfather Hitchcock, trying to make sense of what had happened, thought "Steven was aware, when he was growing up, that his grandfather and his father had been successful in business, and he wanted to be also. Unfortunately, he had rather grandiose ideas. He preferred starting from the top to starting from the bottom. I preferred that he start like me, from the bottom." But the grandfather, who had been too busy recoiling from his fear of failure to guide his own children, now felt that it was the duty of his son-in-law to guide his own grandchildren. "I never told him that [he should start at the bottom], because he had a father living, and he got his guidance from his father," Alas, he did not, for Father was away buying tobacco in Manila or escorting his worshipped daughter to beauty queen contests, not engaging in the unpleasantness of daily family life.[49]

Despite excelling in physics and chemistry, Steven enrolled—at whose request we do not know—in business administration at Franklin and

Marshall College. In any case, his career was brief and undistinguished; he tentatively withdrew from the college several times before leaving in the summer of 1972. To make sure that his parents continued his allowance, he did not tell them of any of his departures. His wife was puzzled by his lack of interest in college: "He's smart," Nancy told Greenya, "but, for whatever reason, he just wouldn't discipline himself to sit down and study." Even here, his parents taught him the wrong lesson: when they learned of his duplicity at college, they applauded it, and described it as an example of Steven's "brilliance." What was most puzzling of all to his bride was his mild obsequiousness to his family; he danced attendance on them, always on call to visit, play tennis, or help with the chores. Nancy remembered that if she complained of this dependence, Steven would merely silently retreat into a newspaper, or turn up the volume of the television. Once she asked him if he was happy. "I've never known what happiness is," he replied. "What would make you happy?" Nancy asked. "*Really* happy?" "To make a million dollars before I'm thirty," Steven told her.[50]

It should not be thought that Steven made no attempt to escape his numb depression. Like all the others in the family, he tried to chart an independent course. But the unloved child lacked the confidence to assess accurately his own abilities, or even to complete a project successfully. He established his own business, Lancaster Landscaping, but he was a poor manager. From the beginning his family was forced to subsidize the business heavily because he purchased expensive new equipment entirely out of keeping with the needs of a struggling new business. In the early 1970s, when he finally gave up and went to work for his grandfather, he left behind a warehouse filled with tens of thousands of dollars worth of unsaleable gardening equipment, a pattern he would repeat many times.[51]

If his family had manipulated his personality to fit the Benson requirements, it is equally clear that he had perfected the art of manipulating them. As his sister later remembered,

It wasn't that no one in the family ever said anything to Steven about the way he managed businesses. My father did, my mother did, we all did, at some time or another. But Steven would just go ahead and do things, and then come and say, "Get me out of it." This was Steven's mode of behaviour all along the way. Steven never had to start a project, work it all the way through, and if he had difficulty, Daddy was always there to bail him out.

And he knew—he learned his lessons well—he knew that if he got into trouble, all he had to do was to go to his parents and they would help him out.[52]

His biographers all note that as the boss's son at Lancaster Leaf, Steven felt the resentment of his fellow workers and, as one executive of the company noted, Steven tried to "do something that he could say he had done on his own." Yet he was incapable even of keeping regular business hours. Moreover, his wife Nancy remembered, his insecurity expressed itself in his reluctance to socialize with anyone other than the lower-status members of the company—"the carpenters and the plumbers, and people like that. Never any of the other executives, the people on his level." One employee liked having Steven as the boss because he would approve any expenditure, no matter how preposterous:

> [H]e spent hundreds of thousands of dollars on security devices and other modernizing equipment, which was great. The company could afford it, but he also put in a whole lot of stuff that we really did not need. He brought his own plumber and electrician from Pennsylvania [when travelling to the plant in Wisconsin], and they all stayed at motels and had rental cars, and Steven drove a big Cadillac or a Continental. None of it was what you'd call cost-effective. He must have spent half a million dollars remodeling the warehouse, alarm systems, new wiring. Some of it was necessary, but not all of it. Yet he was tight with his own money. He used to come in and ask me if I had any money in the cashbox. That got to be a regular thing. But he kept forgetting to pay it back.[53]

Perhaps the most startling aspect of the family's treatment of Steven during his tenure at Lancaster Leaf was that they kept him in a state of permanent ambiguity by refusing to give him a specific position, role, or title. An insightful business colleague, Willem van Huystee, suggested to Benny that he start Steven off with a specific position at the bottom, as van Huystee's own father had done for him in Holland, but the suggestion was dismissed. Consciously or otherwise, Steven was obliterated at Lancaster Leaf. His style a mixture of flamboyant display and petty larceny, the boss's son found his only independence and power in extravagant and unjustifiable expenditures. He would also pretentiously toss off grand suggestions to more experienced employees. Small wonder then that when Benny sent Steven to the Philippines on business, van Huystee received a cable from one of his men announcing Steven's arrival: "The little shit has arrived—and on first class!" Nevertheless, he began to think of himself as a bit of a rebel. He unabashedly told his wife that his first mistress, a working class woman, was attractive to him because "she doesn't represent the establishment."[54]

Within days of his father's death, Steven came into the office to find that his desk had been removed; he took the hint and resigned. With characteristic grandiosity, he thought his business experience was now sufficient to create a rival company that would destroy Lancaster Leaf. But his attention to his newly founded United International Industries Incorporated focused, as always, on inessentials—the design of the logo, the ordering of business cards, embossed pencils and pens. Most of all, he wanted an office commensurate with the status that would soon be his, and he consulted one bewildered Lancaster businessman:

> Steven came into my office, which is good-sized, and told me that he was going into the tobacco business for himself, and that he wanted my advice on decorating and outfitting his office. He said he had been downtown and looked at a floor, *a whole floor,* of the building that was used to house one of the newspapers, but he said that was too small. "Well, how much do you need?" I asked him, and he looked around my office and said, "Oh, maybe about ten times this much space." I asked him if he was planning to hire a large staff, and he said, no, just himself, and a secretary, at first. "But, it's important to look successful," [Steven told him].

Which was why he had budgeted a half million dollars for office decor. Ultimately, Steven did rent an entire floor, with signs on each of the empty offices indicating "Marketing Division," "Electronics Division," and "Tobacco Division." Larcenously, he travelled to the Far East in an attempt to steal the customers of his friend and mentor van Huystee.[55]

Steven seemed to be a hatcher of unrealistic schemes, depending on his family to pick up the pieces after each of his failures. His sister thought that "Steven just had a lot of grand ideas, but couldn't follow them through. For example, he would approach the plant manager with this wonderful idea, go out and purchase all the equipment and all the materials he needed to do it, and then it would never be completed. This was Steven's plan, spend big, then fail to follow through. He did that throughout his life." He purchased a seventeen-acre farm called Norwood with the intention of subdividing the land into a dozen building lots. He raised the five-figure down payment from his mother, promising great profits; but the land was on a steep hill and was quite unsuitable for building homes. He failed to pay the property taxes, and finally stopped meeting the monthly $1,755 mortgage. The land was repossessed. Carol Lynn explained that her parents always covered Steven's losses because they did not want his grandfather to know of his incompetence: "It's a matter of family honor. Everything is done for family honor. There is the family name. You do everything for the good of the family as a whole." But was Steven's consistent incompetence a personal flaw, or some studied incapacity—a kind of submerged adolescent rebellion against what he called "the establishment"?[56]

It was not until he divorced Nancy and married the pugnacious Debra in 1980 that he finally found the instrument through which he could directly confront his family and fight the establishment without appearing to do so. Through their stormy marriage, Debra remained with Steven under the conditions that contact with his family would be minimal and that none of the family would be permitted to visit Debra's home. Steven presented this to his mother and sister as necessary acquiescence to his wife's demands, and they in turn assumed he tolerated these conditions only because of his ambivalent fear and besotted love for Debra. As Carol Lynn reconstructed the period, "My mother, meantime, has been completely shut out of everything. Debby hated my mother. And she *told* my mother that she hated her ... there were incidents where she exhibited violence toward my mother." Ultimately, Margaret was forbidden even to see her grandchildren, or to telephone Steven at home. Not understanding Debra's function as proxy rebel, Carol Lynn "didn't see why Steven couldn't stand up to Debby. I even said something to Steven about it, that I thought he should bring them down, and he got really, really nasty at me, and he told me to shut up."[57]

While Debra was confronting the family, Steven asserted himself in his time-honored fashion. Now having also settled in Florida, he moved to take over his mother's finances in order to create an international financial empire. In early 1983, he created the Meridian World Group of companies, whose subsidiaries included Meridian Real Estate, Meridian Construction, Meridian Security Network, Meridian Technologies, Meridian Property Management, Meridian Marketing, Meridian Legal Services, Meridian Design and Engineering, Meridian Financial Services, Meridian Leasing, and Meridian Condominiums. Undeterred by his previous failure in the Norwood development, he initially envisaged the empire as based in real estate. He ingratiated himself with his mother's friend and real estate adviser, then tried to steal his business: inevitably he fumbled, and was forced to pay a $10,000 monthly mortgage while receiving no income. "And of course," said Carol Lynn, "you know whose money that was. In fact, Steven once told me that for three or four months after he'd told Mother that he was out of the deal, he was actually still paying that money." Meridian World Group was hastily restructured; now its cornerstone was to be Meridian Security, installing fire- and burglar-alarm systems. His grandfather assured Margaret that "electronics is something he knows about. It's something he is competent to do." With that assurance Margaret committed herself to financing her son's schemes.[58]

The advertisements for the new security systems company were characteristically misleading, inviting potential customers to "call for a free survey or visit our showrooms," when there was no showroom. Indeed, his primary customers appeared to be his own family, as when he purchased a thirty-five-foot luxury cabin cruiser for his mother and installed a ludicrously expensive security system. A friend and neighbour told Greenya that Steven "buys this radar and everything, and three months later he's got it all fixed up. A hundred thousand dollar boat with another hundred thousand worth of electronics on it." In the meantime, earning his daily bread through perfected obsequiousness, Steven hovered around his mother. Another neighbour remembered: "We met him at a couple of parties where he was acting as host for his mother—his wife was not there, by the way—and he acted more like the hired help."[59]

One of the companies in the Meridian group, Meridian Marketing, was kept a secret from Margaret; its function was to hide Steven's systematic looting of her estate. Its records were in such complete chaos that after the murders it took the efforts of a court-appointed expert auditor to sift through the morass of unrecorded transactions. After weeks of analysis, the auditor glimpsed the pattern: money was flowing from all of Meridian's accounts to Steven or to Meridian Marketing, the existence of which was unknown to his mother. Between May 1984 and July 1985, $247,130.27 was funneled from Margaret's personal account through Meridian to Steven. For example, when Margaret went on an extended holiday, she left Steven with a few signed blank cheques to cover incidental expenses.

Steven wrote cheques for $60,000, depositing them in Meridian Security's account, then transferred $25,000 to his personal account to cover the down payment on his dream house in Brynwood—the existence of which was unknown to Margaret. While juggling the finances, he was also trying to keep the paper companies afloat: Walton reports that if calls came for Meridian Boat Charter, the customers would be told that the nonexistent boats were all leased.[60]

The moment of reckoning was not long in coming, since Steven was so remarkably careless; he did not even try to conceal his escapades from his employees. Inevitably, a casual remark from a Meridian employee revealed to Margaret the existence of both Meridian Marketing and Steven's expensive dream house. Margaret was furious. The discovery came at a time when she was afraid that Steven's mismanagement of her estate might make it impossible for her to afford her own dream house. Determined to do something about Steven, she telephoned the family lawyer in Pennsylvania and ordered him down to Naples. On Monday, July 8, when Margaret and her lawyer arrived at Steven's offices— now featuring a large sign proclaiming it the FUTURE SITE OF MERIDIAN COMMERCE PARK—they discreetly asked to see Steven's books in order to help prepare Margaret's income taxes. As the lawyer recalled, Steven agreed, but insisted that he first had an urgent appointment: "Wait until I get back, and I'll give you everything you need." Before leaving, Steven admitted to his mother that Meridian Marketing existed. Then he borrowed a baseball cap from one of his employees to disguise his appearance and purchased from Hughes Supply the remaining items for the manufacture of two 27-pound pipe bombs.[61]

Margaret was enraged, her lawyer recalls, upon discovering the expensive new offices of Meridian Marketing, and doubly so upon seeing the luxury home housing her despised daughter-in-law. The Datsun 280Z sports car, which Steven had earlier insisted he had sold to make the down payment on the house, was in the driveway. Upon their return to Meridian World Group headquarters, Steven was waiting for them with the firm's records, but having glimpsed them the lawyer immediately saw they were virtually useless. Margaret demanded that Steven spend the evening putting the records in a semblance of order. Steven said that he would be delighted to do so, but unfortunately, had an important prior social engagement that evening. As Margaret and her lawyer left the offices, Steven telephoned an employee and arranged a social engagement.

That evening he telephoned Carol Lynn to arrange the early-morning family ride.[62]

DECIPHERING STEVEN

This is a terrible ordeal for my family and me.

—STEVEN BENSON[63]

How can we begin to understand this inept man? Should we take it all at face value, as so many have done, and assume he killed his family simply to stop his mother's investigation of his irregular business practices? But even the police knew that—at worst—his mother would only have slapped his wrists. Why then not beg her forgiveness rather than risk killing her? Failing that, why kill his entire family instead of just his mother? Perhaps we should assume that he destroyed the family in order to gain exclusive control of his mother's inheritance and, later, his grandfather's much larger estate. This seems plausible on the surface, but if the prize was glittering, he must have known that the risks were uncommonly high and that his own history of botching all enterprises was perfect and complete. A less commonsensical approach might question the man's sanity; yet curiously, at no time during the trial did anyone, prosecutor or defender, even allude to such a possibility. Insanity appears not to have been an issue.

Perhaps he was driven to the killings, as some family members have suggested, because he was under heavy pressure from his wife. Certainly Debra was assertive, but we have already seen that Steven used this quality, and appreciated it, for it was his only protection against his family. Could his act have been a misogynistic hatred of females, as some radical feminists have suggested? Perhaps, but one of his victims was male. Could he have committed the murders as an expression of long-repressed jealousy of his siblings, bringing a dramatic end to his position as the ignored child? Perhaps, but if that had been the case he certainly would have killed only his siblings, leaving his mother free at last to overwhelm him with adoring eyes. As if to compound the difficulties in deciphering Steven, he has told us nothing. We can therefore base our assessment only on his behaviour; and the most revealing place to begin is with his bizarre actions in the immediate wake of the bombings.

HIS INDIFFERENCE

Did we get any money in today?
—STEVEN BENSON[64]

All witnesses agree that Steven's reaction in the aftermath of the explosions was utterly inexplicable. Some found him profoundly unmoved, while others who observed him later thought he staged a bogus display. In any case, at no time did he attempt to come to anyone's aid. Scott's lover, Kim, testified in court: "I could see the truck engulfed in flames. . . . When I got outside, the first thing I saw was Carol Lynn. She had blood all over, Steven was sitting on the steps and he had his head in his hands. . . . I stopped and told Steven [that] Scott was dead. He wouldn't even look at me or say anything." In court, Carol Lynn remembered "seeing my brother, Steven, standing on the walk. He was facing the Suburban and staring straight ahead. I couldn't understand why he wasn't coming over to help me." Yet moments later, Carol Lynn recalled, Steven "sounded as though he was making lamenting types of sounds," and "his body was extremely agitated." It has been suggested that his unhappiness was not over the sudden deaths of his mother and brother, but the unexpected survival of his sister, and there is no doubt great truth in this. Still, it appears that he lamented whenever he remembered to do so.[65]

Police and firearms officials viewed the scene with a proper professional cynicism. One official, Agent Nowicki, was struck by Steven's "lack of concern. He just seemed concerned for his own situation and what he was going to do next. There his mother and his adopted brother were lying out there in the yard, and he just seemed unfeeling. That's the impression I got. He didn't seem overly nervous, and he didn't seem overly upset. That was the biggest impression that bored into my mind that afternoon, that he didn't seem to have the normal human response to what had happened." Yet when another officer privately interviewed Steven later that day, Steven seemed extremely upset: "It was bullshit nervousness, so to speak. The overexaggerated shaking, is the best way to put it. I've seen a lot of people come out of a lot of hairy situations, and he was so nervous that he couldn't even put a cigarette to his lips, he shook so badly—that's the impression he gave. Then he grabbed his hand with his left hand, to be able to smoke, and I just thought, 'What's this shit?' It didn't look right." Family friend Stephen Vaughan was surprised that Steven appeared uninterested in seeing his badly burned sister in the hospital: "I kept asking him if he'd like to go see Carol Lynn, and his answer was no. And I probably asked him half a dozen times. All he would say is that he wanted to wait for Debra, his wife, to get there." But when Debra arrived with employee Steve Hawkins, Steven asked, "Did we get any money in today?" before Hawkins had time to offer his condolences.[66]

Police thought Steven's obsession with business details inappropriate to the moment. On the morning of the bombing an investigator, Officer Graham, testified, "Steven came up and asked me if he could go into his tan van. I asked why, and he said, 'I've got to get in there and get some equipment out, because I've got an installation in the morning.'" Within hours, Steven's attitude had changed to wariness. When a police officer contacted him at home, Steven declined an interview. "I said, 'How about tomorrow?' and he says, 'You know, I'd rather talk to my lawyer first, before I talk to anybody.' If somebody had just killed my mother and adopted brother," the officer reasoned, "you wouldn't need a lawyer to talk to me. I'd be on your front doorstep, trying to knock the door in to find out what you're doing next and what I can do to help. But he had this defensive posture, and there shouldn't have been one." Two days later, Steven's lawyer told police that Steven had only authorized him to explain his extended stay at the doughnut shop on the morning of the killings. Police, trying to find a motive, asked the critical question: could it be financial gain? "Yes," reasoned one officer, "he was on the verge of losing house, car, and everything. But from the way [family lawyer] Wayne Kerr talked, Momma was going to do nothing more than slap him on the wrist, and he should've known it."[67]

Yet the most extraordinary thing of all was the way Steven dealt with his mother's physical remains that the explosion had splattered along the side of his van. Police watched him in amazement in the Florida summer heat: "His mother," Office Graham recalled, "for lack of a better way of describing it, was kind of spread out down the side of the van. The door was spread with blood, and bone matter, and, ah, skin. And *he never had it washed*." Embarrassed over their crude humor, he confessed that "we even made comments like, 'Well, there goes Steven this morning. He must be taking Mother for a ride and showing her around.' I mean, every time he got in the van he's opening a door *that his mother's spread out on*! But he never washed it off. Now that's cold."

Was this insane indifference, or some kind of private joke and private satisfaction for Steven?[68]

More ominous was the fact that although he did not telephone his sister, he did make one attempt to visit her in the hospital. As she lay there, disfigured in her bandages, Carol Lynn saw him in the hall staring at her. When a nurse suddenly appeared, Steven spoke to the nurse and left. Days later, when Carol Lynn had been transferred to the Burn Center at Boston's Massachusetts General Hospital, her son Travis told her that his uncle Steve had telephoned him to ask about the procedures for having packages delivered to Carol Lynn's room. Police placed an armed guard outside her door.[69]

As striking as his indifference to both victims and survivors was his adaptation in the days that followed. At the funeral of his mother and brother, Steven expressed annoyance at what he thought was the low social status of the pallbearers. Then he asked his grandfather for a six-thousand-dollar loan. When police arrested him on August 22, 1985, and charged him with the murders and attempted murder, he expressed no emotion; he did, however, complain that the yellow Thunderbird in which they drove him to jail was "kind of small." During the drive to the jail, he fell asleep. Officer Graham, who was also in the car, remembers thinking to himself, "Now there's one cold son of a bitch." Shortly after, his lawyer held a press conference and read aloud what would be his client's only statement: "I am frustrated and angry over a crime I did not commit. This is a terrible ordeal for my family and me, but I am confident we have the strength to make it through. I am anguished for the suffering of my children and my wife and wish desperately that I might be reunited with them." He made no reference to the loss of his mother and brother, or to the maiming of his sister.[70]

AN INTERPRETATION

The Bensons were one variation on the social theme of the aspiring family—the corporation. Such corporate families control a major economic resource, the income from which is enough to sustain many or even all family members. Such families have the power to do far more than simply shower their members with largesse. In fact, as the family typically moves to increase its wealth and elevate its position in the social order, it imposes unique stresses and tensions on its members.* These tensions tend to be resolved over time, as the family finds new strategies for dealing with problematic situations and individuals—most especially in coping with variation in abilities and preferences among family members.

Long-established corporate families such as the Rockefellers have managed to seize their place among the social elites, and to develop over the generations specific mechanisms for obviating conflict and maintaining the estate. These mechanisms vary from family to family, but they centre around the assignation of control of the estate to members who are most naturally suited for business, while (often begrudgingly) ensuring substantial independent incomes for those whose character and interests take them in other directions. As one member of the Rockefeller family put it to the family's biographers, "Most of the younger people [Rockefeller heirs] are not interested in going into business . . . with so much to do, you can't do everything, and they're interested in environment, they're interested in philanthropy, they're interested in government and politics." If the corporate family is to survive and prosper, it must learn to accomplish these tasks without making destructive demands on the identities of its members. Established families learn to obviate this potential conflict between individuals and generations with finesse: however unhappy they may be, they do not produce familicides.[71]

However, the newly emerging corporate family—the oft-denigrated nouveau riche—has only recently seized control of a resource. It has not had the time to develop the mechanisms to ease succession, and the family is often riddled with conflict. This tension is not usually just about money, not merely about rivalry and jealousy over suspected or real differential treatment. The social aims of the family's leadership impose special penalties on the family if they aspire to abandon their social origins and take a place among the social elites. Should they seek to place themselves socially among those who are now their economic peers, they prepare themselves for humiliating social rejection. They cannot have learned effortlessly to display those behaviours and techniques for the maintenance of class boundaries that elites typically dignify with the word "taste"—the myriad subtle cues of background and schooling, style and substance. Perceiving this failing, the Lancaster dowagers had placed the tombstone on the Bensons' social aspirations.

---

* See the initial report resulting from my thirty-year study of the Ostroffs, a merchant family of "Cherbourg," published in 1965 in the *Journal of the Royal Anthropological Institute.*

The more cutting a family's rejection by the social group whose membership they covet, the more likely it becomes that the family will begin to turn in upon itself. Too proud to return to their social origins, cut off from the group they wished to join, they resort to the family for the satisfaction of all their social and emotional desires. From the outside, these families often appear to be incestuous—not in a sexual but in an emotional sense. They only dare to establish social relationships outside the family with employees who are their social inferiors, or those with whom they have secure business relationships. This use of the family for all needs can create a regime that smothers all attempts of dependent children to form independent identities and relationships. Those who control the family purse strings may use their economic power to reinforce their position, utterly to dominate the personal lives of their children and grandchildren. Thus lovers and spouses may be tormented or rejected, even violently removed from the scene, if they do not meet the criteria of the family controllers (who may wish in-marrying spouses to be either of lofty social status or gifted in business affairs). Similarly, identities and careers may be selected by the family, not by the developing individual.

Their special place in the social and economic order permits—even encourages—intrusions in the private affairs of an individual which in any other social milieu might be regarded as an intolerable assault. The techniques for the maintenance of this level of control are simple and long-established: the family will offer the dependents a standard of living that they could never hope to attain on their own. (To ensure this, the family may even interfere actively with the efforts of an individual to earn his or her own income or enter a profession.) Once dependent and dominated, they must obey the family's instructions or lose their standard of living. In this manner, the children are kept dancing in permanent attendance: the loss of autonomy in their personal lives is the price they pay for their comfort.

Viewed from the outside, the family may appear to be flamboyant and arrogant, since its taste is uncertain, and its insecurity demands that it flaunt its wealth in ostentatious display. Viewed from the inside, the family may appear to be volatile and highly charged, with a marked tendency to stage scenes and to quarrel vituperatively with one another and with the rest of the world over trivial issues. These are but stratagems through which the controllers express their dominance, and the rivals fight for their priority. In such circumstances, the aspiring corporate family can be a kind of emotional pressure cooker that without the chance appearance of a benevolent dictator can erupt into violence. This appears to have been the case among the Bensons. The founder, Harry Hitchcock, was no tyrant tycoon but he did not provide his children with a set of instructions—a social curriculum—for handling their affairs. Neither did Margaret's husband, Benny—the ambitious son of a railroad employee—have the social wherewithal to correct this omission. In not understanding their social responsibilities, in easing Margaret out of a meaningful career and into the position of failed *grande dame,* the family set the stage for familicide.

If we are to understand Steven, we must integrate his history and social class, his gender and his role, into one biography, since it was a forty-year sequence of social events that led to the explosion of two pipe bombs in July of 1985. Harry Hitchcock, the founder of the fortune, developed his ferocious fear of failure when his blind singer-father lost the family's theatre. Through a combination of hard work and good luck in an expanding market, Harry rose to become a major shareholder in one of the world's premiere tobacco firms. He and his wife appeared to lack the social pretensions that often come with sudden wealth, and their material possessions—the status armor with which people confront the world—were muted and modest. But they did not transmit these aspirations or this style to their daughter and son-in-law.

Harry's daughter Margaret was a woman of some talent and substance who had submerged her identity in her husband's. Benny, ambitious and hardworking, appears to have focussed narrowly on the family's social and economic rise. Neither appeared interested in children in any fundamental way. Benny did not wish to be bothered with their troubles, and Margaret, uncomfortable in the role of mother, had her own task: to break into the establishment. Yet they never penetrated the elites. Margaret was never asked to join the Junior League, and Carol Lynn was not invited to become a debutante, a kind of social death.

The family increasingly turned in upon itself—Benny cashiering his daughter's lovers as if they were mere servants, Margaret cultivating her reputation for ostentatious bad taste. As the rejection intensified, Benny—Margaret's prime source of security—died, leaving her entirely on her own, with only her children for succor. "I'm free," she declared to her friends, but her training had not prepared her for this: the competent-biologist-turned-failed-socialite now yearned vaguely to become her own person, a "Chairperson, or something," as she told her friends. But her only power lay in dominating her children. As she groped to control their lives, she battled endlessly with them. Scott's girlfriend, Kim, described the family's final years with convincing objectivity: "Carol Lynn and her mom fought . . . most of the time. Arguing over just dumb things, like what color they want the drapes, you know, always there was a disagreement on just about everything." Margaret "had a lot of money, and if the kids didn't do what she wanted them to, she'd threaten them, threaten them by saying, 'I'm not going to give you any money.' " With Steven, Kim remembered, Margaret would say, "I'm not going to do something for your business," if Steven threatened to stray. "The kids are not supposed to make a move," Kim said, "without Mrs. Benson saying, 'It's okay.' "[72]

Carol Lynn and Scott, the children who did not kill, both staged their own rebellions—their attempts to construct their own identities. If these personas seemed unrealistic fantasies to some, Carol Lynn was at least attending university once more and aiming at work in television; and Scott was trying, however inadequately, to become a tennis professional. But Steven, the child who killed, the child who never showed anger and never argued (just withdrew), staged only one brief rebellion in his life—his ludicrous attempt, after his firing at Lancaster Leaf, to create a rival company. After that ignominious failure, he docilely followed the family's expectations. Steven could only follow the dreams of others, and the special way he had been taught to fulfil those dreams was through manipulation, exploitation, and duplicity.

But why was Steven so singularly false to his abilities? Was it merely that being a talented electronics technician would have yielded him insufficient status and money? Was it just the failure of his assault on Lancaster Leaf that left him too traumatized to venture outside the corporate family? Anthropologist Nancy Scheper-Hughes has written with great insight on the manner in which a family may quite unconsciously manipulate the socialization of each of its children according to the future role it deems the child should play. Thus a child selected to inherit a despised or undesirable role—such as caring for aged parents, or tending to a tiny and valueless family farm—will be conditioned to feel too worthless, too untalented, to aspire to anything else.[73]

A family controlling a major resource must select at least one descendant in each generation to assume responsibility for the estate. This can be accomplished with a minimum of damage to that person if roles and expectations are clearly assigned. But an emerging corporate family may have special insecurities, especially if it is failing in its social aspirations, and the selected person must therefore be welded to the family. To ensure the strength of this bond, his socialization will concentrate on his dependence; the prospective estate manager will be conditioned to obsequiousness to his parents, grandparents, and siblings. To mold such an adult, the selected child will quite unconsciously be ignored or insulted, given an insufficient sense of self-worth to strike an independent path, and taught to acquire expensive tastes beyond his own ability to afford. A certain recklessness may even be tolerated, for it allows the family periodically to rescue the offender from his scrapes with reality, and intensify his dependence thereby. One unintended consequence of this tactic is that it sometimes teaches him that it is not necessary to learn how to complete a project, or think through the consequences of an act: all he needs to know is how to manipulate the family to achieve short-term goals, as they manipulate him for their long-term aims.

In this sense, Steven was the perfect product of his family. Replaced by his indulged, adopted young brother and relegated to the position of inferior middle child; given the luxury cars and clothing to fit his social stature, but not the information on how to obtain them for himself, his insecurity and his detachment from reality expressed itself in increasingly grandiose fantasies. However, a family's socialization is not a flawless instrument. This role can create terrible tensions within its players, keeping them in a kind of suspended state of perpetual adolescence, forever engaged in a covert war with their parents, manipulating and being manipulated. When cornered, such individuals can be dangerous.

A human being's biography is the process of negotiating an identity. Early in life, Steven internalized his family's expectations that he succeed his grandfather and father as merchant prince. This desire was not some all-consuming love of money—as so many family members, police, and commentators have thought—since there is precious little evidence that money meant much to him. What was important to him, and compulsively so, was *"becoming* a millionaire," assuming the identity his family had allocated him. In his own eyes, he seemed to be close to achieving this lofty goal. His wife Debra, whom he loved because she kept the family at bay, presided over their dream house in Brynwood with its millionaire's tennis courts and manicured lawns, just as he presided over the vast new empire he created. Illegally issuing legal advice on divorce settlements over the telephone as president of Meridian Legal Services; duplicitiously refusing applications for nonexistent boats as oversubscribed president

of Meridian Boat Charters; the founder and chief executive officer of the
Meridian World Group could survey with satisfaction the future site of
Meridian Commerce Park, the ambitious building complex that would be
necessary to house the ever-proliferating worldwide Meridian network of
companies.

The only obstacles in his path were family members who, untutored
in the ways of international commerce, were threatening to interfere with
the construction of both his empire and his identity. He did not, as so
many of his critics have assumed, purchase the pipe bombs' ingredients in
a fit of pique after his mother's discovery of his chicanery: most of the
materials had been purchased *before* his unmasking. In any case, he knew
that his mother's retaliation would be slight. No, it had become necessary
to destroy the family in order to save it, to cease for all time the
intolerable meddling that was holding back the estate from becoming a
giant in world commerce. The family had always rewarded his duplicity,
even calling it brilliant, and the family had always covered up any
shortcomings in his plans: surely they could be relied upon to do so again.
When his remote-control device triggered the bombs, the motive was not
simply a spirit of malice or greed. Rather, it was the action of a young
man socially detached from both morality and reality, determined to do
what was best for his aspiring family and its illustrious new head.

AN ADIEU

Steven seemed to find a form of happiness in prison. Removed from the
necessity to be what he was not, his morbid anxiety seemed to fall away:
he had never been able to control his overeating but now he lost between
twenty and thirty pounds. He seems to have considered suicide, because
his jailers found a cache of sleeping pills in his cell. Curiously, his sister
was disappointed that he had failed to take his own life: "I was actually
angry," she told Greenya. "It would have been the honorable thing for
Steven to do, because it would have spared the family the scandal of a
public trial." That seemed scanty recompense for Steven's heroic attempt
to pass a vastly enlarged estate on to his own children.[74]

Still, he adjusted well in prison, and guards—who called him "Boom
Boom"—thought him a model prisoner. Walton, ever alert to irony,
noted that Steven "was always dressed and shaved, with his bed made—
the sheets pulled skintight—before the 8:00 A.M. deadline. His sneakers
were neatly tucked under the bunk, and copies of *The Wall Street Journal*

were stacked chronologically." Polite to both his fellow inmates and his keepers, he was elected to represent the inmates on his block at liaison meetings with staff; and he spoke ably, if rarely, on issues such as the items that should be carried on the commissary cart. He seemed more of a whole person in prison than he had ever been when free. Through the annihilation of his family he had constructed his own identity: now he was the *retired* chief executive officer of the Meridian World Group, freed at last from the pressures of high office, but still concerned with matters of high finance, staying in touch through *The Wall Street Journal*.[75]

CHAPTER THREE

The Administrator
in Ford's Export Department

Harry William Frederick De La Roche, Jr.*

Familicides rarely tell us much about their crimes. When they do admit to any involvement, it is often to only a small portion of the massacre. They prefer to blame the dead, or evaporated phantoms of the night. This should not be surprising since their deeds lack any of the "prestige" that often comes with other forms of homicide; moreover, it is to their legal and personal advantage to deny the killings. Yet it should not be assumed that they regret their acts or are much troubled by them. Once they have accomplished their task and wiped out the source of their frustration, their lives sometimes take on a curious serenity. Nevertheless, we must not diminish Harry, for he has told us much, even if he would not tell us why. It is left to us to show that the origins of the crime lay in a frantic attempt by Harry's ambitious father, himself an illegitimate child, to use him as the vehicle for the family's recovery of its lost genteel status.

THE KILLINGS

> I phoned one Sunday and said in a broken voice, "Uncle John, this is Harry. I'm at the Montvale Police Station, and Mom and Dad and Eric are dead."
>
> —HARRY DE LA ROCHE[1]

The killings began in the early hours of November 28, 1976, in Montvale, New Jersey, and within minutes his parents and two brothers were dead.

---

* The sources for this chapter include the corpus of letters exchanged between De La Roche and myself; reports and interviews contained in *The New York Times*; but especially the unusual and most interesting biography/

According to his least implausible sworn statement, he had taken the pistol from his father's nightstand drawer at three o'clock in the morning and gone to his bedroom to think. The High Standard .22-calibre semiautomatic pistol lay beside him on the bed with ten cartridges in its fully compressed magazine. He hesitated, perhaps uncertain about his course of action, or merely steeling himself for the task. "I was sitting in my room for a while thinking of what I was going to do," he told the police,

> thinking I can't go back [to military college], and I really couldn't tell my parents because they wouldn't listen. I kept walking back and forth from the entrance to my room to the entrance of my parents' room. I walked in there and said, "No, I can't." Then I walked back in my room and sat down for a little while. Finally I walked into my parents' room and got real close to my father. I must have stood in his room about a half-hour just holding the pistol up. Then finally I said, "I can't go back," closed my eyes and pulled the trigger.[2]

The first two bullets hit his sleeping father, Harry, Sr., in the right eye and behind the left ear. There is some disagreement on whether a third shot missed its target or if the bullet that had pierced the eye also punctured a hole in the pillow and mattress. He moved the pistol in an arc until it was pointing at his mother, who had "just started to stir," he remembered. Both bullets struck the brain of Mary Jane De La Roche who, asleep in her yellow nylon pyjamas, appeared not to have awakened during the seconds that occupied the action. He then walked to his brothers' bedroom: "When I turned on the light, Ronnie was laying on the side of his bed. His eyes were opened, like he was in shock, like he didn't know what was happening—I guess he didn't. Ronnie was just like—I don't know. I don't know. He just saw me there or heard the shot or knew something was on. . . . He was laying on his side with his head out and eyes wide open like he was staring at something. I shot him." He put a rag on Ronnie's wound to "keep him from bleeding all over the place."[3]

He had shot Ronnie the moment he turned on the light, but his youngest brother, Eric, had a few seconds to begin to resist.

> I shot him twice, and I figured it's all over. He's not feeling any pain at all. Then he started getting up and I figured, "Oh, God,

autobiography, *Anyone's Son*, by Roberta Roesch (with Harry De La Roche, Jr.). According to a personal communication from Ms. Roesch, all quotations attributed to Harry are from letters or taped conversations, and are either reprinted "verbatim" or "lightly edited" for stylistic reasons.

what was he going through? What am I going through?" He was getting up and trying to get out. He was saying—he was saying something, I couldn't hear him. I put my hand over his eyes and said, "Eric, go to sleep, go to sleep. It's just a dream," trying to calm him down. Then he got up and he started screaming, and I hit him with the pistol butt in the head. Then he went down to the ground. I hit him again. He was still breathing. The next time I hit him he wasn't breathing anymore.

Yet the memory of this assault did not trouble him unnecessarily. At his trial, he later dispassionately remembered, "I could see a few of the jurors wince when Dr. Denson went on to say that Eric survived two bullets fired at close range and died when his skull was cracked open by a blunt object. He said powder burns on Eric's face showed he was shot with a gun held less than two inches from his face. Then he added that there were superficial wounds on the back of Eric's hands which indicated he had been trying to fight off an assailant."[4]

In what is a common practice among murderers, perhaps to initiate the process of wiping the deed from their minds, Harry then began to tidy up the mess. He carried the body of his brother Ronnie upstairs to the attic:

I tried wiping down the stairs to the attic. There were a few drops of blood there. There was blood on Ronnie's bed, so I took my father off his bed and put him on Ronnie's bed. Then I was just sitting there, like what am I going to do. The shirt had some blood stains on it from when I hit Eric, blood splattered up. I had some blood on the long johns from when I was carrying my father and Ronnie. I took them off and threw them in the back of my closet in my room. I went into the bathroom, showered off, and then I put these clothes on.[5]

He admitted that he moved the bodies in an attempt to fool the police, "to make it seem like I didn't do it." He stuffed Ronnie's body into a metal closet because "that was the only place I could think of putting him." But his intention had been to hide the body: "I was going to put him in the back of the car and bring him out to Seven Lakes with the pistol and hide him out there." He carried his father to his brother's bed because "there was blood on my brother's bed. How could I explain Ronnie did it if there was blood on his bed?" At first he tried to hide the pistol in the metal closet upstairs: "I put it there, but I said, 'that's going to be too easily found,' so I put it downstairs in one of the drawers."[6]

At 4:10 A.M., a police officer observed Harry driving past a stop sign without stopping. The officer followed and he later testified, "Harry stopped and jumped from his car in front of Davy Jones Locker, a local tavern and hangout. 'Quick, come up to my house,' he hollered. 'I've just found my parents and younger brother dead and my middle brother missing.' " The officer followed Harry to his home, and told the court that "when I entered the first bedroom on the left I noted a bed with a large amount of blood on the pillow. Mrs. De La Roche was lying there, apparently dead. I noted that the other half of the bed also had some blood stains. As I looked down the hall into the other bedroom I could see a twin bed and two human legs. Harry, Sr. was dead on the bed. He was lying face down. Eric was face down on the floor by another twin bed."[7]

As police began to crowd into the house, Patrolman Olsen took Harry, Jr. into the kitchen to obtain more information. Above the kitchen table he saw a plaque that read, "What little boys are made of—frogs, and snails, and puppy dog tails." Harry was not considered a suspect until noon, when investigating officers climbed the steps to the attic, opened the brown metal locker, and found Ronnie's body stuffed inside. It could not have been a suicide, for the gun was nowhere to be found, and boxes had been piled on top of the locker. Harry's facile attempt to cover his tracks had purchased him less than nine hours of freedom.[8]

TRUTH'S KALEIDOSCOPE

Familicides are not only among the least likely of all multiple murderers to confess their crimes: they are also among the more likely, if they have confessed, to retract that confession. Harry was no exception to this rule. When he first showed police through the murder scene, he denied all knowledge of the murders, telling police he had no idea who might have committed such an act, but hinting broadly that it might have been his brother Ronnie. "I don't know," he replied to police questioning. "All I can say is my father learned that my brother used drugs. They had a big fight about it and Ronnie told my father he'd bury him under his bed." This amateurish attempt to shift the blame—quite pointless, since Ronnie's body lay upstairs in the attic, crushed into the metal locker—developed into a story that Harry, Jr. had returned home from an evening's entertainment to find "the light by the door was off. And this was very strange." He recounted his shock at the discovery of the bodies of his family, and the absence of his brother Ronnie.[9]

THE FIRST TALE: OBFUSCATION

His first version of events pursued this theme. Shortly after eleven that morning, in Montvale police headquarters, he gave police a statement dwelling on the alleged conflict between his father and brother, and claiming he had been "disgusted" when he had learned that his father planned to report his brother to the police for smoking marijuana. "The thing that really bothered me was my own father would turn in my brother and I was thinking I just had to get out of there, I couldn't listen to that . . . 'I can't let you turn him in.' " He said he discovered the bodies when he entered the house later:

> I had to pass my parents' room to get to mine and I happened to look inside my parents' room and I noticed only one person was laying in bed. I knew my father wasn't in the upstairs bedroom, so I decided to take a look and see what was up. I turned on the light and I found my mother in bed. I then went into my brother's room, found my father laying in my brother's bed and my youngest brother Eric lying on the floor with no sign of my other brother Ronnie . . . when I found that and when I saw my brother I thought I was going to get sick.[10]

Bergen County Prosecutor Joseph Woodcock was struck by Harry's lack of emotion, remarking to *The New York Times* that the boy "did not appear to be visibly upset. He was very civil, he seemed extraordinarily calm." But the interrogation continued through the morning and Harry later wrote that it seemed to be "growing endless, and the constant grilling and interrogation added to my state of shock. I was starting to get confused." When asked if he had checked if any of the victims were still alive, he told police: "I went to see my father. When I touched him he was cold and I couldn't feel any pulse at all. I did not want to try getting a pulse around his neck because it was all bloody. I tried his arm, tried to get any sign of life and I saw Eric on the floor and I knew."[11]

Harry insisted that his brother Ronnie and his father had been arguing. He denied that the dispute had become violent, but said that Ronnie had threatened his father: "He said he would bury my father under his, Ronnie's bed. . . . When my father did hit him on different occasions he said he would get even or he would run away or something, but this was a while before. My father had not done any hitting for a while." Harry then claimed that his father had confided in him that he intended to turn Ronnie over to the police: "I said I did not want to hear it, that my father would turn in my own brother. I was going to come back today and say, 'If you turn Ronnie in I'm not going back to The Citadel and that's money wasted . . .' [but] I did not have a chance to tell him." Shortly after this statement was made, Ronnie's body was discovered along with the pistol and a bloodstained Citadel T-shirt.[12]

THE SECOND TALE: CONFESSION

Following these discoveries, Harry was given a polygraph examination, and as the intimidation increased, his version of events began to alter. The test apparatus, he later recalled, "seemed as formidable to me as an electric chair. I said to myself, 'I don't like this—I don't like this at all.' " Nor did he like the polygraph operator, Allmers, because "I felt he was using psychology on me." Having completed the test, "I turned and looked at Allmers and said, 'How did I do?' He quickly snapped, 'Don't you know?' Then he told me I was lying and that I had hurt them all. He also said—since the test was over—that Ronnie had been found. The hands on the clock said 3:30, and my attitude was 'Fuck it.' " In a second sworn statement, he admitted killing his entire family, and he was formally arrested at five-thirty P.M. In the course of that day he smoked eight packages of cigarettes.[13]

Surrounded by journalists and police, he was taken before the court. "As usual people commented that I showed no outward emotions when the warrants were handed to me. But in my spaced out condition I would have taken anything without even batting an eye." Harry expressed concern only for his dog, Lucky, as police drove him to jail, and he was relieved when the officer "assured me that someone would take care of our dog." When they asked what he had done with the empty cartridge cases, "I told him I'd collected ten empty bullet casings and put them in my desk." Still, he had not yet found peace. "When I awoke on Monday after an on-again, off-again sleep, induced by the trauma of Sunday, I was in such a stupor that I felt out of it . . . life had fallen in on me. I was locked out of my skull." He did not say a word at his arraignment in court that day. It was left to his insightful aunt Arden to ask the critical question and expose the nature of his personal trap: "If things were so terribly bad," he remembers her asking, "why didn't you run away? You're eighteen. You could take off. Lots of people do." " 'But where would I go?' I responded. 'What would I do if I split?' When she asked if I'd like to send flowers to the funeral home and church I told her 'Yes—and I'd like them placed right by my mother's head.' "[14]

Of all the deaths, it was the murder of his youngest brother, Eric, that bothered him the most. He asked that the cross he always wore be placed in Eric's coffin. Eric's death "was imprinted most vividly," Harry later said. "He was a victim of something that he had nothing to do with, so he shouldn't have suffered in any way. And he shouldn't have been beaten so badly. 'Put the cross in Eric's hands,' I told [Pastor] Roy. 'That's where I want it to be.' " But of what crime did Harry consider Eric innocent and his family guilty? "Lonely and scared inside, and often, very depressed," he later admitted, he often contemplated suicide. Once he asked his guards to place him in the detention room for his own protection.

> Nobody wants to go there, but on the day I requested it one of the cell mates near me had threatened suicide. The whole thing was getting to me, and I didn't want to be there when the suicide happened. I also wanted to blow off steam and be by myself for a while, so when I went there for the night I cried a little while. I wouldn't have wanted my cell mates to see me doing that. While I was there my arms were strapped to a bunk the officer brought in. Again they feared I'd kill myself and were taking no chances of that.

Nevertheless, if he felt lost and alone, nowhere in his account does he indicate unhappiness for his family.[15]

THE THIRD TALE: RETRACTION AND FABRICATION

Within weeks of his confession, as he put it, "I started to come to my senses." He asked his relatives to contact the family's clergyman, Pastor Roy Nilsen: " 'I have something to tell him,' I said. 'It's urgent I see him right away.' " When the pastor appeared on the following day, "I was anxiously waiting to see him, too, because I had something to say to a person I knew I could really trust. Roy Nilsen was that person." At their meeting, "I was itchy to get started, so I opened the conversation with, 'I want you to hear this story.' "[16]

" 'I know this will come as a shock,' I warned, 'but I didn't kill my family alone. Ronnie shot Eric and my parents, and I shot Ronnie in a rage. There are plenty of gaps in my memory, and it's like a twilight zone. But I'll tell you what I remember.' I can still see the look on the pastor's face. But he listened and said very little. 'As I said in my two statements both the light by the door and the light in our living room were off when I got home,' " he explained, drawing attention to perhaps the only consistency in his various tales.

> I went upstairs without lighting the lights, and if you've been upstairs in my house you know we have a L-shape hallway with my parents' room at one end of the L and Ronnie and Eric's at the other. When I got to that part of the hallway I looked down toward the boys' room and saw Ronnie sitting on the side of his bed. His feet were dangling over the side, and he had a dazed look on his face. I started down the hall to speak to him. Then when I got to his door I saw Eric to the right of me. He was half lying on the floor and half propped up by his desk. The back of his head was bloody with something white around it, and blood was all over his bed. I can't describe what was in my mind, and I don't know what I said except, "Where are Mom and Dad?" He answered, "In bed," and when he spoke it was like he was in a trance. He didn't talk in his normal way, and his voice was a low monotone. I turned and ran to my parents' room. But even before I snapped on the light I knew what I would find. There was blood all over their bed. I touched my father and checked his pulse. When I didn't get any from him I figured Mom was gone too, because if something was wrong with my father she wouldn't have been just lying there unless she was dead herself.[17]

When an astonished Pastor Nilsen asked him what he had said to Ronnie, Harry's memory wavered:

> I'm not sure now. I think I said some common thing like, "What happened?"; or, "What is this?" I then went on to tell Roy how Ronnie kept on looking dazed and didn't answer at first. Finally

he said in an abnormal voice, "Dad discovered me with drugs and is going to turn me in." I don't think Ronnie believed that, though. I think he feared Dad might beat him—maybe shoot as he'd threatened—since nothing had ever made him as angry as discovering this. As I try to piece things together, maybe Dad had postponed taking any action because I was still on vacation or maybe my mother had said, "Let it slide till Harry leaves tomorrow."[18]

Thus Harry struggled to distance himself from the murders. When Nilsen asked him when Harry, Sr. had discovered Ronnie's drugs, Harry, Jr. remembered saying that

Ronnie didn't say. But if my father had discovered it and known about it before supper, I don't think that Dad would have let him out when he went to collect for his papers, and I don't think Ronnie was in the house when my father asked about Ronnie and pot when I went back to change cars. I guess sometime after 6:30 or 7:30 my father must have found the green G.I. Joe box that Ronnie used for his drugs, scales, and baggies. He would have seen some empty baggies since Ronnie liked to keep them so he could smell them sometimes. Dad must have been on a spring cleaning spree or he might have been looking for something under Ronnie's bed, since Ronnie was sleeping in his own room while I was home from school. At any rate, Ronnie was scared for his life as he said in a dazed monotone, "I shot Dad and Mom, and then I shot Eric."[19]

When Nilsen wondered where Ronnie had obtained the pistol, Harry remembered saying,

"I think he must have taken it when he came home from wherever he was before my parents went to bed. I don't know where he was that night, and I don't know what time he came in." I couldn't begin to tell Roy the feeling I had at that moment, and I can't describe the state I was in when Ronnie said in quick succession, "I shot Dad, I shot Mom, I shot Eric." I'll never know why he killed Mom and Eric unless he cracked once he started. We talked for a little while longer—I really don't know how long. Then I heard Eric let out a groan. I also saw he'd been beaten and bludgeoned in the head—I don't know [why]. Ronnie might have hit him because he didn't die immediately. Or possibly he hit him before he went to my parents' room to make sure Eric didn't run. Maybe he hit him before the shootings. Or maybe it was afterwards. All I know is when I saw Eric it really set me off. I wasn't sure when I heard him groan whether he was dead or alive, so it's true that I went over to him and put my hand over his face [thus "explaining" any blood on his hands]. Then I said, "Eric, go to sleep" [thus finding another consistency with his previous stories]. I wanted him to think it was a nightmare because there was no way he was going to live. When he slumped to the floor I just flipped. It's in my mind that he died in my arms since I had blood on my forearms and hands. After that I wasn't accountable. I screwed up an awful lot [thus transforming his self-serving murders into a mere excess of righteous wrath].[20]

His revised reconstruction of events continued to exonerate himself.

There was nothing I could do for Eric, so I moved back toward Ronnie's bed. Then suddenly I had an impulse to kill him for what he'd done. When I began to approach him Ronnie lay over on his side. His eyes were wide open as he pleaded, "Please help me—get me out of here." I could have called the cops right then, and I don't know why I didn't. But I saw the pistol on the window sill at the end of Ronnie's bed, and when I saw some blood on the butt that freaked me out even more. I picked it up and held it. Ronnie's eyes were closed. Then I whispered "Ronnie" and quickly pulled the trigger. There was only one bullet left and that shot killed my brother. After I shot Ronnie I freaked out totally, and the first clear thought that came to mind was "Now I'm going to get the blame for all four of the deaths," so what I started to do at that time was completely illogical.[21]

When the pastor asked, "Why didn't you turn and run for help when you saw Ronnie that night? Wouldn't that be a natural reaction when you walked in on that scene?" Harry answered this eminently reasonable question with his now-customary vagueness. " 'Who can know how they'd react?' I replied. 'People can't put themselves in this spot until it actually happens. And look at the way I was brought up and, also, the way I lived. I had taken an awful lot, and you know how I control my emotions.' Roy looked at my face, and I looked at his, as he took out his pipe. 'I just went nuts,' I told him, 'and I know I did a lot of things that I should never have done.' " Harry moved then to explain his attempt to clean up the house and hide the evidence as merely a natural reaction to his shock. "I know I did a lot of things that I should never have done. I moved some stuff around the house just to keep myself going. But now I don't remember getting from one spot to another. I wiped up certain spots of blood with long johns and a shirt on Ronnie's floor, and I even wiped off the light switch since there was blood on that. Later I chucked those clothes in my closet, and that was illogical too."[22]

Harry was then able to explain previous lies and to complete the complicated reconstruction of his story.

> My next concern, I related, was what to do with the bodies in order to protect myself from looking as though I was the one who had shot the entire family. I know that I was loose in the head, but my next move was to strip to the waist and leave only my long johns on. Then I put a towel around Ronnie's head and dragged him upstairs to our attic. I really can't remember putting him into the chest, but I guess my reason for doing this was personal survival and a half-assed way of setting myself up to say I didn't know where he was. When I told the story that Ronnie had said he'd bury my father underneath his bed that was erratic and stupid. But it provided a reason for why Dad was in Ronnie's bed. After I moved the two bodies I went in the upstairs bathroom and washed up in the sink. Ronnie had told me when we talked that he had used the shower. That Sunday the cops kept asking all day whether I'd used the shower, and when I had it up to here I finally said what they wanted and told them that I did. When I finished with the washing I put on the clothes I had taken off—the ones I'd been wearing that night. Then I went out to my mother's car. You know the rest of the story.[23]

Typically, Harry took the time to worry over relatively minor inconsistencies in his various stories. "We have a bit of discrepancy in Patrolman Olsen's statement that he saw me go through a stop sign and pulled me over for that. Instead I pulled him over when I came east on Grand Avenue and turned right at the intersection." He even volunteered "proof" for this assertion: "There's no way you shoot through a stop sign when you make a right turn. I cut around his car right away and spun my tires to stop him. What are the chances of his looking in his mirror and seeing a car run a stop sign at that time in the morning?" His lack of preparation was converted into proof of his innocence with, "People have said I was planning to escape when I encountered Olsen. But if I'd been trying to run from the house I would have loaded my car with food, camping stuff, clothing, and guns, and any money left in the house in addition to what I had on me." Now equipped, he thought, with a satisfactory explanation for all his behavior, he concluded: "If I'd been the criminal the cops said I was I could have headed for Route 304 and upstate New York. I could even have dropped the car I had, and stolen another one. Or I could have set my car on fire and then just kept going. But I didn't do any of that. I went right to the cops. And I went there instead of calling because if I called at 4:00 A.M. and told them my family was dead they'd think I was drunk or something."[24]

When his pastor asked why he had given so many conflicting stories, Harry reached for new depths of implausibility. In doing so, he convicted his brother of the murders, and himself on charges of poor punctuality. "There are several reasons," he said.

> I'd shot my brother. My family was dead. And I had no one and no place to go. They had me for Ronnie anyhow, so I figured I'd be a martyr and take all the blame myself. Ronnie and I were both guilty, it's true. But I feel more guilty myself because things might have been different if I had talked to him about drugs or if I had come home earlier instead of going for those beers. I blame myself for not doing more, since I knew about the drugs. I also found out he was getting money to buy some of his drugs by selling coins from the coin collection Pop Pop [grandfather] kept at our house. Now I hear I'm getting blamed for stealing from that collection.[25]

With a transparent cleverness that revealed the habits of his thought and the patterns of his rationalizations, Harry laid the foundation for the suggestion that he killed his brother in self-defence, as a form of preemptive strike.

> There was the matter of the pistol, too. As I told you, there was one bullet in it when I picked it up from the sill. Now this gun was a semiautomatic one that's a ten-shot clip. You can hold an

eleventh shot in the chamber, but this isn't always too wise. After I cleaned and reloaded the gun earlier in the week there were ten shells in the clip. I've learned from conversations that eleven bullets were fired that night [this was mere speculation], so, since I only loaded ten, the pistol had to be reloaded with an eleventh bullet. "It *had* to be reloaded," I explained to Roy, "because you could tell from the pistol butt that Eric had been hit on the head with that. When you hit someone with an automatic the gun is going to fire, especially when you hit hard enough to get some brain matter out. That brings up the question—who reloaded it and why? I've thought about that a lot this week, and if Ronnie opened the chamber and slid in that extra shot was he going to use it on himself or was he thinking of me? The bodies were warm when I found them so I feel the family must have been shot about fifteen minutes before I arrived. If I had been home earlier would something have happened to me? No one will ever know. But that extra bullet was strange, so now I've had a change of mind and instead of playing the martyr and taking all of the blame I want to tell the story to a few of the people I trust.[26]

We have dwelt at length on this splendid example of jailhouse logic, and barrack room law, because it reveals his ineptness and guilt. Obviously he told the story first to Nilsen in the hope that it might be believed. But why should he wish to construct such a palpable falsehood and stick to that story through the trial and throughout his years of incarceration? His own explanation for this verged on admitting that he had come to believe it himself. "Some believed me, while others discounted it. But this is the picture I have in my mind and the recollection I'll always have, no matter what anyone says." Then in what would be the closest he would come to a second confession, he remarked that "all the while I was in jail I had one ongoing wish and that was to go to the grave sites the day I got out of jail. I knew I'd have a time of remorse when I actually said farewell. But I had to control my emotions in jail, or I wouldn't have been able to survive. I'll never forget I killed Ronnie, though," he said, curiously half-acknowledging that he had already forgotten he had killed the remainder of his family.[27]

PSYCHIATRIC ASSESSMENT

I'd rather go to a funny farm than be killed in a state
prison.

—HARRY DE LA ROCHE, JR.[28]

Harry quite naturally would have preferred to be placed in a mental
hospital. This desire initiated that peculiar encounter between psychiatry
and the courts—admonished by many individual psychiatrists such as
Willard Gaylin, as well as by the American Psychiatric Association—in
which psychiatrists argue what is essentially a legal or even political case.
Dr. Joseph Zigarelli was the court-appointed psychiatrist for the prosecution; and he argued the prosecution's case most effectively, denying that
Harry was insane.[29]

Zigarelli first interviewed Harry on December 18. In his report to the
court on their one-hour session, he noted that Harry "preferred not to discuss
anything about the episode for which he was placed in jail," but was quite
willing to "discuss his entire background." Zigarelli noted that Harry

> tells how he was interested in going to a military college [and
> how he did ultimately] accept admission to The Citadel.... He
> states that he was home on a visit in November from the school.
> He informs this examiner that he intended not to return to the
> school because he felt that he was not making a satisfactory
> adjustment there. He describes in detail how he became involved
> with some of his fellow students in certain altercations where he
> felt he was being picked on. He also describes certain episodes
> which occurred in which he injured his head and describes how
> since that time he has had some dizzy spells. He states that he
> has not been examined or treated for these dizzy spells since
> their onset at school.[30]

This did not conflict with newspaper reports from The Citadel, in
which the vice president of the college had described Harry as an average
cadet who had been experiencing difficulties with his studies. However,
he added that Harry had asked to leave The Citadel early, claiming his
mother had terminal cancer, and Harry's difficulties at the college had
"accelerated a little at the time he announced to his superiors that his
mother had this illness."[31]

Regardless of these half-truths and fantasies, Zigarelli emphasized to the court that Harry's behaviour during their interview was "appropriate."

> He expresses no psychotic ideas. The area as to whether he is depressed is probed deeply and he denies any suicidal ideation or attempt. He prefers not to discuss the episode and states that he had been able to accept what did happen by feeling *that it did not happen*. Occasionally he finds himself thinking about the episode and that he wanted to speak to members of his family and then realizes that they are no longer there. He describes how he spends most of his time while in Bergen County Jail. He has been reading but has limited activity. His intelligence is estimated as slightly above average.[32]

Zigarelli's neurological examination of Harry found him to be "within normal limits except for his visual difficulty." He concluded that "we are dealing with an underlying personality disorder and possible neurological involvement (post concussion syndrome with sequelae) which warrant further study and evaluation." He emphasized that "there is no evidence of any overt psychosis in this patient and it is my considered neuropsychiatric opinion that he is not dangerous to himself or others." He recommended that Harry be placed "in a secure, controlled environment pending further study and evaluation," and suggested that he be given "a program of some activity which should include occupational and recreational therapy and some counselling." Essentially, he had determined that Harry was a mildly troubled young man who was not seriously mentally ill. He did not pursue the possible post concussion syndrome, perhaps because this theory is usually reserved for defence psychiatrists.[33]

A few weeks later, Harry's lawyer entered not-guilty pleas to all four charges of murder, but he reserved the right, pending further examinations by a defence psychiatrist, to alter the pleas to "not guilty by reason of insanity." Defence psychiatrist Dr. David Gallina's battery of psychological tests and his early diagnosis made no mention of severe disturbance, but during the actual trial his scientific testimony became more appropriate to the defence's needs, and the spectre of psychosis was raised. Still, the psychological tests revealed only mild disturbance. In the Rorschach test, "Harry gave an adequate number of responses to each of the cards with which he was presented and gave no indication of psychotic responses at any time. He gave a good affective response which included both color and form to all the responses and seemed able to spontaneously respond." In the Thematic Apperception Test, "Harry tended to respond in a guarded fashion. The chief defenses of denial and repression were indicated in the somewhat concrete descriptive answers which he gave to each of the rather emotionally stimulating pictures presented to him."[34]

However, the tests revealed "no psychotic responses," and "none of the situations elicited from Harry an extremely strong affective response." Harry scored 117 on the IQ test, and his testers commented that "there were no signs of organicity or severe depression during the course of taking the ten subtests." They also noted his good concentration and memory, and the fact that "he was able to direct his attention to the tasks required in an adequate manner." In the sentence completion test, observers saw "the same process of guardedness and the defenses of denial and repression." For example, when asked about his greatest worry, Harry said, "I am not worrying about anything," an improbability given his circumstances. His completion of the sentence, "Most women . . ." yielded the banal, "are average citizens." The testers thought "such sentence completions reveal little or nothing about his inner emotional life and tend to keep his correspondence with the outside world on a level which is designed and prone to cause as little interpersonal conflict as possible."[35]

Six months later, on June 9, 1977, Harry was examined again by both Drs. Zigarelli and Gallina. "In this interview," Harry later wrote, "Dr. Zigarelli asked me what I recalled about November 28. I told him how I walked in and found Ronnie and what I did after that. He wrote at the end of the June interview: 'We are now seeing an individual who is in his own way attempting to control much inner emotional and mental conflict. The exact psychodynamics of this conflict still warrant some psychometric evaluation and some further probing into the actual experiences that Harry had at the time of the episode.' " Zigarelli reaffirmed his position that "there is no evidence of any overt psychotic reaction in this individual," and concluded that "he is mentally competent, is able to consult with his counsel in his adequate defense and is legally sane according to the McNaughton standards." He urged that the previously recommended neurological and electroencephalographic examinations be carried out.[36]

At that time, Dr. Gallina essentially concurred with Zigarelli that Harry was not insane, that he "was mentally competent to stand trial and that he could and would cooperate in his defense," and was therefore legally sane. Gallina found "nothing in his mental status examination or psychological profile to indicate that he was prone to crimes of violence or that he was a danger to society." He merely noted that Harry was extremely guarded about revealing himself in an open fashion, which might produce a conflict with his environment. He is rigid and holds to a perfectionist view of himself, which is not flexible in adjusting to changing situations in his life or in his immediate environment. Acknowledging problems is seen by him as a weakness, which was the view held by his father, and is held to be unacceptable. He has a great need to be strong, capable, and completely invulnerable and has built his defense system to comply with these needs. He is, however, highly defensive and many of his actions and outward appearances are not, I feel, indicative of his inner emotional life.[37]

Gallina thought that Harry's chief defences "are the primitive ones of denial and repression, although they are *not utilized to a psychotic degree.*" He found it

extremely difficult to engage Harry in an intimate interpersonal relationship, although he has the social skills to be outgoing and sociable, although always quite guarded. He has a tendency to take on too much responsibility and is burdened by such responsibility but will not recognize the extent of the burden. His anxiety level tends to be quite high because of the lack of resolution for the many conflicts in his life and this can lead him to being impulsive. He ultimately does have a hard time in adhering to duties or ways of doing things which are imposed by others, and he will tend to resent such activity as he did adherence to the unreasonable demands of his father.[38]

Gallina concluded that Harry was

afraid of being in a passive and what he determines an effeminate state of non-competitiveness and will compensate for these fears with rigid patterns of behavior which will deny the existence of any soft, passive, or effeminate feelings in him at all. The application of these character traits to the incidents which led up to and culminated in the deaths of the members of his family can only be conjectured. The family situation certainly was an inflexible one in which conflict was not resolved among the various members through discussions or reasonable behavior. Rigidity was the hallmark characteristic, particularly of Harry's father, and such rigidity could not live with conflict. One side or the other had to comply. Harry seemed continually torn by the mixed loyalties that he felt to himself as an individual and to what at times were the unreasonable demands of his family. His actions on that evening appeared to be impulsive and not of the deliberate, premeditated type, but rather explosion of emotions which resulted from internal conflicts that undoubtedly went back many years.

Neither psychiatrist mentioned Harry's ominous fabrication of the imminent death of his mother from terminal cancer.[39]

As the trial approached, Dr. Gallina and Harry's lawyer prepared him for what lay ahead. As Harry remembered it, "We went through everything that day and he tried to shake me up with Christmas pictures of my family that would call back memories. Both John [the lawyer] and the doctor wanted to see if I would break when I saw them because they knew that the prosecution would barbecue my hide. I talked and I looked, however, and I didn't break a bit," Harry admitted, without quite apprehending the significance of what could be interpreted as either strength or indifference.[40]

During the trial, however, lawyers and psychiatrist for the defence changed their strategy and raised the issue of insanity. The defence had first asked for a verdict of not guilty on three counts of murder, and not guilty because of temporary insanity on the count of Ronnie's murder. Now they surprised the court by changing their defence to one of "general insanity on all four counts." The psychiatric diagnosis now took a rather different form. Dr. Gallina observed that "everything is black and white to this boy. He sees his growing up in only one of two ways, either he does what his parents want from him or he doesn't do what his parents want from him. There's no middle ground. There's no bending. There's a rigid, fixed kind of person . . . it doesn't bend, it just snaps. This is the rigidity of this boy's basic personality structure. He's a very distrustful and guarded type of person. No one really knows what his feelings are until the feelings just explode and come out."[41]

Harry quite naturally preferred this version. As he later wrote,

when Dr. Gallina began to talk about the night of the murders he said that at that time I was psychotic, emotionally trapped, and residing in a pressure cooker of fear. As he talked directly to the jury he described a personality conflict that developed between my father and me over my education at The Citadel. He testified that during Thanksgiving vacation I became obsessed with the thought that I couldn't return to school, but I was torn between my desire to leave and my desire to stay and please my father and work out what I was supposed to do. The conflict between these desires was intense, and the problem was I couldn't bring myself to confront my father because my father would withdraw his love. I couldn't contend with the impulsive and violent reaction I anticipated, and I wasn't equipped to deal with this stress.[42]

When both judge and prosecutor complained that Dr. Gallina had reversed himself, the defence lawyer made the fine distinction that the original diagnosis had only referred to Harry's ability to cooperate in his own defence, not to his state of mind at the time of the killings. As Harry later recorded, Dr. Gallina testified

that at the moment of the deaths I was no longer in control and unable to make judgments. He said that emotions were running my life and that my mind was not registering such external facts as what's right, what's wrong, what the law is, what might happen to me, or even what the consequences were of what I was doing to the people involved. "I don't think Harry would have available to him at that time of the killings the intellectual process to know what he was doing, or even to realize the concept of death," he pointed out. "Before his emotions exploded he was hopelessly trapped between two hopeless situations." Then he went on to explain to the jury that the acts after the murders might be the result of a person coming out of psychosis, a person who is frightened because of what had happened.[43]

Gallina tried to explain to the court why he had reversed his position. "The report was written in an attempt to give a fair and complete appraisal of Harry De La Roche's character structure and personality," and he insisted that his initial diagnosis had not required him to assess Harry's mental status at the time of the murders. Thus Harry could write,

Dr. Gallina went on to reemphasize that the report only dealt with my state of mind during the psychiatric examination and that at that time I did not suffer from a psychosis. He said the psychotic behavior was presently in remission but held it could be triggered by any stressful situation at any time. "His prepsychotic personality has been with him for many years, and it could not be ruled out that he could be suicidal," he declared. "This is a person who under pressure such as prison is capable of doing harm to himself. He could reach such heights that he could again become psychotic as he did on that night. He needs long-term hospitalization, drugs, and psychotherapy."[44]

Harry seemed well-pleased with the defence lawyer's summation which

> pictured me as a dazed psychotic who couldn't sense right from wrong on November 28, and, as he paced in front of the jury, he said I was sick and in need of help. He mentioned my life at The Citadel—and my desire to quit—and declared I had lived in two private hells, one, the hell at The Citadel and two, the hell of not being able to talk to my father. "Then the clock ticks and it is almost time to return to his hell," said John. "The pressure cooker builds. Harry comes home, and he sat there with a gun. He walked back and forth in his parents' bedroom, and he finally screams out 'I can't go back' and then Harry starts firing the weapon, and his family is gone. A rational boy," he told the jury, "could have said, 'Pop, I'm not going back ...' He was psychotic," John stated. "You can't tell me that anyone who killed his family is not mentally insane."

The lawyer also argued that Harry's clumsy secretion of both the pistol and Ronnie's body in the attic was further evidence of his psychosis; he closed his argument with an emotional plea that his client "can be salvaged. While ill now, there may be a future for Harry De La Roche."[45]

The prosecution's psychiatrist reached precisely the opposite conclusion. Dr. Zigarelli insisted that Harry understood the nature of his acts and had the ability to distinguish right from wrong: he was therefore quite sane under the McNaughton Rule. Harry was offended by Zigarelli: "I thought he was patronizing on the stand and sometimes it seemed he talked as much about being a major in the Second World War as he did about my case. He said he'd examined me on three occasions and testified I was not psychotic when my family was slain."[46]

Harry thought the prosecution lawyer's rebuttal of the defence case agreed

> that I was sick and in need—but contended I'd weighed the four murders. "Of course, he's sick," he [the prosecution lawyer]

stated. "You'd have to be sick to do what he did. You may think he needs hospitalization. You may think he's crazy. But that doesn't mean he's legally insane. If anything, Mr. De La Roche is not out of touch with reality," he declared. "If he was, he could not have given this statement. It tells us what he was thinking. That's the key word: what he was thinking. He knew what was going on when he was doing it. You don't come up with details like this unless you were there. What he did subsequent to the murders is indicative of knowing. He said he switched bodies and hid the gun twice. These are thought processes."[47]

After Harry's trial and conviction, the psychiatrists took less political stances. Gallina said the real issue was not Harry's role in the murders, but

the family pathology that's back of everything. If by any chance two brothers were murderers that night the focus on the family pathology is even more intense. But the fact that anyone pulled a trigger has to say something about that family. I believe that all five members had a very limited ability to communicate with each other and express and share their emotions and feelings. Harry is the perfect example of a psychological breakdown—of a person who says, "I can't take it any more." But, still, he was tied to his family with bonds that kept him from running away.

An experienced local psychiatrist, Dr. Alan Tuckman, put the matter more succinctly when he observed that people had to be able to release pressure: "I think the lesson to be learned from this case is that you cannot repress or oppress people in a family and not expect them to react with rage."[48]

SOCIAL HISTORY OF THE FAMILY

We looked like the ideal American family people thought we were. But beneath this pleasant picture a war raged in our home.

—HARRY DE LA ROCHE, JR.[49]

It seems such madness. A young man, from a family of modest means, does not wish to return to his military college. His father wishes him to do so. The young man is tied to his family neither by the promise of great wealth nor love. Yet rather than simply leave home and become an independent person, he murders his entire family, condemning himself to years in prison. We have already seen that some commentators on the case assumed Harry to be psychotic at the time of the killings; but other, equally qualified, psychiatrists have dismissed this notion. Other observers of the case have assumed that something in The Citadel was so vile and terrifying that Harry would do anything to avoid returning, but there is no evidence whatever that more than routine adolescent harassment and cruelty was Harry's lot at the military college. Moreover, as he has himself admitted, many of his contacts at the college were exceptionally sensitive and kind. There seems to be no sense to this story, no explanation for the family's remarkable rigidity, unless we look elsewhere. The origins of this familicide lie neither in the college nor in Harry, Jr.'s psyche, but in the social history of the De La Roche family.

Scrutiny of the De La Roche family tree reveals an extraordinary story of radical downward social mobility and frantic attempts to reclaim that lost status. One of the major insights of sociology has been its awareness of the corrosive insecurity generated in individuals by any dramatic rise or fall in the social ladder; and a thousand studies have demonstrated how that class-generated insecurity reveals itself in diverse ways, from the embrace of the production of racist or sexist attitudes, to delinquent children. The family was distinguished on the maternal side: Harry, Jr.'s maternal great-grandfather, George Bronson Howard, was a well-connected and celebrated popular author and playwright at the turn of the century. The family's biographer, Roberta Roesch, tells us that by the time Howard was a young man, he was writing popular magazine stories. Later, he wrote romances, essays, plays, criticism, and musical revues, served as a vaudeville impresario in Paris and a librettist for the Winter Garden in New York, collaborated in two plays with Booth Tarkington and David Belasco, and worked with the original Follies Bergère. His most famous work, *The Red Light of Mars,* was published in 1913. When he and his wife separated, she moved to an artist's colony in Edgewater, New York, while Howard and their daughter Margaret (Harry, Jr.'s grandmother) lived together in Greenwich Village. Here, Margaret was raised in a cultivated and literary atmosphere, and father and daughter shared their company and their literary interests. Margaret's fate, however, led in other directions: while visiting her mother in Edgewater, she met Ronald Greer, a traffic manager. The unsuitable romance shocked her father and when Margaret married Ronald her father disowned her, mortified that she had married so much beneath her. Their daughter, Harry, Jr.'s. mother, Mary Jane, graduated from high school in 1943 and took a position teaching sewing in a Singer sewing machine shop, where she met Harry, Sr.[50]

If the maternal side of the family had fallen precipitously in the social order, the paternal side was struggling to rise. Harry, Sr. was the illegitimate child of Johanna (Honey) De La Roche, and she raised him on her own until she married Ernie Ebneter when Harry, Sr. was an adolescent; Harry kept his mother's maiden name, De La Roche. Harry's mother and her mother shared in rearing him, and Roesch notes that while both mother and grandmother were proud of Harry, their pride "couldn't protect him, however, from the taunts he got because he had no father, and some made it a point to mock him and call him a bastard." According to Roesch, Harry began to carry a knife. Harry's mother had two brothers, but he had no relationship with these maternal uncles because he felt that, as an illegitimate child, they would not accept him. Harry, Sr.'s childhood friend Steve Madreperla remembered watching him nervously approach his uncles' house for the first time when he was twelve.[51]

Harry, Sr. graduated from high school in 1950 and went to work in a factory that manufactured Christmas tree balls; he enlisted in the Navy in 1952 and served on a destroyer in the Korean War. When he returned to civilian life he took a position as a serviceman with the Singer Sewing Machine Company, where he met his wife, Mary Jane, seven years his senior. The Greers did not approve of the match any more than the grandfather had approved of Margaret's choice, even though Mary Jane was by the standards of the time well past prime marriageable age. According to family lore, Mary Jane's father passionately opposed the match, telling his daughter "there's something about that man." The young couple moved to a little home on Avenue F in Lodi, a grimy New Jersey industrial town. It would not be long before Margaret, the daughter of the internationally celebrated playwright, would be reduced to a kind of beggary.[52]

Struggling to raise a family on a sewing-machine serviceman's salary, Harry, Jr.'s parents jumped at the chance for a form of social mobility when Mary Jane's mother, Margaret, needing someone to live with her to help with housing costs and her medications, invited them to share her more substantial home in Montvale, New Jersey. Under this new arrangement, everyone would save money, Margaret's personal needs would be attended to, and the young couple would enhance their comfort and social status in the better home. According to Roesch, the family drew up a formal agreement, which made the three adults joint tenants of the house and specified that the young couple would inherit the house when Margaret died. Harry, Sr. converted the home into a two-family dwelling with a separate apartment for Margaret.[53]

As Harry, Jr. later wrote of the period,

> on the surface our lives appeared to be good, and in our Christ-mas picture for 1964 we looked like the ideal American family people thought we were. But beneath this pleasant picture a war raged in our home. On our side, my father, as I've said, disliked my Grandma Greer's ways. From her side she objected to how he was bringing us up. His word was law and when we'd ask "Why?" he'd say "Because—and that's it." Sometimes he'd throw me down the steps for doing what he didn't like, and once when we visited Uncle John and Aunt Arden he swung at me and missed. But he swung with such strength his hand was bloody from the impact of hitting the wall. In fact, the ring he was wearing made a permanent hole in that wall. Sometimes his temper got so out of hand we'd be punished for something we didn't do just because we were there. Later, if he felt that he'd been wrong he'd try to make up for it, and just by the way he did something for you you'd know that he was sorry. He never said "I'm sorry," though. That wasn't in his nature. Because of their differing set ideas he and my grandmother fought, and soon there were constant conflicts—and open battles—between them. My mother, in a passive way, tried to keep peace in the house.[54]

But the conflict between the daughter of the internationally celebrated playwright and the illegitimate sewing machine serviceman inevitably intensified. Harry remembered that within two years of the move to the new home,

> hostilities grew so bitter my grandmother conveyed her interest in the property to my Uncle John. This complicated financial matters, and there were even more fights. My father openly disliked Uncle John for standing up for my grandmother, so as relationships dwindled, Uncle John always visited us when my father wasn't home. My father also refused to keep on getting my

grandmother's medications, so either Aunt Arden or Uncle John had to do that again. Eventually my mother yielded completely to my father's wishes and I'd hear my grandmother on the phone asking Aunt Arden to take her to the doctor's because my mother had indicated she couldn't continue to do that. Sometimes she'd call Aunt Arden for food and on those times she'd say, "Mary Jane 'forgot' my things when she shopped today."[55]

Even when Harry, Sr. found a position processing orders for the Ford Motor Company's international sales division, family relations continued to deteriorate. "I was too young to do anything," Harry, Jr. remembered,

but I wasn't too young to see that, slowly but surely, Grandma Greer was being forced out of the house. I heard more fights than my parents knew, and later, when I was older, I learned that on one Saturday night my uncle and aunt were served with a summons instituted by my parents, stating my mother and father were taking my Grandma Greer to court to get her out of the house. There were many legal hassles I didn't understand. But I know, among some other things, my father itemized his expenses for taking care of the house from the time we moved to Montvale till he started the legal action. Finally the matter was settled without going to court. But the day my black-haired Grandma Greer, with her wise and loving ways, went out of the Montvale house for good, something went out of my life.

Clearly, what had departed was the only love in Harry, Jr.'s life: the family was to pay dearly for her exit.[56]

With the triumph of Harry, Sr.'s maneuvering, the last adult not under his absolute control left the familial orbit. "Uncle John found an apartment for her close to where he lived," Harry, Jr. remembered,

but my parents wouldn't take us to visit and I never saw her again. She used to phone my mother and beg her to bring us down, and after she died—with a broken heart—one closet in her apartment was filled with wrapped-up presents for Eric, Ronnie, and me. There were gifts for every occasion since she'd moved out of the house, in the hope my mother would change her mind and let her see us again. That day never came, however, and when she died she said in her will: "I leave nothing to my daughter for reasons known to her and to me." Everyone but my father went to her funeral, however, and for a short time after that we occasionally saw Uncle John and Aunt Arden.

The final excision of all family took place after a conflict-ridden Christmas visit: "my parents never called them again. For years I didn't see the Greers and they never heard from me—until I phoned one Sunday and said in a broken voice, 'Uncle John, this is Harry. I'm at the Montvale Police Station, and Mom and Dad and Eric are dead.' "[57]

THE EVOLUTION OF A FAMILICIDE

> As roots the tree, close clings the vine
> So doth my heart to thine entwine
> Charming Prince Hatchy, be my Valentine.
>
> —FROM HARRY, JR.'S BELOVED GRANDMOTHER[58]

Like Steven Benson, Harry, Jr. was the obedient little boy whose obsequiousness and inappropriateness lost him the respect of his peers. As one family friend commented, "Harry, Jr. had a difficult time making friends. It's true that everyone would pick on him." As Harry told his biographer, "I was the butt of first-grade jokes, and the kid who was always picked on and beaten up by others. When I had to wear glasses—by third grade—the kids mocked me even more. I wasn't one to fight, however. Instead I tried to please. But no matter what I did or said I got the reputation of being a whipping boy." Later in the Boy Scouts older campers teased and tormented him, once tying him to a tree and leaving him there. Ever dutiful, he rose to the rank of junior assistant scout master, and was a member of both the Leadership Corps and the Senior Patrol.[59]

If his father's rigid paternalistic rule appears to have obviated much kindness, Harry, Jr. received encouragement from his church's pastor and basketball team coach, who "more or less rooted for me." Harry, Sr. was coach of the Little League baseball teams and manager of the Montvale Athletic League. Harry, Jr. said he "wasn't the natural athlete that my two brothers were," but obediently, "I went out for Little League to comply with my father's wishes. I didn't really like it, though, because, as my father's son, I sometimes felt I got the brunt more than anyone else." One of his father's interests that he did share in was firearms, "which my father always encouraged. Guns represented power to him, but my mother really despised them and tried her best to ignore the four my father kept in the house. As always though, she deferred to him, so his rifle was usually under their bed. His 9mm automatic pistol was always under the mattress, and a loaded High Standard .22-calibre pistol was in his bedside table." Harry became a skilled marksman, and an instructor at the gun club.[60]

The De La Roches were not narrowly athletic in their aspirations for their sons, and scholarship was also demanded. "School marks came first," Harry later said, "and if our marks were low my father made us stay in at night until the next report card. He always wanted to pull us up to our very best and highest, so whenever we had a low mark he'd give us work on his own and then he'd check on us every night and keep track of the progress we made." At school, Harry, Jr. retained his unassertiveness. Bullied by the school's athletes, Harry remembered a friend shouting, " 'Fight back,' he begged, 'at least just once. Let them know that you can!' " But he could not: he had been conditioned otherwise, and by the eighth grade he had folded inside himself, deciding "once and for all to work problems out on my own and never let anybody know how I felt inside." He continued trying to please his father, dressing in the unfashionable clothes he demanded: he played his father's preferred game of baseball for three years before, in a tiny assertive gesture, he switched to soccer.[61]

Yet it seemed to the emerging person who was Harry, Jr. that nothing he did was appreciated; that no matter how intense his efforts to ingratiate himself with his father, they came to nothing. His father always found and dwelt upon, the flaw in any achievement. When Harry, Jr. landed his first after-school job, "a high point in my life, and a really big day for me," and proudly broke the news to his father, "my father was furious when he found out that all I knew was I had the job—and no further information. 'Why didn't you ask questions?' Dad hollered. 'Why didn't you get details? What about insurance and raises? Didn't you ask *anything*? There's a right way to get a job if you want to get anywhere,' " admonished the man who had not gotten anywhere.[62]

The family was ruled by a regimen of complex and arbitrary rules and regulations. As the eldest son, Harry was subject to the stiffest rules: "We lived by rules at our house during my high school years," he remembered. "One of the rules I hated most was having to get in early when my friends could stay out later. In my freshman year at Pascack Hills I had to be in at 8:00. Yet when Ronnie was a freshman he could stay out till

11:00. As always, I was a proving ground and subjected to the stiffest rules." His father would invariably refuse to explain the rules and regulations, intensifying their apparent meaninglessness. "Our conversations through the years would usually follow this pattern: 'Dad, is it all right if I do this?' 'No, I don't want you to do it.' 'But why?' 'Because.' 'But because why?' 'Because—and that will be it.' "[63]

Harry, Jr. typically deferred to these rules. "As I grew older I understood how ambitious he was for us and so when he said I had to do something I usually complied." Only occasionally does he remember asserting himself.

> I particularly remember one evening when I asked for the car. "Absolutely not!" Dad told me, not looking up from his paper. "The weather is bad, and it's raining. You're not going anywhere." At that point I showed my stubborn streak and answered with "Everyone is going—and I'm going too." "Oh, no you're not!" he retorted. "Oh, yes I am," I answered and I went out of the door. I walked to where I wanted to go and when I returned in two hours he didn't say anything. Ronnie and Eric stayed scared of Dad. But I wasn't as afraid after that, and eventually, as I grew taller, he couldn't pick me up by my hair. In fact, the last time he hit me, the most he could do was grab my shirt and pull till the buttons ripped off.[64]

Despite his one successful, if tiny, act of rebellion, Harry remained wrapped in his submissiveness. A brief period of happiness as a senior in high school, when he "felt like a top person," was ended by the pressure to select a suitable career. One family friend remembered how "his parents felt it would be the best thing for him to go to military school, but he just hated it and began rebelling." For the aspiring family, The Citadel would open to their son a commission in the armed services. According to Harry, Sr.'s acquaintances in the athletic leagues, Harry, Sr. had a "Prussian aura," "was always telling Harry, Jr. how to run his life, and he wasn't realistic in what he expected from the boys. He tried to make the decisions about everything Harry did." Acting under these orders, the passive son agreed to go to the college to please his father: "My father was terribly proud of The Citadel acceptance, and he wanted me to go so much I wanted to make him happy instead of letting him down."[65]

"My father has my whole life planned," he complained to a friend. Perhaps the awareness that he was living another man's life accentuated his customary social ineptness: in any case, within a few weeks of residence at The Citadel, he was the butt of jokes and humiliations as he had been in high school. Moreover, the primitive coping strategies of withdrawal and foolish remarks that he had developed within his own family merely served to intensify his alienation from his fellow cadets. He remembered "crazy table games . . . like eating just with your mouth. About once a month we'd have cream puffs, and then there would be a contest in which you were told to turn your plate over, put the cream puff on the plate, and, while sitting on your hands, eat the cream puff solely with your mouth." An adolescent at peace with himself and his environment might enjoy these harmless diversions, but Harry merely withdrew: "I said I wouldn't do it, and when cadre members persuaded me with threats I clammed up and didn't acknowledge they were even talking to me."[66]

As his perceived isolation increased, he doubled his inappropriate reactions: "When more and more things got to me I became more defiant. I developed a habit of explaining things which pissed everybody off, and instead of answering, 'Yes, Sir' or 'No, Sir' I'd add something else, too." Yet he did not hate The Citadel: "I made some friends. . . . But even with those good times I had many troubled moments, and as early as mid-September I thought of changing schools. I didn't hate The Citadel, but I hated a few people in it." What he hated most, of course, was that he was there. As early as mid-September, he began to think of leaving the school, but to do so would mean defying his parents' will. "What would I tell my parents? It would hurt them badly if I mentioned dropping out, especially since they'd taken a loan to cover my first year's expenses."[67]

He began to raise the matter in letters to his parents. As one family friend remembered, "I talked to his mother a couple of weeks ago and she said he was having a difficult time adjusting but that she thought it would take just a little more time." After an extended series of letters, reprinted in *Anyone's Son,* Harry capitulated as he had done all his life: "In the end I decided to stick it out and stay for the rest of the year. . . . On campus I started to stay in my room as much as I possibly could." Harry proposed to his parents that he be allowed to transfer out of The Citadel the following year, so as not to waste the tuition monies, but "when they gave me a solid 'No' I decided there was no further point in staying at The Citadel. But I couldn't write back and tell them that if I couldn't transfer I was leaving school—and I wasn't ready to mention that maybe I'd even move out of the house and work and pay for another college as soon as I got enough money. My father wouldn't like that. But

I'd tell him, 'This is my choice,' and if I were paying for it myself he couldn't do very much." Alas, this was impossible bravado.[68]

By November, the internal conflict generated by this dispute with the family was made flesh in a series of psychosomatic complaints. "I wasn't feeling well so I went to the infirmary and stayed for three days for diarrhea, plus nausea and vomiting." He tried out his rebellious plans on his few friends: "As I mentioned to more and more people that I might not return from Thanksgiving everyone started saying I ought to do everything I could to try to come back till Christmas so I could get credits for a semester." Even then, he found his resolve "wavering, because, while I told some people 'I may not be back from Thankgiving,' I also told some others 'I'll probably stay till Christmas.' I decided to keep the door open and not take my property home." Besides, he added with characteristic timidity, "if I had my things with me my parents would think it was funny, and I'd have to tell them right away that I was planning to leave."[69]

What had accentuated the conflict was the series of letters from his parents. On September 17 his mother had written, "Uncle Steve and Aunt Dorian seemed awed by your going to The Citadel. It has a wonderful rating. People are quite impressed when they hear you are there." Having emphasized Harry's familial role as status-bearer, she admonished: "Now about changing schools. Forget it. On every count it would be the wrong move. You would lose too much of what college is all about. You have money in uniforms that would be wasted. To go to a school two years here, two years there you belong to nothing. A Citadel man is one who went through four years, not an in-and-outer." Two days later, his father wrote to emphasize that he would be "nothing" if he left: "You would end up being nothing. You wouldn't have the true Citadel education or background and you need that to have your great life." Thus both father and mother reaffirmed that he would be invalidated as a person, become a "nothing," if he followed his own preferences. By November 9, his father was confident enough that his will would be obeyed that he could write, "When you graduate [from the Citadel] will you get a commission in the regular army or in the reserves? I think it would be better in the regular army if you can."[70]

When Harry returned home for the Thanksgiving holidays, his habitual fearful deference to his parents forced him to delay discussing the matter. "I didn't say much about college while riding home in the car, and when my parents asked questions, I answered, 'I'll tell you later on.'

Later there wasn't much chance for this, since I wasn't home a great deal." When his friends asked about his plans, "I kept pretty quiet, and I usually tried to make it appear that I'd be going back. I often just said, 'It's okay' when people asked me about it, though I told certain people— like Steve and some of the others—some of the things that happened and how hard it really was. Steve and a few of the others knew I planned to pack it in. But even they weren't exactly sure whether I'd quit after getting my things or whether I'd stay till Christmas. I guess you couldn't expect them to know when I sometimes wavered myself." He seems to have been still uncertain when he spent one morning listening to music and cleaning the High Standard pistol, loading its magazine with ten cartridges before putting it back in the drawer. He may even have believed what he said, that he intended to take the pistol out to the shooting range.[71]

As the holidays drew to a close, the pressure to take his stand grew intolerable. Yet he could not bear the possibility of a confrontation with such overpowering personalities.

> I knew the time was getting short for talking about my plans. But, still, I couldn't bring myself to say, "I'm leaving The Citadel." There was always Sunday morning. Maybe I could say it then. I also had in the back of my mind that if I was questioned at supper I'd say, "I'm still on vacation. I'll tell you about school at Christmas, I'll tell you everything then." I didn't have to say this, though, because I was able to get out of the house before any questions arose. There was never a confrontation about my leaving school. . . . In my week with my family there was never a time that we ever discussed the big things on our minds. None of us knew what the other was thinking, and we left it at that.

Indeed. They had always done so.[72]

DECIPHERING HARRY

> As far as Harry doing it, Harry wouldn't have had the
> guts to do a thing like that.
>
> —STEVE MAHONEY[73]

The more people knew of Harry, Jr., the harder they found it to believe that he had annihilated his family, and his closest friend, Mahoney, could not believe it at all. Yet others glimpsed the truth. "The lid blew off for Harry," said one high school friend. "If only he'd been able to let off steam and come to an understanding about his relationships with his parents." Another schoolmate thought that "basically he's taken care of, so I don't think the death of his family is any great loss to him. He has alleviated the problem, and the pressure is off." One student speculated that Harry "might have shot his father not only to get out from under him but also to keep him from being hurt because he was leaving school. Then he had to shoot his mother because he couldn't face her after shooting his father. The same thing would be true of his brothers. How could he look at either of them after shooting his parents? He may have thought when everyone was gone he'd really have his own life." In an important sense of course he was right, for Harry's identity was so squashed by authority that, one sergeant at The Citadel recalled, if he praised Harry "he'd beam and grow eight feet tall. But when you told him he was doing something wrong, it made him feel he could do nothing right."[74]

His remarkable, and typical, indifference to the killings expressed itself in a number of ways, not the least of which was his occasional "forgetting" what had happened. Being driven to court by the police, what he "wanted most," he thought, "was to get out of jail and go home. But, then, when I'd think of the red frame house and mention, 'I want to go home,' I'd suddenly realize what I'd said and remember there was no home." But his indifference was primarily characterized by the absence of emotion that struck the spectators at the trial. One experienced journalist remarked, "It was incredible to watch and sketch him while he read his dead mother's letters and recounted the gory death of his younger brother without the slightest show of emotion. Whoever was responsible for creating what I felt was a zombie perhaps received the full penalty for their efforts." Harry was aware of the response he was generating in the courtroom, and commented that "people in court kept saying I seemed too cool and calm." But any passion he felt was about his punishment, not about the loss of his family; thus it was only when the judge ruled Harry's confession admissible that "I reacted so strongly I wanted to throw the water pitcher [at the judge]."[75]

Harry, Sr.'s lifelong friend, Steve Madreperla, gave a generous assessment of the father's motives: "He wanted strength and security for his sons, and while some people thought his approach to this was a too-stiff discipline, others might call it a dedication to what he thought was right.

His family was everything to him. But there was something about his discipline and Harry, Jr.'s chemistry that didn't mix." A thoughtful neighbour echoed a more widespread feeling when he exonerated the perpetrator: "Personally, I think Harry, Jr. was a victim of his own family life. He's also his own worst enemy—and he doesn't know how to change this. . . . Did they contribute to their own demise by failing to be responsive enough to what was best for Harry? And in trying to do what they felt was right were they going by *their* plans for Harry instead of Harry's plans for himself?" Undoubtedly this was the case; but it still leaves us without an explanation for the parents' creation of a stultifying regime, or the child's homicidal acts.[76]

AN INTERPRETATION

I'm not a cold, heartless bastard, and a lot of people know it.

—HARRY, JR.[77]

The formation of a relatively mobile society, whose members may in the process of realizing their individual potential rise or fall in the social order, has been one of the great achievements of modern civilization. To a remarkable extent, this creative act has freed us from the humiliating rituals intrinsic to societies based on inherited class and caste. Yet however progressive a social development may be, it carries with it an unintended side effect; few liberations fail to present the newly unchained with a different set of fetters.

One of sociology's earliest insights focuses on the personal anguish that may be provoked in some individuals by radical social mobility. Intense anxiety and insecurity can be the lot of those who rise or fall dramatically in their own lifetimes. A similar status-induced anguish can grip those who desperately desire such a rise, or those who cling to the bottom of a class they once occupied in confidence—the "genteel family in reduced circumstances." Such anxiety is a consequence of a morbid fear of status deprivation, and may be experienced by the individual as a terror that achievement might never come, or having come might be lost. These fears often manifest themselves in an extraordinary rigidity of thought and expression: thus it may be felt that only one race or gender is worthy of respect; or there is only one correct way to hold a fork; or only one career that could be acceptable to a family.

Harry, Sr. was raised as an illegitimate and working-class child, feeling he was shunned by his own family in a society which at that time was obsessed with procreative "purity." Yet for an aspiring young man, there was more to overcome than a spurious social stain: there was a real absence of information on how to negotiate a social rise. Just as Steven Benson was not taught how to run a great corporation but was merely encoded with a frantic desire to be a millionaire; so Harry, Sr. was not given the middle-class tools to ensure his family's rise but was merely inculcated with an intense desire. He demonstrated his social ambitions when he married a woman who was much older than himself: by the demeaning standards of the time, one of Mary Jane's primary attractions was her high-status background, for she was the granddaughter of the internationally celebrated playwright who had lived in Paris, London, and New York.

The street gangs among whom he roamed as a young man must have taught Harry, Sr. the use of that class's primary resource—physical force. Thus once the tactics of violence and intimidation are learned, it can be carried over into parenting, as his son has testified. Harry, Sr. was no better or worse than any other human being: he had his dreams and he could harness to them only what knowledge he had. From the beginning, Roesch wrote, the prevailing goal of his life "had been upward mobility." Moreover, he struggled for what he perceived to be the correct social credentials, winning "kudoes for his community work with the Boy Scouts, Masons, American Legion, Christ Lutheran Church, and Montvale Athletic League." At least one neighbour thought the De La Roches "did more for these activities than anyone else in Montvale. They're going to be missed by a lot of people." If his humanity seemed consumed by his desire to achieve, if he disciplined his sons with insensitivity and harshness, his friend was still correct to insist that "in many ways he should be admired for his hopes and aspirations for his family."[78]

In such an angry and intimidating familial milieu, however, a sensitive child who is failing the family's evaluative index may begin to feel entrapped as his or her needs are swept aside by the overwhelming force of the dominant parent. Some children learn to cope with this intense molding by cynically rejecting it in private while publicly seeming to go along with it. Others submissively struggle to internalize their parents' expectations. Yet some, for reasons that social scientists understand no better than anyone else, refuse to tolerate this daily assault on their integrity. This invasion of their persona eats away at their self-esteem and engenders great anger, which struggles for supremacy with their fear of their parents. In this manner Harry, Jr. stumbled dumbly toward a refusal.

For someone with substantial personal resources, this refusal might have led merely to a small rebellion. But Harry did not have these resources. Reared to be the vehicle for his family's claim to loftier status, he struggled for his parents' approval in a regime of iron discipline. Despite his many reservations, he enrolled at The Citadel, offering his life as hostage to the family's aspirations. However, his social awkwardness ensured that he would come to feel alienated from the college milieu. Moreover, his suppressed desire to be his own person clashed with his agreement to give the family the officer and gentleman they expected. The internal conflict thus generated personal confusion and the variety of psychosomatic complaints: only decisive action would cure his headaches and diarrhea. Yet his profound insecurity made him prevaricate. At home for the holidays, he found himself fabricating any excuse to avoid confronting the family.

Families are the entire world to their children. Even children in late adolescence may fail to grasp that there is a world outside into which they can escape. From this warped perspective then, the adolescent in turmoil may come to feel that the only escape from the family is to destroy it. They do not kill only the dominant parent, but the entire family. Harry, Jr.'s family all played a role in his suppression, since his mother and brothers backed his father. One neighbour had commented that, "The family didn't work together, and I always felt that the brothers teased Harry, Jr. a lot. I was in that house just twice, and I never wanted to return. Everyone was on young Harry's back. Nothing he did was right." As French historians Peter and Favret wrote of a nineteenth-century familicide, his killings smashed through his immobility so that "something should happen, start to live, to move, to question, to disturb. The event was freedom; it cut like a blade."[79]

Thus there can be an underlying rationality to the insanity of familicide. Since Harry could bear neither the prospect of living out someone else's life at The Citadel nor the fear of confronting his family with his defiant refusal, it made a certain sense to take the one bloody course that would solve both problems. In annihilating his family, he took a decisive step that would allow him to claim his own identity and, in eliminating any possibility of a confrontation with his family, spare him the agony of trying to seize his manhood in the face of his omnipotent father. Nor would he be forced to explain his acts to any of them, for he would dispatch them all. He would not even have to explain it to himself, since his memory would graciously yield, allowing him to forget any negative role he might have played. In his own terms, and given the interaction between the regime of fear and his own limited imagination, there was a certain logic to the killings.

AN ADIEU

At this writing, Harry still sits in prison in Yardville, New Jersey, awaiting his first eligibility for parole in the early 1990s. He and I exchanged letters through much of 1984. His concern then appeared to be proving the truth of his innocence in all but Ronnie's murder. "Don't judge," he admonished me, "unless you have all the facts." Simultaneously, he insisted on exploring various stratagems—while discussing homicide in academic terms—for gaining parole. He asked if I had considered the well-known Twinkie Effect: "I believe it was a case in Florida (or maybe California) where the defense blamed the high sugar content of junk food on a particular murder." When I replied that "I believe in the Twinkie Effect exactly as much as I believe in the Easter Bunny," he seemed to lose interest in our correspondence. Certainly he never wrote to me again. That was a pity, but any sympathetic and insightful parole board will surely see how he was deformed enough by his family to do what he did.[80]

The Buick Dealership's Service Manager
Ronald Joseph "Butch" DeFeo, Jr.*

> I wouldn't kill anybody for money. If I wanted money,
> I'd rob a bank.
>
> —RONALD DEFEO, JR.[1]

The killer is the grandson of a Buick dealer on Coney Island and the son of that dealer's service manager. He worked for the dealership in a menial position, taking home some $80 each week in salary, but this modest income was supplemented by as much as $500 each week in gifts from his remarkably generous father, whose own source of income remains unclear. Members of the family were mortified when the press publicly connected them with prominent figures in organized crime, but they did not explain their extraordinary incomes. Of equal interest was the suggestion, which emerged during the trial, that the father may have been cheating the grandfather as much as the son was cheating the father—the father overbilled the grandfather's dealership and pocketed the difference, while the son staged bogus robberies of the firm's payroll. All this took place in a family atmosphere so violent that their fate seemed sealed in an unconscious mutual suicide pact. In this sense, "Butch" merely declared his manhood by executing the pact.

---

* The material for this chapter is drawn from *The New York Times*, from Jack Levin and James Fox's *Mass Murder*, and from the prosecuting attorney's retelling of the case in Gerard Sullivan and Harvey Aronson's most useful book, *High Hopes*.

THE KILLINGS

Nothing can happen to you as long as you wear this
[statuette of St. Joseph].

—RONALD DEFEO, SR.[2]

Butch gave so many differing versions of the events of the night of
November 13, 1974, so many fabrications and conflicting stories, that we
will never know precisely what happened. What we do know is that he
murdered his mother and father, his two younger brothers, and his two
sisters, with a .35-calibre lever-action Marlin rifle. The most reliable
reconstruction of the killings appears to be that of the prosecuting attorney (and family biographer), Gerard Sullivan, who concluded that at
three A.M., Butch loaded his rifle and walked to his parents' bedroom and
fired twice into his sleeping father's back. Both shots, the autopsy later
noted, struck Ronald, Sr. in the lower back, one piercing the kidney and
the other striking the base of the spine. The shots seem to have awakened
Butch's mother, and she was turning in bed towards the doorway when
two bullets pierced her chest and back, "shattered her rib cage" and
"destroyed most of her right lung, diaphragm and liver." Butch then
crossed the hallway to his younger sister's room and, from a distance of
less than two feet, shot her in the face. The angle of the bullet's path
suggested that Allison, like her mother, had awakened and turned her
head towards the doorway. The bullet entered her left cheek and damaged her brain and skull before passing through the mattress and coming
to rest on the floor.[3]

Butch moved towards the bedroom of his younger brothers. Both John
and Mark—an eleven-year-old who could move only on crutches due to
an injured hip—were still asleep. Standing at the foot of each bed, Butch
fired into their backs: John's spinal cord was broken, and both boys'
livers, diaphragms, lungs, and hearts were damaged. The only survivor
was now his oldest sister, Dawn, who must have been awakened by the
gunfire on the floor below, and who may have heard Butch reloading
as he moved up the stairs. In any case, Butch fired into the back of her
head, the bullet destroying the left side of her face.[4]

Butch then began methodically to collect the expended cartridge cases
from the victims' bedrooms. According to his own later testimony, he
took off his soiled clothing, bathed, and put on fresh garments. Con-

cerned that the soiled clothing might incriminate him (for he had no intention of confessing his guilt), he stuffed them into a pillowcase, along with the towel he used to dry himself, and the eight spent cartridges. He hurled the rifle some thirty feet out into the waters not far from his canalside home, then drove to work in Brooklyn, stopping only to stuff the pillowcase and its contents into a sewer.[5]

He was initially treated as a witness, not a suspect, when he called police at 6:35 P.M. to report the discovery. Indeed, his broad hints about Mafia involvement in the murders made the police fearful for his safety—so much so that they felt it necessary to provide a cot for him in police headquarters so that he could sleep through the night in protective custody. Still, Butch was a known heroin and "speed" user and had been involved in several brushes with the law on charges of petty theft and suspected burglary: when police learned that he personally owned a .35-calibre Marlin rifle, he became their prime suspect. The following morning, when Officer Harrison awakened him and Butch asked if they had been able to find the Mafia assassin, the officer remembered replying: "Butch, we have guys out on the street looking for him, but to tell you the truth, I think you're the guy we want."[6]

DENIALS AND CONFESSIONS

It all started so fast. Once I started, I just couldn't stop.

—BUTCH DEFEO[7]

THE FIRST TALE: THE MAFIA EXECUTION

When first interviewed by police at the scene of the murders, Butch had claimed that the family had been well when he had left for work early that morning, and that he had been out of the house at the time of the killings. When asked if he had any idea who might have committed the murders, he offered the name Falini (a pseudonym). He said Falini was a Mafia executioner with a grudge against the DeFeos, and that he, Butch, had survived the assault only because he was out of the house at the time. Butch freely admitted to the police that he was a heroin user with several felonies in his background and, according to his biographers Sullivan and Aronson, he was "equally frank in discussing his family's criminal connections." His granduncle, Pete DeFeo, had been linked with the underworld by the press, and a visitor to the Buick dealership allegedly worked for Carlo Gambino. Butch's rather weak story was that his father and Falini had been close friends until he, Butch, had argued with Falini and called him a "cocksucker." After the argument, his father had told him that Falini was a professional killer: "He's a hit man, that's how he makes a living," Butch claimed his father told him. "You don't realize what you've done when you called this man these names."[8]

Detective Gozaloff interrupted this story to observe that since this argument had taken place years before, why should Falini now go after the DeFeo family? Butch said that it was related to the robbery—purportedly by two gunmen—of himself and another dealership employee when they were taking several thousand dollars to the bank. Butch's father had not believed the story of the two gunmen and, Butch claimed, had said, "Not only do I have to worry about you as far as this phoney robbery, but I've also had to lose a good friend." Butch said that although his father threatened Falini that "if anything happens to my son, I'll kill you and your whole family," his father blamed him for the destruction of his friendship with Falini, and said, "I have to watch [out for] Ma and the kids now." The police, impressed at first by the sheer professionalism of the killings—"a real neat job," one of them told *The New York Times*—were initially inclined to believe this story.[9]

THE SECOND TALE: INNOCENT BYSTANDER

Within a few hours of skillful police interrogation, however, Butch admitted that the murders had taken place between two and four A.M., not after he had left the house as he had originally claimed. At first he denied hearing the shooting, even though he admitted he was in the house. Then he capitulated: "I was scared. I was really scared. I did hear something. I heard two shots. I didn't do anything. I was scared. I was scared shit. I stayed in the room, in the TV room, for about twenty minutes. I hid in the closet behind the door. All I heard was two shots." Butch told his interrogators that he had waited a few minutes after the shots, and had then driven into the city, too frightened even to look at his family. "Put yourself in my position," he told the police. "I just got out of the house. And that's it, man." But when Detective Rafferty insisted that he must have heard more than two shots, he retreated once again: "I did hear more than two shots. Let's see, I heard one, two, then there was like a hesitation, and I heard a third shot. Then there was another hesitation, and I heard two more shots. And then a longer hesitation, and the last shot. That was the furthest away."[10]

Relentless pressure from the detectives cracked this story still further, until he admitted that in fact he had looked into some of the bedrooms after the shooting. "I did check my mother and father. I saw my father was shot in the back. He had the hole in his back. There was a little blood, but I didn't see any blood around my mother, but I could see she was dead. Then I left the house. I was just scared." But under closer questioning, he admitted that he had also examined the other bedrooms. "Well, after I checked my mother and father's rooms, I went down and I checked Allison's room, and she got it in the head. Then I checked Mark and John's room. They both got it in the back. And John's foot was shaking and twitching. Then I went upstairs and I checked Dawn's room, and she got it in the neck. Then I was just so scared, I got dressed and I left."

Butch first denied that his rifle could have been the murder weapon, but began to cry when questioned and replied: "You won't believe it. You won't believe it. Well, when I was going into Dawn's room, I didn't have any shoes on, I was in my stocking feet, and I stepped on the gun and I looked down and sure enough, it was my gun. My rifle. Well, I knew I'd been framed. I knew I had to get rid of everything. I had to get rid of the evidence." He then admitted collecting the cartridge cases and soiled clothing, and disposing of them along with the rifle.[11]

Not surprisingly, Detective Rafferty was still unsatisfied. "Butch," he said, "it's not logical. It's incredible. Every time we go into another area of questioning, you change your story." Butch's reaction to this remark was to change his story yet again. "You won't believe me. You won't believe me. Give me time to think. You won't believe it. Louis Falini did it. He was there." Butch now claimed that Falini and another man had awakened him at three-thirty A.M., holding a pistol to his head and taking his rifle.

"You're going to live with this the rest of your life," Falini told me. "This is for what you did to me." They went into my mother and father's room, and Falini shot my father twice. He shot my mother once. Then they went to Allison's room. Yeah. I had to go with them. I had to see the whole thing. Falini opened the door and shot her [Dawn] right in the head, and her head was like blown away. That Falini loved it. He loved it. . . . You should have seen him. He was like a mad dog. The gun was smoking and the barrel was hot. You asked me before about the [family's] dog. The fucking dog was screaming while this was going on. The dog was screaming.[12]

THE THIRD TALE: CONFESSION

Too experienced to find Butch's story credible, the detectives applied rather more interrogative pressure until a third tale emerged. Detective Dunn cleverly suggested, "I think they must have made you shoot some of them. If they didn't, you can testify against them. They had to make you a piece of it. They must have made you a piece of it. They must have made you shoot at least one of them—or some of them." Astonishingly, Butch concurred: "They did. They made me shoot my father and Mark." When the detectives found that combination unlikely, and Detective Rafferty remarked, "It didn't happen that way, did it?" Butch retreated once more. "Give me a minute, give me a minute," he asked. "Butch, they never were there, were they?" Rafferty asked. "No," Butch admitted. "It all started so fast. Once I started, I just couldn't stop. It went so fast." However, when police asked if he would commit his statement to writing, he refused: "No, if I put that in writing, my grandfather will see it. My grandfather has a lot of connections with cops. If I put that in writing and sign it, he'll have it twenty minutes after I sign it. I'm not putting it in writing." His concern, he said, was that his grandfather would have him murdered.[13]

THE FOURTH TALE: BAD FRIENDS AND BRAVE DEEDS

Once Butch knew that the police understood his guilt, he devoted a great deal of energy to embroidering different versions of the truth. Imprisoned while awaiting trial, he befriended a jailer named DeVito, and blurted out yet another story. When DeVito asked him if he had committed the murders, he remembers Butch replying: "Mr. DeVito, you ought to know I did it. But I didn't do the actual shooting." According to DeVito, Butch's story was now that his best friend, Bobby Kelske, his girlfriend, "Sherry Klein," and another couple, had been searching the house for hidden money when they were surprised by Ronald, Sr. One of Butch's friends killed his father, then his mother, then the siblings. They did not find the cash.[14]

If Butch told his jailer one story, he told his cellmate, Kramer, quite another. In this version, according to Kramer, there were no accomplices: Butch had done the killings himself (thus inflating the prestige of his deed according to the values of jailhouse culture). Now he claimed he had stolen several hundred thousand dollars in cash and an equal amount in jewelry from a hiding place in his father's home. Unfortunately, his father had discovered the theft, and Butch had been forced to kill him in order to silence him. Following the killing, however, he went "berserk" in a manly sort of way and annihilated his entire family.[15]

THE FIFTH TALE: AMNESIA AND GRIEF

Speaking to the psychiatrists, Butch played a different game. When Dr. Zolan asked him if he had killed his family, he replied: "I don't know. I can't remember certain periods of time in that night. . . . I don't know what I did. I can't remember taking a gun and shooting my family. I can't remember none of that. . . . I don't see how I could have did it, but it looks like I did do it." When asked if he had retained any memory at all of the shootings, he said: "No, sir. I try hard—it's hard to believe; I have my family's pictures upstairs. I still, to this day, don't remember taking that gun and shooting anybody in my house with it. Like I said, I must have did it, but I can't place myself doing it." When Zolan asked if he grieved for the loss of his family, he said: "Yes, sir. I loved my family. I'm never going to get another family."[16]

THE SIXTH TALE: THE EVIL SISTER

Butch showed more creative imagination in constructing this tale—and more tenacity too, for he repeated it at his trial. In this version, he had been at home listening to his family engaging in one of their frequent fights. "They were all fighting again. My sister again with the knife. Every time with the damn knife. I went down there. She was trying to kill my father. Honestly, I wanted them to kill each other . . . but I couldn't take the noise. So I went down there and tried to break it up." However, his altruistic efforts as peacemaker were in vain, he claimed, because he later overheard his family plotting against him in the parents' bedroom: "They were all going to get me that night. They were saying, 'We'll wait until he goes to sleep,' this and that. You know, I couldn't hear too good because of the war picture [on television]. I was hearing, you know, words."[17]

Despite the "fact" that it was his family that had been plotting against him, his eldest sister, Dawn, decided to kill everyone in the family. Dawn "came down the stairs and said something to me. She said, 'I'm going to get him [Ronald, Sr.]. I'm going to get Mommy. I'm going to get you. I'm going to kill everybody in the house' . . . and then she went back upstairs." Hours later, Dawn awakened him when "she came down the stairs and kicked me and woke me up, she had the .35-caliber Marlin in her hand. . . . She put the gun in my hands. And I don't remember what I said or what I did. But I wasn't angry or mad. I was calm. Just very, very, very calm." Almost as if he were carrying out her unspoken orders, he suggested, he walked to his parents' bedroom and shot his father and mother: "I remained calm. But the thing that bothered me, I fired the gun but the gun didn't make any noise when I fired it. And then I dropped the gun—I didn't throw it—just dropped it and left it there."[18]

His sister Dawn, he surmised, must have then picked up the rifle because, "I heard shots. And then when I went and got up I seen my sister . . . running up the stairs with the gun." "Realizing" that she must have killed their siblings, he followed her up the stairs:

> When I got to the top of them stairs and I looked at my sister, she was putting a shell in the gun. I took the gun away from her, and I don't remember. . . . What I believe is I wanted—I told Dr. Schwartz I wanted to throw her out the window. . . . Even though in my own mind I felt my whole family was a threat to me. I felt what she did wasn't right. Now I felt that she was a threat to my life and that she was going to kill me in fact with this gun that she just killed them with. . . . I remember taking the gun away from her when I pushed her down, and I shot her. But again the gun didn't make no noise.

To strengthen his argument that his acts had been a kind of self-defence, he added that his sister had had an accomplice: "I seen somebody running across the lawn. If I didn't kill Dawn, she in turn was going to kill me. She was going to kill me and tell the police 'he [Butch] was drunk or stoned on dope or something and killed everybody and we had to kill him.' "[19]

THE SEVENTH TALE: EDITED FOR FAMILY LISTENING

Whenever he was speaking to his own relatives, Butch insisted on versions that distanced him from the actual killings. He told his sympathetic aunt, Mrs. Procita, that he had been awakened by gunshots and had hidden in the crawl space in his room until the real killers had left. "After they left," his aunt testified, "he went and he looked around and it was a mess. He said his sisters were hit bad. He said to me it was just awful; he was scared. And he asked me if I ever heard the sound of screaming children." Mrs. Procita said Butch did not reply when she asked him why he had not saved Dawn's life by bringing her into his hiding place. When she asked him why he had not telephoned for help, he told her that the phone was dead.[20]

Three weeks later he gave his aunt yet another story. In this tale, a friend had come to visit him the previous night, and they had both fallen asleep in the television room while watching late night television. When Butch awoke in the morning his friend was still asleep, and his family was alive and well. He asked his sister Dawn to awaken his friend, and left for work. The next time he saw his family, they were all dead. "And when I would question him—that didn't make sense, like, he wouldn't answer," his aunt reported. A few weeks after that, he returned to blaming Falini: "He said that Falini did it, that Falini wanted to kill his father, and I said, 'Why should Falini want to kill your father?' And he told me," Mrs. Procita continued, "that I didn't know what was going on in that house. He said my brother was no angel; he talked to people in organized crime; his mother had a boyfriend. I said, 'Why wouldn't Falini just kill your father on his way to work? He could do that.' And he said that he always went to work with his father."[21]

Later visits with his aunt generated still more stories, variously blaming a friend, an older man, or his sister Dawn. As Mrs. Procita struggled to comprehend her nephew, "I asked him another time if he would cover up for somebody and take the rap himself, and he said, 'Why not?' And he says, 'What makes you think I'm not covering for someone in the family?' His sister, Dawn. And I thought that was just ridiculous. And I thought—I said, 'I don't know why Dawn didn't just fight for her life. She was big enough to give anybody a good beating.'" The common theme underlying all these infinite variations, Mrs. Procita recalled, was Butch's own innocence: "He would say to me that he was no angel and he was involved in different things, but he said he never killed his family. . . . I asked him many times if he did it and he said that I would never hear him say he did it."[22]

THE EIGHTH TALE: POLICE BRUTALITY

In this tale, Butch moved to exonerate himself. He claimed that the police had not read him his rights at the initial interrogation, and had taken him to the police station while giving him the impression that they were taking him to see his paternal grandfather, Rocco DeFeo. Moreover, to force a false confession out of him, they had violently assaulted him once he was in their custody. He claimed police first subjected him to intense deprivation, denying him permission to eat, drink, or visit the bathroom. The detectives threatened him with violence if he would not sign a confession, and when he refused to do so, three detectives—one of whom was six feet, four inches tall and weighed 260 pounds, he claimed—punched and kicked him in the stomach and back. After that, they forced him to sit in a chair while they slammed a telephone book on the top of his head. This brutal torture continued, he claimed: they covered his head with a paper bag, then shoved his head into a filing cabinet and poked him unmercifully. When he could take it no longer, he began to cry: he said whatever they wanted him to say, including his admission of guilt.[23]

THE NINTH AND FINAL TALE:
INSANITY AND SELF-DEFENCE

By the time of his trial, he had arrived at a final draft of events, the function of which was to diminish his responsibility by pleading both insanity and self-defence. When his lawyer asked if he had killed his father, he replied: "Did I kill them? I killed them all. Yes sir, I killed them all in self-defence." He developed this version in some detail, complete with phantom figures darting across the lawn, but concluded, "As far as I'm concerned, if I didn't kill my family, they were going to kill me. And as far as I'm concerned, what I did was self-defence and there was nothing wrong with it. There has been a lot of people who have been threats to my life. I tried to find them and kill them. And if I couldn't find them and kill them, I couldn't do anything about it. I might have killed a dozen people before this, I don't know. . . . When I got a gun in my hand, there's no doubt in my mind who I am. I am God."[24]

PSYCHIATRIC INTERPRETATIONS

I can beat this case ... I been going to psychiatrists all
my life.

—BUTCH DEFEO[25]

While still awaiting trial, the garrulous Butch told a number of people
that he intended to feign insanity in order to escape both conviction for
murder and incarceration in prison. Fellow inmate Kramer claims Butch
told him that once he had beaten the case, he would have all the money
he had looted from the house, plus his inheritance and an additional
$100,000 insurance policy. In addition, he was certain that his family
would place him in an expensive private mental institution that would
soon release him as miraculously cured: "I'll be free, like a bird." Kramer
also recalled Butch developing techniques for demonstrating his insanity,
including sitting on a shelf and whistling strangely, throwing his mail
through the cell bars or flushing it down the toilet, and starting a fire in
his cell. Corrections Officer Ross noted similar behavior: Butch questioned him about the behaviour of another inmate who had been declared
insane, and told him that he, Butch, would accomplish the same. Officer
D'Augusta noted that DeFeo would hide in his bed or try to climb the cell
bars—or complain of poison or broken glass in his food—and then
formally request that his outburst be recorded in prison files.[26]

DeFeo's biographers, Sullivan and Aronson, noted that the prison's
sickbay log recorded a number of such attempts. On the morning of
March 31, 1975, Butch threatened to "blow this place up," and soon after,
"DeFeo starting to burn his person[al] prop[erty]. Control notified." Two
days later, Butch threatened to commit suicide. The log read: "In[mate]
DeFeo is shaving. Changed his mind and said he might cut his throat."
He repeated the threat on April 15: "Inmate DeFeo is threatening suicide
in a joking sort of way. We are not sure how serious he is about it.
Notified Control. We must assume he is serious!" Butch intensified the
general effect by threatening violence to others, and one note in the
logbook reads: "Above inmate said if he gets out of jail he will get even
w[ith] all his neighbors and friends of his sister for saying things about
him."[27]

PSYCHIATRIST FOR THE DEFENCE

Butch and his attorney wished him to be declared insane, and their psychiatrist made the appropriate diagnosis. Dr. Daniel Schwartz testified in court that it "is my opinion that as a result of mental disease the defendant at that particular time [the night of the killings] lacked substantial capacity to appreciate the wrongfulness of his acts." Schwartz quite reasonably emphasized Butch's upbringing in a violent home—a childhood that left him aggressive towards others, but fearful of expressing this anger towards his father. "As wild as he could be with others," Schwartz said, "he could not respond in kind to his father. But the anger had to go somewhere.... His came out, among other ways, at most of his teachers and school authorities, who for many children quite naturally stand as parental figures."[28]

Schwartz saw Butch as an explosive young man, apprehensive about his own aggressiveness, and overindulged with gifts of money from his father. Butch's paranoid delusions, Schwartz thought, stemmed from a 1973 incident in which Butch had pointed a loaded gun at his father, and thereafter become confused by the ambivalent love and hate he had expressed. "He began to get the feeling that—and the belief that—there were people who were going to kill him and that his only recourse was to kill them first." If these delusions were developed to spare Butch the danger of expressing his anger to his father, Schwartz thought that they were ultimately ineffectual since Butch had begun to feel that his father was among those who were trying to kill him. "There was a birthday party held for him [Butch], and he went around at the party and kissed all of his family and felt love for them. At the same time, the delusions were eating at him, that these people were going to kill him."[29]

On the night of the killings, Schwartz thought that a fight between Butch's father and his sister Dawn had intensified his internal conflict, and that a violent film he watched on television created the ideal emotional conditions for an impending catharsis. The film, *Castle Keep,* Schwartz said, was

> a movie about ... our army in Europe in World War II. And the culmination of it is that our troops are forced or ordered to defend a hopeless position, and amidst incredible violence and explosion, every one of our soldiers are killed. The defendant, the patient, told me that he was moved by the bloodshed and the

violence in the picture. It's also clear to me that the picture had other meanings to him, too. There is a significant theme in the picture of some soldiers who have renounced violence and who walk through this town in Europe preaching religious nonviolence, but it's to no avail.... The violence will out. And I think this was a significant message to the defendant, that nothing he did was going to prevent this final showdown.

Schwartz did not believe that "the movie caused the actual killings," but he insisted that what "I am saying [is] that it was the straw that broke the camel's back. And now in a paranoid psychotic state of mind, he proceeded to do what he thought was the only thing he could do, namely kill those who were out to kill him."[30]

Anticipating charges that Butch was malingering and faking insanity, the defence attorney asked the defence psychiatrist for his opinion. Schwartz said that the possibility of faking mental illness during his interviews was so remote that "I don't consider it as having any likelihood in this case." For Schwartz, the proof that Butch was genuine in his "psychotic state of mind" was the dissociation he displayed when he could not hear his rifle firing. This denial of sensory reality was a certain symptom of psychosis, Schwartz insisted: "I don't believe that someone with his limited education and sophistication and lack of familiarity with psychiatry could have invented this particular symptom of dissociation."[31] Yet anyone with any experience in these matters would know that not hearing gunfire is one of the most common sensory peculiarities generated by the tension of combat or competition—it is a function of total concentration, not psychosis.

Schwartz found further proof of psychosis simply in the familicide's typical calm good marksmanship: "The other thing that comes through with such striking strangeness in this case is his calmness throughout the killings." An explosion of anger, Schwartz thought, would have resulted in random shots and much damage throughout the house:

Every one of them was fired with an almost eerie accuracy. This was the act of an absolutely calm, cold person who had no feelings at all at the time. This is exactly how he coped with his feelings. He just turned them off. I don't mean intentionally. Psychologically, unconsciously, without his awareness, all his feelings were turned off completely; and now in an eerie, calm, machine-like way he goes about executing the closest people in the world to him, but the same people who he believes are the greatest threat to his life."

However, it is as plausible to argue that he made a professional job of it because he had no love for his family.[32]

Schwartz also reinterpreted Butch's eminently rational attempt to hide the evidence—gathering up the incriminating cartridge cases and bloody clothing and disposing of them along with the murder weapon—as further evidence of Butch's *irrationality*. The prosecuting attorney asked him if this was not "indicative of a person who has gone to very careful lengths to remove evidence of the crime, that would connect him to that crime?" The psychiatrist responded with the assumption that such behaviour was disordered:

> It's evidence of somebody who is trying to remove evidence from himself, too, that he has done this. We are now speculating as to the motive for the cleaning up. If you are familiar with Lady Macbeth's complaint—"What, will these hands never be clean?"—she's not hiding a murder from anyone, but she can't live with the imagined blood on her hands.... My considered psychiatric opinion, Counselor, is that he's not hiding this crime from anybody by picking up the shells. The bodies are there. The bullets are in the people. You don't use the shells to prove the origin of bullets. You use the bullets themselves. He knows this. The cleaning up is some kind of neurotic, inappropriate act on his part. It's not a concealing of the crime.

Thus by painting Butch as a kind of sensitive, Shakespearian soul, the psychiatrist tried to bury the fact that it would have been impossible for anyone to conceal the crime for any length of time. What Butch in fact was eliminating was not evidence of the crime, but evidence linking him to it—especially the rifle, which was the only link between him and the bullets in the bodies—and doing so in a most rational way.[33]

PSYCHIATRIST FOR THE PROSECUTION

The prosecution wanted the maximum legal penalty for Butch, and therefore wished him to be declared sane and culpable. The prosecution psychiatrist provided the appropriate diagnosis. In court, Dr. Harold Zolan began by distinguishing psychosis or insanity from the less serious form of mental disturbance known as antisocial personality. He defined psychosis as "a form of mental illness in which the patient has lost the capacity to deal with reality, to distinguish between reality and fantasy," a form often associated with delusions and hallucinations. Antisocial personality, however, was a simple "personality disorder, as opposed to a mental illness." In Zolan's diagnosis, Butch was an antisocial personality, not a psychotic: he was therefore sane in the legal, McNaughton, definition of sanity, which is to say he was capable both of distinguishing right from wrong and understanding the consequence of his acts.[34]

Zolan concluded from his interviews with Butch "that there was no mental illness, and that the symptoms that were being presented as a form of mental illness constituted a form of malingering." First, he noted that Butch's violent behaviour was inconsistent with mental illness since the presence of authority figures would stop the violence: here, Zolan referred to an incident in which Butch had carried a hand grenade into a bar because he claimed someone there was poisoning him, but had aborted his planned assault when he discovered police in the bar. Zolan thought a true paranoid would have ignored the police and gone ahead with his attack. Similarly, he felt Butch had too *many* symptoms of mental illness: "I don't mean to be facetious, but I would say that he was too psychotic. He had everything. He was hearing voices all the time. Now, even psychotic people don't hear voices all the time. Everybody was against him—everybody. Even people with paranoid delusions don't believe that everybody is against them."[35]

Zolan also argued that Butch's removal of critical items from the crime scene indicated that he had a clear and precise idea of what he was doing, and was not therefore insane. "He, as I recall, mentioned that he subsequently put these in a pillow case. The gathering of all this material, which would have been identifiable with the gun he owned and with which the crime was committed, demonstrated the awareness of and appreciation of the wrongfulness of the act." The psychiatrist argued that "by eliminating your connection with a crime—you must first be aware that it is a wrongful act or there would be no purpose in eliminating evidence. So when evidence of a crime is removed . . . for the purpose of dissociating" the perpetrator from the crime, this constitutes a sane and rational act. Butch's purpose in tampering with the crime scene, Zolan thought, was "furthering the alibi that he was setting up for himself; that here he had come upon this tragic scene and now he was overwhelmed."[36]

Zolan saw the relationship between Butch and his father as one of enforced dependency: the father used his money to control the son, which gave Butch a great need to appear to be independent and assertive.

Butch was "fully aware of the value of money, of his own lack of any real capacity to earn money, because he's held many jobs and he's never been able to keep a job, and the only source of money is his father, who doles it out and doles it out very, very generously. But there is always a string attached. And it's that string which ultimately becomes strangulating to this defendant." Thus Butch was "attempting to build himself up into a big man" to compensate for the feelings of inadequacy derived from his dependence on his father. "You know, the macho image, the man of great strength and virility. This is the image which is very understandably diminished and even prevented from developing when your father can reach out and pull you back each time you make an effort to become independent of him."[37]

This "macho" syndrome was reflected in both Butch's sexual impotence and his pugnacious behaviour in court. His growing impotence "played perhaps not a key part, but certainly an important part in having the defendant reach a point where he just had to be his own man and be free of all restraint." Ultimately, only heroin released him from the sexual impotence which undoubtedly stemmed from his social impotence. "He was really not at all a free agent. There was only one way that a personality type like this could resolve this problem, and that is to eliminate the source of these restraints, which he proceeded to do." Zolan argued that Butch's "bravado outbursts in the courtroom, indicating his contempt for the proceedings," and shouts "to the effect that I would come down there and kill you," were all part of his attempt to present a macho image. "All of this adds up to the strong individual, the individual who cares about nothing, is afraid of nothing. In fact, he repeatedly states ... that he's not afraid of anything. He has no fear. And this is essentially what he was trying to convey in the courtroom."[38]

Zolan noted with great insight that Butch

was seen by a psychiatrist and a psychologist when he was somewhere between the ages of fourteen and fifteen. He is noted to be a passive-aggressive individual ... [and] is being urged to assert himself. . . . [T]his defendant *did* become more and more aggressive, attempting to make impressions on people that he was a big man, an important man, and that the various things that he did to start fights to produce the image of the macho were all for the purpose of attempting to overcome what started out as a passive-aggressive individual and now is becoming more and more overtly aggressive to the point where he finally reached a point of aggression where he committed the ultimate crime.

Zolan found no evidence "whatsoever" that Butch was suffering from any serious mental illness.[39]

The defence attorney pled for clemency, but did so on the peculiar grounds that although his client was admittedly "an animal," that "in ten or fifteen years he may be rehabilitated and possibly make a contribution to society." This statement gave less credit to the client and more credit to the rehabilitative powers of state prisons than is customarily expected from defence attorneys. In any case, the jury dismissed the insanity plea and found DeFeo culpable and guilty on all six counts of second-degree murder. On December 4, 1975, Butch was sentenced to twenty-five years to life on each of the six counts. In passing sentence, the judge said, "I am of the belief he is a real danger to society in that he may kill again and the law provides for certain sentences to insure the community's safety." Nevertheless, since the law allows the sentences to be served concurrently, Butch will be eligible for parole as early as 1999, when he will be forty-eight.[40]

THE VIOLENT FAMILY

I have the devil [Butch] on my back.

—RONALD DEFEO, SR.[41]

We know very little about the social history of the DeFeo and Brigante families. We do know that the families were the subject of many rumors connecting them with organized crime, but more revealing than the rumors is the reality that few service managers at automobile dealerships are in a position to offer their sons a weekly $500 in spending money. Such largesse certainly suggests alternative and unusual sources of income. Yet if we know little about the family's origins or economic relationships, we know a great deal about its conception of itself, its notions of appropriate child-rearing techniques, and its attitudes towards the expression of aggression. If one of our sources of this knowledge, the killer, is a self-serving and confirmed liar, much of it nonetheless has the ring of truth—and much more is confirmed by outside sources.

"High Hopes", the DeFeos' splendid waterfront home on Ocean Avenue in Amityville, Long Island, with its yard backing on a protected canal, was a small-boater's paradise and an expression of the high social aspirations of the family. The home, which the DeFeos occupied for the ten years prior to their murders, was notable not only for its fine setting and unpretentious architecture, but also for the religious shrines that dotted the property. Ronald, Sr., who had in recent years become an enthusiastic Catholic, was sometimes seen saying his rosary in front of a shrine of St. Joseph and the Christ child that he had built in his yard. The home's interior decor, with its expensive furnishings, crystal chandelier, and alabaster fireplace, expressed the DeFeos' distance from their natal Brooklyn and gave substance to their solid middle-class family life. These images were made explicit in the family portraits that lined the staircase wall: in one, father and son, Ronald, Sr. and Butch, sit side by side smiling at the artist while father pours a glass of wine for his son. In another, the two daughters pose on a love seat, half smiles on their faces. In a third painting, the two young brothers pose with Mark's arm on John's shoulder. Appropriately for such a paternalistic family, there was no portrait of the mother, Louise.[42]

But if the physical plant the family presented to the outside world was a tasteful expression of middle-class family values, the actual relationships within the family were otherwise. Indeed, violence and aggressive display appeared to be the lingua franca in which most social interaction was phrased, interpreted, symbolized, and expressed. Even the family's English sheepdog, with its fey name, Shabby, was both cause and provocation of further violence: Butch appeared to despise the dog and not without reason since the dog would occasionally attack him. Still, his father warned him that if he injured the dog, a similar punishment would be visited on him: "If the dog ends up in the canal," his father is reported to have said, "you're going to end up in the canal."[43]

Certainly the coarse Brooklyn emigrés seem to have caused a stir in their adopted genteel neighbourhood. Some of the neighbours found the DeFeos "loud" and "showy," and one remembered that "they all screamed at each other." Although most respected the family—but not Butch—both neighbours and friends remembered numerous incidents of violent clashes, especially between father and eldest son. Butch's friend recalled driving up to the family home with him. Butch's mother had snapped at her son for enjoying himself when there were chores to be done; Butch lunged at his mother and threatened to kill her, doing so with sufficient conviction that the friend wrestled Butch to the ground. Similarly, a maternal uncle remembered an incident when Butch was two: "I believe we were all sitting down in the basement, watching TV, and I don't know, the boy had did something, and all of a sudden he stood up, the father, and just pushed the boy this way into the wall, and the boy banged his head or part of his shoulder or something."[44]

Butch's friend, Frank Davidge, recounted a battle that he witnessed when he joined the family for a meal. While Butch and his father were eating with the children, Mrs. DeFeo was doing the laundry. The children grew noisy and Mrs. DeFeo shouted at them several times to be quiet: each time she shouted, Ronald, Sr. shouted at her to be quiet so that he could eat in peace. Ultimately Ronald left the table and punched his wife, knocking her down the stairs. He slammed the door behind her and said, "Now we'll get some peace and quiet while we eat." Butch began shouting at his father for hitting his mother in front of his friend but instead of running downstairs to help his mother he bolted upstairs to his own bedroom. "He'll get over it soon," Ronald reassured Davidge. A nine-year-old neighbour described another encounter: Butch "asked for some more money and he wanted a new car. Then his father said no, and [Butch] punched him, and then he punched him back, and then we went upstairs." According to Sullivan and Aronson, Butch's grandfather, Michael Brigante, Sr., tried to punch a newspaper photographer who appeared in front of him at the funeral of the DeFeo family.[45]

Curiously, it was this seemingly unending violence that brought Ronald to religion, following the incident in which Butch had pointed a loaded gun at him and it had miraculously misfired. As Butch later described the incident,

> My mother and father had—this the truth now—since I've been a young kid, very, very bad fights. I'm talking about with the hands. I have seen my father beat my mother so bad—I mean she's bleeding and black eyes. This is all the truth. And when I was younger was one thing. As I started getting older, you know, it was getting kind of, you know, bad. . . . Like I said, about two years ago when this started—I don't remember the night—but they were having these bad fights again. And I happened to be in the house that night, and the kids were all in there, and everybody. And they are all screaming and they are all yelling and fighting.
>
> The kids were yelling, "Butch come down and break it up.

Come down here. Daddy is killing Mommy," or something like that. And my sister, Dawn, is down there trying to break it up. Now, I got sick of this. I got sick of my mother and father fighting. . . . I had a twelve-gauge shotgun on the wall, Doc. I put a shell in the gun. It was a single-shot gun. I took the gun and came down the stairs and I said, "Listen, that's it." And I pointed the gun at my father. I told him I was going to kill him. "Leave that woman alone. I'm going to kill you, you fat fuck. This is it." I took that gun and pointed it at him and I pulled the trigger, and the gun didn't go off. I snapped the handle [sic] again, and the gun still didn't go off. Yes, sir. He looked like he seen a ghost. He shit. I dropped the gun. I didn't do nothing. I just walked away. It's very lucky for him, my mother and everybody else in that house that I didn't have any other guns at that time in my presence because I would have killed them all. That's the way I felt about it. See, you don't understand. I didn't want to be bothered. I was upstairs. My family and brothers and sisters come up there, and they were bothering me.

The incident provoked no reduction in Ronald's violence; it could hardly have been otherwise, given the nature of the family culture.[46]

Duplicity and theft seemed as integral to the family's style as violence. According to Butch, just as he stole from his father, the service manager, so his father stole from the dealership—Butch's maternal grandfather.

My father used to rip my grandfather off a lot. I was involved. . . . The body shop next door, it was our building. But this guy from the street was in there. He used to do all our work. And my father would tell him how much like to charge the company. Like, say, if the job was five hundred, he'd charge maybe eight hundred, a thousand, and that extra three or four hundred would go into my father's pocket. He'd send me over there to get the checks from the body shop and I'd take the checks down the street to the loansharks and I'd cash the checks, and they would take so much out. There was that body shop. There was another body shop off of Coney Island Avenue. Those two. And there was some other work they did on the stolen cars. . . . My father was the one that was running the show.[47]

Money and jewelry of uncertain origin seemed to flow through the house—so much of it that Butch and his father chiselled a secure hiding place out of the master bedroom's closet floor. "We hid a cash box there," Butch remembered. "It's always full of money and jewelry." In one of Butch's less implausible versions of the night of the murders, he claimed that his father had discovered that he had stolen cash and jewelry from the hidden box: Butch, endangered by the discovery, had gone "berserk" and began killing. If he was certainly stealing from his father, there is some evidence that he was also stealing from his mother. Indeed, he told his cellmate he accepted hush money from her to keep secret her alleged adulterous affair.[48]

Police tape recordings of the family's telephone calls hinted at the possible source of these monies. During a wire tap investigation by Brooklyn police, Butch's maternal grandfather had referred to Butch: "He's a nut job. This guy is crazy. If somebody killed this kid, he's better off." In another conversation with an alleged organized crime figure, the grandfather remarked: "You I'll talk to . . . because you understand my language, and I understand your language. They want to kill if he killed, go ahead. . . . But you better find out what's going on. And if they kill that kid in prison . . . you better get it squared away, boy." The tape also seemed to confirm Butch's story of his thefts: "Where's the rest of all that other jewelry?" Brigante is reported to have asked. "That's what I want to know. I want to know where the hell it's at. Naw, the detectives didn't take all that stuff, that's bullshit. And Butch told them where the box was, you know. . . . And, ah, who knows, this fucking kid may have walked in, you know, he used to come in at all crazy hours. He may have saw his father with the thing out. This kid can hang everybody. That's right, he knows what was in that house. That boy had my . . . had my daughter crazy." "Well," observed Brigante's confidante, "that's why she had all them aches and pains." "Jesus Christ," Brigante agreed, "she was living with a torture."[49]

In sum, the family's reputation for conflict and violence was so well established that few who knew them were even surprised to learn of the killings. On the night of the murders, when one police officer was told merely that a homicide had taken place at the DeFeo home, he immediately asked: "What'd Ronnie do? Blow his father away?" After the murders, Butch's rage towards his family continued unabated; and he even rebuffed attempts by his gentle aunt, Phyllis Procita, to calm him. She remembers him accusing her of stealing from him: "Butch said that all you people are interested in is the money from the estate and that we have probably hired Siegfried [the defence attorney] to take a dive and then we could have the money. He also asked what right we had to sell his car. I said it wasn't his car since it was under his father's name. Butch then demanded the twelve hundred dollars that we got for the car."[50]

THE EVOLUTION OF A FAMILICIDE

I couldn't care less what happens to me or the rest of my life.

—BUTCH DEFEO[51]

We have no way of knowing why Louise DeFeo tolerated the assaults on her person. What we do know is that her husband's assaults on Butch were more than merely physical, and led inexorably to their conclusion. First, the father stole the child's legitimacy and his birthright. When the prosecuting attorney asked Butch how much he remembered of his childhood, Butch told the court: "I was twelve. Somewhere around there." He was remembering the day he was expelled from parochial school. When he told his father of his expulsion, "He said to me that I wasn't even his son, that he had to marry my mother when she was pregnant with me, he had to marry her six months early ... and then he started with my mother." After this savage revelation, which hinted at many private contracts between his father and his maternal grandfather, they argued heatedly until his mother attacked his father with a knife. "My father picked up a chair and threw it. I got hit with it and it knocked all the teeth out of the front of mouth. That's why I remember that incident because the teeth in front of my mouth are all caps."[52]

His childhood was riddled with denigration and violence, both within and outside the family. He was stabbed in the back at school during a fight with two other students; he claimed his father had beaten his younger brother, Mark, to the point where stitches were required to heal his wounds; and in an explosive display that reads like a rehearsal for familicide, the fourteen-year-old Butch attacked and severely beat his eldest sister, Dawn. "It was a crazy house. I couldn't take it. I couldn't take it back then; I couldn't take it before this happened." To drown his anxiety and depression, he turned first to daily doses of amphetamines and crystal Methedrine: "Sometimes I snorted it. Sometimes I put it in a drink, Coke or a Pepsi, to kill the taste. Once in a while I would shoot it, put it in my arm and shoot it up. You move around fast, you talk a lot, you are always awake, you couldn't sleep, you couldn't eat. You had to force yourself to close your eyes."[53]

Then they stole his personality. He was born on September 26, 1951, in Brooklyn to a twenty-year-old textile worker and his nineteen-year-old wife, the first of the family's five children. The pressures in his home were reflected in his early obesity and his consistent failure at school; but it was the attack on his sister when he was fourteen that forced the family to take Butch to a psychiatrist. There, in an extraordinary value statement, Ronald complained to the psychiatrist not that Butch was obese, inadequate, and violent, but that he was insufficiently aggressive! The family's biographers gained access to that psychiatrist's notes on Butch's visits during the year following March of 1966. According to Sullivan and Aronson, the psychiatrist "described the fourteen-year-old DeFeo as a withdrawn child who bought protection from hostile peers and got other kids to throw his snowballs. His mother told the doctor that 'Ronald used to ask me if I loved him,'" a question she appeared to find strange—which tells us a great deal about Louise DeFeo. In any case, Ronald insisted that his son learn to be more aggressive. The astute psychological report recommended family counselling: "Impress[ion] is that Ronald, Jr.'s problems serve family needs, preserving a familial balance, albeit maladjusted. Father projects hostility re: authority figures who mistreat Ronald, Jr. Enables father to project, and yet vindicate himself via his beneficient efforts for Ronald, Jr. Parents see Ronald, Jr. as problem; they have, by their attitudes toward him, *written out a script for him to follow*. Which he does, playing the role of the bewilderingly bad boy."[54]

At the trial, the prosecution psychiatrist summarized Butch's adolescent personality with no little insight.

> This defendant was seen by a psychiatrist and a psychologist when he was somewhere between the ages of fourteen and fifteen. He is noted to be a passive-aggressive individual. A passive-aggressive individual is an individual who never manifests overtly aggressive behaviour, but feels aggressive, never expresses it directly, gets other people to do it for him. . . . Now, on the other hand, this passive-aggressive individual is being urged to assert himself. His father tells the doctor, "Dr. Y, I wish he

could become more aggressive." I have no doubt that this father told this not only to the doctor but to the defendant as well. And not only that, but displayed a perfect model for aggressive behaviour. And this defendant began to follow this aggressive model which was provided for him, and he began to assert himself; he began to be aggressive. But of course, always with the awareness, always with the knowledge, that there was one figure in the background that could prevent all of this from continuing. . . . So the father was saying to him, "Be aggressive, but don't be aggressive." Nonetheless, despite his father's attempts at suppression, this defendant did become more and more aggressive, attempting to make impressions on people that he was a big man.

In this manner, Butch fleshed out the family's self-fulfilling prophecy.[55]

Then they stole his independence. In this emotional maelstrom, Butch did not develop an ability to fend for himself. His marks at Amityville Memorial High School were less than mediocre and he left school for good at the age of sixteen. After that, he went through a succession of unskilled jobs: he claimed he was fired from these jobs for manfully fighting with the boss or his fellow employees. However, those who knew him insist there were no such problems; in fact he was fired either for consistent absenteeism or for cheating on his accounts. Unable to cope, he capitulated and joined his father in the family's Buick dealership. Like Steven Benson in the family's tobacco firm, Butch was given no specific position or responsibilities, and was overpaid to keep him dependent. The psychiatrist Zolan argued that all the while "this defendant was attempting to build himself up into a big man. . . . You know, the macho image, the man of great strength and virility. This is an image which is very understandably diminished and even prevented from developing when your father can reach out and pull you back each time you make an effort to become independent of him." Zolan noted that Butch would have been acutely aware "of his own lack of any real capacity to earn money, because he's held many jobs and he's never been able to keep a job, and the only source of money is his father, who doles it out and doles it out very, very generously. But there is always a string attached. And it's that string which ultimately becomes strangulating to this defendant."[56]

Then they stole his sexuality. Inevitably, his sexual performance began to mirror his social impotence: soon, only heroin gave him sufficient tranquility for sexual potency. "Doc," he told the court psychiatrist, "I'll be honest with you about everything. I was not like a sex maniac or nothing. I went out with a lot of girls and I had a lot of sex. Women just started to turn me off right before this happened. I couldn't have sex. I just couldn't do anything. Like you know, I thought it was me. Then I thought it may have been the girl I was going out with. But I kept going out with all these girls. I mean a lot of girls. It wasn't the girls; it was me." Only heroin had the power to calm his fears of his personal inadequacies:

> [W]hen I was on heroin, I could still have sex, do whatever I wanted. . . . When I wasn't on heroin, in fact, I was having a lot of trouble. . . . When I was on it, I could do it. . . . It's just when I was on heroin, I had sex with women. I had no problem. . . . The heroin kept me calm. It kept me mellow. When I was on heroin, I was a nice person. It didn't put me in another world or anything. Just like downers would, it kept me mellow. I tell you, when I was on medication, like heroin, anything like that, I never did nothing to nobody. I was fine. I was calm.[57]

He held the job at his grandfather's dealership for more than a year, longer than he had held any other, but he was trained for nothing but passivity and dependence and was assigned no specific responsibilities. As he told the psychiatrist, "Nobody could tell me what to do because my father was the boss. I did what I wanted to do." It was not very much. "Some days I have to do work, you know, tune up the car or grease and change the oil, or take one down and have it washed, a new car, that was about it, mainly. I just hung around." His father's lavish gifts allowed Butch to cruise the nightclubs with as much as several thousand dollars in his pocket. He could stay out late, since he often left the dealership by noon.[58]

Despite this apparent laxity and generosity, he made no secret of the fact that he hated his family. So intense was this hatred that immediately after the murders, when he was not yet under suspicion, he shocked the detectives when they had innocently asked why he had not eaten at home that day. "My mother was a lousy cook," he told them. "She cooked up some brown stuff in a bowl. It looked like shit and it smelled like shit. Yeah, if you guys had to eat it, it would taste like shit. My brothers is a couple of fucking pigs. I often used the same bathroom that they used on the second floor. And I go in there and sometimes there is toilet paper hanging out of the bowl. Sometimes there is shit in the bowl and there is no toilet paper. The fucking pigs don't even wipe their asses. A couple of times, there was even shit on the back of the seat." Waxing inappropriate, he referred to his late sister as "that fat fuck, Dawn. Dawn is nigger music, fucking nigger music, nigger music. All fucking day and night. And I can't even tell her to turn it down, because if I tell her to turn it down, I get my fucking ass kicked [by] my father." As for his grandfather/employer, "That cheap bastard; I'll rip him off every chance I get. I'll go to work late, and I'll come home early."[59]

Even when trying to exonerate himself of the murders, he could resist neither blaming others for his predicament nor insulting his family. In the first of two letters he wrote from jail to his maternal grandparents:

> I know you hate me and don't care what happens to me but, I figured I beter write to you, and let you know a few things. Ive don't a lot wrong in my times, pleanty to a lot of people but I never killed nobody. Nobody loved my parents more than me or the kids. . . . There's a lot of things that were going on that none of you's knew about, and the ship was sinking quick. My Father is the one responseable for getting them all killed, but my mother some of the blame to. . . . My father hated you and you hated him, and the only one you didn't hate was my Mother. Ive been reading the newspapers and I know you don't care about me at all. All you care about is your share of the money.

Although he closed that first letter with the vow that "you'll never see or hear from me again," he wrote once more nine days later. "I'am very fedup with you's people, because you all think I did it. All of you's are either sick or money hungry. I don't under-stand how you think that I am capable of doing what has been done. I may have been a theif and alot of other things but am not a murder. . . . My Mother your daughter made things bad for every body in that house. My father is fulley responsseble for the death's of the family. Its a shame that the kids had to die for them."[60]

He seems to have mastered aggressive display in the year before the murders. When he was arrested in 1973 for stealing an outboard motor, a friend remembered Butch threatening to "blow the head off" one of the police officers (although not to the officer's face). Later, fearing that they might be overheard through police microphones installed in the house, the older DeFeo told Butch to be quiet, and to underline his request he hurled a silver pitcher at Butch. Similarly Butch told Dr. Zolan after he had been drinking he went to a girlfriend's house:

I got to her house and started smashing the place up, took a chair and I put the thing through the ceiling—the legs went through the ceiling. The landlady came down. I don't remember what I did to her, started arguing with her, dragged my girlfriend out of the house in her pyjamas and I took her in my car to the bar and I don't remember, my father came down there.... He had to come down there and drag me out of the bar, started a big scene in the neighbourhood and all. I don't know. All my friends had to jump on me.... I was using heroin and acid, not acid too much, heroin.

In a similar incident, when yet another girlfriend was fired from her job in a bar, "I went down there with a gun. I mean, I have a twenty-five caliber automatic, and I went down there. Boy, and I was going to kill the owner. That's the guy I wanted. I was going to blow him away. And I took that gun, got out of the car and two of my friends, or three of them, jumped on me and took the gun away from me.[61]

Despite the manly bluster towards all and sundry, it was the familial arena that provoked the most intense conflict and left him most unsatisfied.

It seemed to be, Doc, everyone in that house—I don't know. They were trying to kill each other, always do harm to each other. It was like a bunch of animals. You know, these people wanted to do harm to me, Doc. They wanted to kill me. This is why all this led up to this in the end.... Yes, I wanted to say one other thing, Doc, about this bit with the shotgun with my father. What happened right after that was that my father, I went to work with him one morning—my mother came—and he told me he wanted me to drive them to New York to take my mother to the doctor, and he wanted me to sit in the car. Now, I went to New York with them and we got to this place.... I didn't want to go in. When I got up there, it turned out it was a psychiatrist.... The guy called me in the room. He's asking me all these questions about different things leading up to this incident. Yes sir.... He came right out and said, "Mr. DeFeo, you got no business being in the street. You belong in a mental institution." I said, "What do you mean?" He said, "You are a sick man." I had an argument with him and I left. Now I was told this a number of times before this by other psychiatrists that I didn't care for. And apparently my mother and father went in, and the

man told my father that he was a psychotic or a psychopath, and
your son is going to wind up killing all of you. This is what the
man told me. He's going to wind up killing all of you. He told
me and he told them too. They were warned ... these people
were warned. When the doctor told my father that he was sick,
my old man laughed at him, paid him his money and he left.[62]

Curiously, this devastating and eerily prescient diagnosis provoked a
new camaraderie between father and son.

Beside telling me I was sick, you know, after he was through
talking with me. Told my father he was sick. My mother is
crying and my father is laughing. He said, "You are not sick; this
doctor is sick." You know, passing the buck over on everybody.
And it sort of became like a buddy-buddy. You know, we
became friends but we could never be friends. Yes sir. As long as
he was alive, he was a threat or a danger to my life. And I had
more respect and never hit my father with a hand. I never hit
him with a hand. He hit me. He did all the fighting. He's the
one that beat me up. I never hit him back. I tried to wrestle and
hold him. I ain't never punched the man.[63]

Inevitably, such a rootless friendship was short-lived. Butch could see
only threat from his father, and experience only violent fantasy and
reality.

The man [his father] told me he was going to kill me. Yes sir. He
told me he was going to kill me. He told me he had a silver
bullet in his gun and he was going to blow me away. My mother
told me she was going to get me. My sister is with these knives,
running around the house. I broke up a fight. . . . And I told
everybody in that house that I would kill them. A number of
times I had told my friends in the street that I could not take no
more of them. They are—my old man, I'm going to wind up
killing them all. And they were warned and warned and warned.[64]

He made one last weak attempt to stake his independence and, he
claimed, avert the violence. "Now, what I tried to do to prevent this is I
left my house. I got—and I just packed up and I left [several weeks
before the murders]." But his idea of asserting himself was merely to
move in with his girlfriend. His parents were able easily to use their

financial power to force him back into the house, despite his solemn vow that "this time, right, I wasn't coming back. This was it." Several days after he had left home, he emerged from his apartment to find that his car had disappeared: he would soon discover that his father had stolen it. "I thought *somebody* stole it. . . . I found my car in the [family home's] driveway. And now I had my keys and I went to take it. I got in the car. He [had] pulled all the spark plug wires and coil wire. So I said to him, 'What is going on? You took my car.' He said, 'I want you to come home. If you don't want to go to work, you don't have to go to work.' You know, but he wanted me home. Now he told me he wasn't going to give me any more money. He took my car, took everything. So I still didn't come home."[65]

Ronald's need to dominate his son allowed him to use duplicity, violence, and financial intimidation to force Butch to return home. "Then he stops my salary. He wouldn't give me any more money. Well Doc, there is a little more to what the Buick dealership is. I honestly—for the last two years, every Friday, Doc, there is some weeks the least I had was five hundred dollars, some weeks I had two, three thousand dollars every week. . . . Money, I never had any problems with money if I wanted money. I could be home and ask my father for five thousand dollars, and bingo, it was there. I have done it many times." Butch capitulated and returned to High Hopes. He remembered his father telling him, " 'I don't care if you come to work or not. You could have your car back. You can have everything back. Just come home and live there.' And I told the man, 'I can't live in the house with you people. I'm going to wind up killing you all.' He thought it was a big joke. As bad as I was getting, every night something was happening. There was trouble every night. And he still wanted me to come home." When asked why his father should want him home so desperately, Butch was baffled: "I thought about that, but I don't know. I think they wanted me in that house so they knew where I was so I couldn't get them. That's what I started thinking about but it doesn't make no sense."[66]

Indeed it does not. But neither does the much longer "Death List" he had drawn up, unless it was to manufacture material for the defence's claim of insanity.

> I had my grandparents [on the death list], not my grandmothers, my two grandfathers; Peter DeFeo; my uncle, Vinnie Procita and his wife, Phyllis Procita; one or two of my sister's girlfriends;

some of my friends. There was a lot of names on it, a good fifty. Took me a long time.... Why do they want to get me? I imagine because of what happened, just to start with. Because maybe they feel that I got it in for all them, too. If they don't get me, I'm going to get them, or vice versa. To be truthful, I told Dr. Schwartz exactly what I'm telling you. I told him if I got out of here, my aunt's own daughter—and she was on the list—I have full intention of killing every one of them.

Despite his dubious motives regarding the purported death list, it made a certain warped sense for him to extend his killing ground since annihilating his family had given him such peace: "I felt good that they were dead. I didn't believe there was nothing wrong with it. As far as I'm concerned ... what I did was self-defense because if I didn't kill them they were going to kill me. It's just who got who first.... You know, I got on the stand [at the pretrial hearing]; everything I said was the truth. I didn't lie about anything. Mr. Sullivan got me mixed up, you know, with words in themselves. I think that's the only thing I'm really afraid of in life is words. You know, people get me mixed up."[67]

What remained of Butch's humanity was at least partly revealed when Dr. Zolan tried to stir him to express his private feelings. "My feelings, it's like my feelings got out of my body and left. Crying—I could never cry. As far as hurting somebody and feeling bad, I can't feel bad. As far as having a conscience, I have no conscience. To this day, I honestly believe— you might laugh about it—I honestly believe sometimes that I'm a secret agent for God.... So I feel with a gun in my hand, the way I was going lately, I feel that I am an ultimate supreme being. I was God when I had a gun in my hand." Considering his circumscribed future, he told the psychiatrist: "I want no part of the world out there. As far as I'm concerned, out there, there is nothing but trouble, disease, animals. I want no part of the world. In here at night when we lock in, they lock us in the cells. I feel safe, that nobody is going to get me. I feel fine. I really like that." Undoubtedly he spoke the truth.[68]

DECIPHERING BUTCH

Maybe I like blood.

—BUTCH DEFEO[69]

What was there in the experience of Butch DeFeo that rendered his universe so unlivable? What made his social landscape so barren that he saw only turmoil and corruption? Why could words hurt him so deeply, and a gun in his hand make him a kind of god? Why should he decide that the only worthwhile escape (short of suicide, which he does not seem to have considered) was to ensure that he would be shut up safe and secure in a prison cell? As with all our cases, on the surface at least, the act makes no sense whatever. Here was the wildly overindulged child of a wealthy suburban family, living in a gorgeous home, who was allowed plenty of time and money to pursue any interests he might have. If he found the terms and conditions of employment—the social contract with his family—unacceptable, he need merely have left home and constructed his own life, as so many others have done before and after him. Yet he could not do so: his attempts at rebellion were weak and insubstantial, and his only realizable goal was escape—into alcohol and heroin and prison.

The facts do not speak entirely for themselves. They might have done so if Butch, responding to endless goading and assault, had simply murdered his father. Such a patricide could be explained in practical, even commonsensical terms—as the prosecution attempted to do when they argued that Butch had killed when he was discovered robbing the family's cash box. Such an explanation makes a certain sense but if it were true, Butch would have killed only his father. He could have then gone on to disguise the murder so that it appeared to be a bungled robbery, or retaliation by an unnamed Falini for some supposed violation of the underworld code. But this is not at all what happened. Butch killed his family coolly and energetically: as he put it, "once I started, I couldn't stop," and his enthusiasm did not wane until his entire family was annihilated. Alternatively, the defence psychiatrist and attorney claimed Butch killed because of bizarre psychological pathology. But what was there in the nature of this "personality disorder" that would cause him to kill his family? Perhaps the answer lies neither in the pragmatic elimination of witnesses to a crime nor in vague and unsubstantiated notions of mental illness.[70]

Butch appeared not to cooperate with the authorities in their attempt to understand the bloody event. Both in prison and in court he told so many conflicting and palpably false stories—all of which could be compared easily with one another by his interrogators—that had he been more intelligent we might conclude he was merely toying with us for his own amusement. However, the texture of his confessions does not suggest amusement: rather, it suggests a series of pathetic attempts to impress whoever he was addressing. Moreover, it reveals a colossal indifference to what he had done and the consequences of the deed—for others and for himself. This was certainly the way he presented himself before, during, and after the trial. Even before such a pose would have yielded him a certain élan, while police were still searching for the missing murder rifle and, unaware of Butch's guilt, making hurried plans for the family's collective funeral, Detective Gozaloff was puzzled by Butch's disinterest in events. When the detective snapped at him, "The least you could do is ask about the burials," Butch responded: "Oh, is there anything that I was supposed to do?" When the detective testily said that a relative would take care of the funeral arrangements, Butch was provocatively crass in asking if he was now eligible to receive the family's insurance. Discussing the immediate aftermath of the murders with the psychiatrist Zolan, he remembered that he had simply cleaned the house and gone to work, feeling no sense of loss: "I felt good that they were dead. I might have felt a little bad, but I felt good that they were dead." Butch structured each response either to impress his audience or please himself.[71]

Yet the same indifference towards his family was evident in his attitude to his own future. As he said during the trial, "I couldn't give a shit what these people find me, guilty or innocent. It doesn't make no difference. I either go to the prison for the rest of my life or a mental institution. What's the big thing? And you keep harping on me." Even at this critical juncture in his life, all he seemed to care about was that people stop bothering him. Yet these blasé qualities contrast sharply with the intense hatred he expressed for his family. The rage is baffling indeed, for surely his mother and siblings were innocent of any crime against him. If they did not deserve to die—and they most certainly did not— what was the process that channeled such aggression in their direction?[72]

TOWARDS DEATH IN LIFE

Anthropologists have built a major academic discipline in the study of culture—that coherent totality of beliefs and behaviours that members of a civilization transmit from generation to generation. This insight into a fundamental mechanism regulating human behaviour is one of the major achievements of the social sciences. But if it yields rich analytic profit in the understanding of small-scale primitive societies, its use in complex, large-scale, stratified industrial nations is more problematic. The difficulty is the heterogeneity of such societies: here, rival ideologies and beliefs jostle one another in the marketplace as they compete for public attention. Here, each family becomes a distinctive culture of its own, transmitting its own beliefs, values, and behaviours (however ineffectually) from generation to generation.

Like the larger, national cultures, familial cultures have their own official and mythologized versions of themselves—concocted for both public and private consumption—which may contrast with or even contradict the informal messages that are transmitted to the children. For example, a family may pretend to the world and to itself that it is both noble and spiritual when in reality it may be the arena for terrible physical and emotional abuse. But in the DeFeo case there was no contradiction. Both formal and informal texts broadcast the same message—rewarding aggressive display, approving violent behavior and illegal action. When Butch was a child, the family "bettered itself" by leaving the urban clutter of Brooklyn for a suburban home whose very name, High Hopes, reflected their social aspirations. But they took their family culture with them, and Butch was raised to kill.

Only two members of the DeFeo and Brigante families were able publicly to register warmth or dignity. Butch's aunt, Phyllis Procita, made strenuous attempts to understand the enigma who was her nephew and the tragedy that had befallen her family. Butch's uncle, Michael Brigante, Jr., showed a measure of real dignity when he protested that he and his family were being slandered. "I am a Catholic," he told the prosecuting attorney, and "I'm very perturbed. I am being slandered and my father is being slandered by testimony that father and I are part of organized crime and we have associations. I have never been arrested. I was in the Armed Services for eight years. I don't understand that people won't talk to me because they saw articles that I'm associated with—I have strong criminal links to the underworld. I don't understand what's going on. Are you trying to slander me as an individual? I don't know what's happening." Still, none of the other persons in the family issued such declarations.[73]

The social history of the Brigante and DeFeo families suggests quite clearly that both father and son, Ronald and Butch, were singled out for specific roles within and outside the Buick dealership. We have no way of knowing if this outside activity was illegal, nor does it matter to our analysis. We cannot state with certainty that we know from mere testimony that Butch was not the natural child of Ronald, Sr.; but if he was not, it raises important questions. What for example was the content of the marriage contract between the twenty-year-old textile worker, Ronald, and his father-in-law, in which a marriage was forged with a young woman pregnant with another man's child? Is it possible that Ronald was brought into the family less for his attentiveness to his new bride than for any role he might be groomed to play in handling the monies and jewelry that passed through his home? We will never know the source, or legality, of these valuables, but it is not important that we do. What matters is that Ronald re-created in his own family a culture and a milieu in which violence and duplicity were taught as virtues, and that both Ronald and Butch played economic roles and functions beyond the confines of the Buick dealership.

Anthropologist Nancy Scheper-Hughes has described the manner in which families occupying certain economic and social niches find it expedient to train one or more of their children to fill specific roles in their business. As Steven Benson was made passive and dependent in order to become a useful manager of the Benson estate; as Harry De La Roche, Jr. was regimented to become the officer and standard bearer for the family's social rise; so Butch DeFeo was indoctrinated from the beginning to occupy a menial role as delivery boy and go-between in his father's extracurricular business activities. In order to make him passive, they taught him he was worthless: thus his father told him at a tender age that he was a bastard, and failed to encourage any natural skills he might have had. Dependence and incompetence are *necessary* qualities in someone who is to occupy a menial role in an industry requiring loyalty and secrecy. To assure his dependence, he would be given far more money than he could possibly earn on his own, and far more influence (whether to avoid conscription or the penalties of parole) than he could possibly wield. The heroin addiction may have marred his suitability, but it did not eliminate it—indeed, it increased his passivity, dependence, and incompetence.

But the family's "job description" contained contradictions. If dependence was necessary to ensure loyalty to the business, survival in that world required an opposite quality—aggressiveness. That world was filled with violent men and women, and no one could survive without being aggressive. Both father and grandfather did their best to condition Butch in these qualities: Butch's grandfather would chase him through the house demanding vengeance for a crude remark; Ronald, Sr. would assault Butch or Louise with remarkable brutality. Similarly, the father would instruct the son in duplicity by rearranging the firm's bookkeeping to his own advantage. Unfortunately for their enterprise, they encoded in the adolescent Butch too much passivity and insufficient aggression; so troubled were they by their failure that they took him to a psychiatrist for help in making him more aggressive. The mother, whose apparent honor-staining pregnancy had precipitated this match, demanded treatment for her son's strange need to be told he was loved. Having initially failed to transplant their desired aggressiveness, in the end they succeeded all too well.

The family is "the crucible of every human identity," wrote anthropologist Thomas Belmonte, and through it we trace our first "connections to the universe." If the family is the central mechanism in the formation of individual character, it is programmed by the social and economic niche it occupies to have certain requirements, needs, and roles. These are idealized and affirmed in family culture, and indoctrinated in each generation by the family's socialization techniques. Sometimes, however, the niche the family occupies requires contradictory qualities, and the family's rulers may not be aware of the potential explosiveness of the ingredients they are stirring. In the case of Butch, in stealing his identity and legitimacy, his independence and his sexuality, yet insisting throughout his adolescence that he was insufficiently aggressive, the family unwittingly created the agent of its own destruction.[74]

Nevertheless, we have still not answered the fundamental question: Why did Butch destroy his entire family instead of his father alone? Because he came to see them, as did all other of our familicides, as indicted coconspirators, each family member playing a role in trapping him in an emasculating and tumultuous web that left no room for him to move. To escape the awareness that he had been unmanned, and to flee from the continuous battles in their noisy home, he sought refuge in heroin, the drug that calmed him and kept the world at bay. But the family culture was steeped in romanticized notions about underworld connections and their sinister powers, and in explicit denials of love and belonging. As the pressure on him intensified, as he was denied the right to flee to a new apartment or a new job, when his father did not believe his bogus story about the robbery, a simple means to quiet all discordance in his life emerged. He could cure his social and sexual impotence by becoming a kind of god, meting out divine punishment while demonstrating manly rage, and in doing so, give himself the precious gift of peace.

Small wonder then that he appeared well-content to spend the rest of the century in prison, locked safely away. Other women and men have escaped similar traps by building independent lives, but Butch knew that such bold action was beyond his capacity. Trained for subservience and dependence, caring nothing for himself or for others, Butch seems singularly well-adapted to his life in the correctional facility at Dannemora, New York.

CHAPTER FIVE

The Salesman's Salesman
Marlene Olive*

I'm evil, I'm so evil
I'm darkness in disguise
I know just what to do to steal
The color from your eyes.

—MARLENE OLIVE[1]

The murders were planned, organized, and commanded by the Olives' adopted daughter, Marlene, but they appear to have been actually carried out by her utterly subservient sex slave, Chuck Riley, who mindlessly followed her orders to kill her parents. Marlene's notable creative intelligence—revealed in the dozens of her poems reprinted in *Bad Blood*—had been reduced in her suburban San Francisco high school milieu to an empty dabbling in drugs, casual sex, occultism, and unfocussed rebellion. Thus to the public the case seemed to be a morality play demonstrating the dire consequences of unconventional behaviour. In fact, it was the opposite: it clearly outlined the pitfalls of conventional middle-class culture and behaviour, in which tensions and hostilities may be ignored rather than resolved, and harmony assigned a priority secondary to public image and economic success.

Nevertheless, it seems odd that the Olives became victims. Marlene's adopted father, Jim, was an optimistic but struggling salesman whose career was a series of failures and unfulfilled dreams. Get-rich-quick

* This chapter is based on the splendid reconstruction of the case in Richard Levine's *Bad Blood,* and on extensive coverage in *The San Francisco Chronicle, The San Francisco Examiner,* and *The New York Times.* Levine's book, which combines literary sensitivity with a rich social imagination, must rank among the finest of all portraits of individual homicides—with Gaddis and Long's *Killer,* Foucault's (ed.) *I, Pierre Riviére . . . ,* Klausner's *Son of Sam,* Michaud and Aynesworth's *The Only Living Witness,* Robins and Aronson's *Savage Grace,* and Frank's pioneering *The Boston Strangler.*

schemes inevitably succumbed to reality, and proposed books—a popular history here, an adventure novel there—were never quite written. Marlene's adopted mother, Naomi, was herself a foster child who turned to alcohol to soothe the anxiety generated by her troubled childhood and her husband's peripatetic career. To launch his final bid at success, the beloved father turned his attention from Marlene to his business while the despised mother accelerated her angry and demeaning assaults on Marlene. A significant irony is that almost from the beginning of their unhappiness the Olive family received care and treatment of the highest quality from psychiatrists, psychologists, social workers, juvenile counsellors, and police. Although most of the mental health professionals perceived with startling acuity the direction in which the family was moving, they were as powerless as the Olives to alter the course of events.[2]

THE KILLINGS

My mind is being blown to pieces,
My feelings are engulfing me.
They are going their own way.

—MARLENE OLIVE[3]

We will never know precisely what happened, since both Marlene and Chuck had self-serving motives for obscuring the truth, and Chuck's memory was further tainted by a number of sessions under hypnosis. What we do know is that Marlene had often broached the subject of killing her parents with her friends and especially with her enthralled boyfriend, Chuck Riley, with whom she shared her darkest thoughts. We do have her testimony of the final argument with her detested mother, in which her mother called her "trash," a "swine," and a "gutter tramp," whose natural mother was a "whore" who "gave you away." Marlene remembered shouting at her adopted mother, "I hate you," and her mother repeating the sentiment; this was followed by an exchange of "bitch" and "shut your damn foul mouth." Moments later, Marlene gave her instructions to Chuck over the telephone: "Get your gun. We've got to kill that bitch today."[4]

After the murders, while in a hypnotic state, Chuck recalled Marlene's last-minute speculation on the method of despatching her parents. "She is talking about putting some kind of pills in the food, in some soup. . . . I

want to get around it somehow. But I have to do it because she says so. I
can't avoid it. She told me I had to do it. . . . That's all we talk about. She
asked me on the phone. . . . 'Where do I hit my mom to kill her? How
hard do I hit her?' I don't know. I don't know. I tell her I never hurt
nobody before. I don't know how to. 'Just tell me where. That's all.
Where to hit her.' " Marlene then asked, " 'What if we use a hammer?'
No, not a hammer. A rolling pin. Something heavy. 'How hard do I have
to hit?' She kept asking that question all day, all day. I didn't say nothing
then. Later, I did."[5]

Marlene's final decision was a hammer and a pistol. While Chuck
dutifully went to purchase ammunition for his .22-calibre Ruger, Marlene
spoke to her friend, "Sharon Dillon," on the telephone.* As the blasé
Dillon later told police, the conversation had been a "casual" one, "nothing important. She said she'd had just about enough of her parents and
was getting tired of them and that she was going to bump them off. She
said she was gonna put sleeping pills in her mom's soup. . . . I didn't believe
her." Marlene dropped a number of Darvon capsules into her mother's
soup, but her mother disliked the taste and only ingested a small amount
before taking a nap. When her father had gone to his own bedroom for a
nap and had fallen asleep, Marlene carried a claw hammer into his room:
"I stood over him," she later recalled. "I started to bring [the hammer]
down and pulled back. And tried it again and pulled back." She could
not complete the act, which made her still angrier.[6]

The Olives had not approved of their middle-class daughter's relationship with working-class Chuck and they had banned him from their
home. In order to kill Naomi, it was thus necessary for Chuck to hide
near the Olive home until Jim had awakened from his nap and left the
house in the family car with Marlene. Chuck entered the home and found
the claw hammer that Marlene had set aside for him. Later, in a hypnosis
session, he said: "I am terrified to walk in the house. It has been so long
since I have been there. And I was really unsure about being there. Mr.
Olive was going to kill me if he saw me enter that house again. Yes. He
told me so. I was afraid of Mr. Olive. He was making me do without
Marlene a lot. He was driving me hard. Looking around . . . I stood there
for a couple of minutes. It was so quiet . . . I walk back down by the
bathroom, and there is a door. And it was closed. It was Marlene's
bedroom." Naomi lay asleep on the bed there and, as he told his arresting

---

* Throughout this chapter, I follow Levine's system of names and pseudonyms.

officer, "I just hit her. I don't even remember. My mind went blank and I don't remember anything after that." He struck her repeatedly in the forehead with the hammer: with the final blow, the hammer lodged in her skull.[7]

> I had to touch her to take the hammer out. It was really hard. It wouldn't come loose. I just about broke the hammer. Blood. Blood. No. No. It is burning my hand up. My left hand. Blood. There was blood everywhere. It shot out when I pulled the hammer. It spurts out as soon as the hammer came out, all over my hand. Fire. I have to do something to get the blood off. I'm flinging it off my hand like you do with a paintbrush when you're cleaning it. I can't stand it, I can't stand it. It's burning my hand. Then I saw the hem of a dress and I picked it up and wiped my hands on it. . . . She wouldn't die. She wouldn't die at all. Please, God, let her die. I just couldn't see her living like that. It hurt so much to see that. So much.

He told the jail nurse that he then stabbed Naomi in the chest with a steak knife, but that she still would not die: he was trying to smother her with her pillow when he heard the Olives' car pull up to the house.[8]

Marlene paused in the doorway to allow her father to enter the house first, warning him, she later told a psychiatrist, "Don't go in there. You're going to die." Her father "just giggled and walked in." Chuck's account continued:

> The car's back. They're home. Mr. Olive's home. What do I do? I don't know what to do. I run up the hallway, look around. There's nowhere to go, nowhere to go. I'm trapped. I'm trapped in the house. There's only one way out—through them. . . . I see Mr. Olive. He is walking towards me. He looks in the room and sees Mrs. Olive. He screams. He runs over towards her. "Oh, my God, Naomi. Oh, my God." I can hear that screaming echoing in my head, just echoing. And then—no, no—he sees me. He sees me. "I am going to kill you, you bastard! I am going to kill you!" There's a knife right there on the nightstand by the bed. "Don't pick it up." No, no. He is picking up the knife. He comes stepping towards me, lunging. I shoot him. I shot him. I shot him. I just pulled the trigger, never even took the gun out of the bag. He didn't even know I had it. I shot him. He spun around,

facing me again, and I shot him three more times before he hit the floor. I couldn't stop pulling the trigger.

Chuck walked to the living room and sat there, "staring into the fireplace. Just staring, staring." Marlene joined him, he said, and assured him that "everything's all right, Chuck. Everything's all right. Don't worry. Everything's all right."[9]

Chuck and Marlene made love. Then they turned their attention to the bodies: they emptied Jim's pockets and removed the gold wedding ring and jade school ring from his fingers. Marlene took the credit cards and a checkbook from her mother's purse, and removed her mother's watch and rings. With the valuables confiscated, they tried to disguise any evidence that there had been a killing, scrubbing down the blood-spattered furniture and walls. Marlene was infuriated when she noticed that her mother's blood was dripping on her favorite oil painting: "Curse that bitch! Getting her blood all over my picture," Levine records her shouting. Drawing a blanket over Naomi's face, Chuck remembered Marlene turning to him with a "mocking grin," and remarking, "that's the last time I'll ever have to look at her." They wandered casually through the local shopping mall, pausing to view the merchandise on display and to chat with friends, before making their way to Chuck's family's modest tract house. After a brief visit, they continued on to a friend's, where they ingested marijuana and cocaine and made love, at Marlene's insistence, in the friend's bathroom. They went out to eat at a local Chinese restaurant.[10]

After dinner and a film, they returned to the Olives' home to dispose of the bodies. Dumping them in the back of the family's Vega, they drove to an isolated rural clearing where hunters often barbecued poached deer. They placed Naomi and Jim side by side on a concrete firepit, covered the bodies with a waist-high stack of branches, emptied a gas can over them and struck a match. They returned to the Olive home to sleep, but awakened early at six A.M. to return to the firepit and check that the fire had done its work. It had not: Naomi's body was almost completely incinerated, but Jim's torso and head remained virtually intact. They made a larger fire, which reduced both corpses to ashes, and then hurried home: Chuck did not wish his parents to learn that he had been out all night.[11]

One week later, Jim's business partner Colonel Phil Royce was sufficiently disturbed by Jim Olive's uncharacteristic absence from work and failure to return telephone messages that he asked the police to make a "welfare check" on the house. The police obliged, but found nothing suggestive of foul play. Nevertheless, they continued their investigations and when police and a psychiatrist interrogated Marlene for fourteen hours, she gave them a series of contradictory and implausible versions of what had happened to her parents. Suspicious police officers continued to press matters until one of Marlene's friends blurted out the story of the killings and led them to the firepit. Professor Rodger Hagler, a physical anthropologist at San Francisco State University and an experienced forensic scientist, was able to identify the remains of at least two humans in the firepit. Marlene and Chuck were arrested and charged.

CONFESSIONS

I have no guilt feelings at all about my folks. None.

—MARLENE OLIVE[12]

Before her arrest, Marlene had made the mistake of telling the truth to two of her friends. The night after the murders, Marlene had slept over at Leslie Slote's. Slote remembered Marlene looking "emotionally wigged-out," and ultimately breaking into tears and crying "I don't have a mom." As Slote remembered, "I go, 'What do you mean?'" and Marlene replied: "My dad was going to take me to the [Juvenile] Hall that afternoon and turn in all of us for smoking dope. He said he had a list. We couldn't let that happen." Slote did not know whether to believe her, but Marlene "gave me the impression it was just a split-second thing. Also that Chuck did all the dirty work." The following morning, Marlene visited Sharon Dillon, who later told police that she had felt "weird vibes" from Marlene and asked her, "Did you croak your parents?" Marlene admitted that she had and told Sharon the whole story, showing her the bloodstains in Naomi's room and asking for her help in cleaning the room more thoroughly.[13]

To the authorities, however—indeed to all adults—Marlene feigned ignorance of her parents' whereabouts. To support her intended alibi that she had been in Tahoe at the time of the killings, she left a note by the telephone in her father's office: "Sun.–Wed. Tahoe. Wed. concert, out night. Thurs. Home. Fri. S.F., movie, dinner." Responding to an enquiry from her father's business partner, she telephoned him and asked, "Colonel Royce, where are my folks? What's happened? Their clothes and luggage are here but I haven't seen them since I got back from Tahoe on Wednesday." She maintained this story with an enquiring juvenile officer who, impressed by Marlene's apparent concern, assumed that the Olives had simply gone on a sudden vacation. "Sergeant Hool," he remembered her pleading, "can you help me find my father?" Detective Stinson, a more seasoned interrogator, grew suspicious when Marlene described quite different weather than had prevailed in Tahoe when she was supposedly there. At first he assumed that the lie was to cover Marlene's theft of her parents' credit cards, but his disbelief increased when Marlene invented yet another alibi to explain her use of the credit cards. He remembered telling her, "You know, I find it very hard to believe anything you've said. Even your second story is not plausible to me." Marlene responded to this by replying, "What I should really do is just sit down and think."[14]

In tears, she began to tell a story of a vision she had had. "Every time I close my eyes, I can still see my father standing over my mother in a pool of blood. He's yelling, 'Nomi, Nomi, Nomi.' I know something terrible has happened to my parents. I know they're dead. I've been seeing this vision ever since I came home Monday with Sharon and found so much blood on the carpet in the sewing room and on the wall behind the couch where my picture is." This convinced Stinson that violence may actually have occurred, and Marlene was escorted to the hospital for a psychiatric evaluation: there, an intern thought Marlene had some "neurotic fantasies," but found her healthy enough to be released.[15]

When Officer Nelson resumed the interrogation, Marlene told him seven separate and contradictory stories. In the first, her mother had killed her father and fled; in the second, her father had killed her mother. In the third, her parents had both been killed by a burglar; in the fourth, a hired gunman had murdered the Olives; and in the fifth, an angry Hell's Angel client of Jim's had murdered them. In a sixth version, the police transcript records, Marlene said: "They're dead. That's not bullshit. I saw their bodies. . . . I tell you they're dead and you don't believe me. It's true." In her seventh story, she denied the previous six and said that her parents had been quarrelling and must have decided on an impromptu vacation. Shortly after this, police intercepted a note she had written to Chuck: "I said my parents went on a trip as far as I knew. I said we had an accident in room with glass table. That's why blood. Even when I did say something true they didn't believe it happened or I'd do it or anyone would do anything. . . . They think my parents will be home tonite or tomorrow. I hope you get to Sharon [Dillon] before they do. I have no guilt feelings at all about my folks. NONE. NEITHER SHOULD YOU! *Relax. . . .*"[16]

When police interviewed Marlene's friend, Sharon Dillon, she confirmed Marlene's fears by telling them what Marlene had said. Chuck listened to Sharon's taped remarks and immediately capitulated: "I did it! I did it! I didn't want to do it. Marlene made me do it. She kept asking me and asking me, begging me and begging me for months. Telling me to do it or she wouldn't love me anymore. And I finally did it. I loved her so much I didn't think I would get by. Please help me." Under further questioning, Chuck added that

> she wanted me to [kill]. I don't know. She said they were going to take her away from me. I don't know. She told me her dad's going to take her away from me forever. She said I had to do it. . . . All the time they were messing me up. They were always hurting my head, always hurting my head. She just told me to do it, so I did it, that's all. I don't know what I did. I really don't. Help me. Please help me. I have to see her and talk to her. I have to. Please. I have to. I don't want to be by myself. I didn't want to do it. I didn't. She told me to. . . . She kept telling me a long time, a couple of months. She kept telling me to do it. Find someone to do it. And I said no, I don't want to. I'm afraid. She just kept telling me to do it and finally she said that I had to do it or she wouldn't love me anymore.[17]

Within months of her admission to Juvenile Hall, Marlene had exonerated herself of all involvement in her father's death. In a letter to her new boyfriend she wrote, "I hate to say it, but I hope that the man who killed my parents pays. He broke my heart, killed part of me, took what I loved most in life—my father—and now smiles. I can't forgive him. I am sorry." By the time she appeared in court, she had decided to deny all participation in the murders. In this revised version, Marlene claimed she had heard her father shout, " 'Oh my God, Naomi. What's happened to you?' " and then heard shots. After these "blasts from a weapon," she was "frozen in place" with fear. When she saw Chuck, "He was just a madman. His eyes were bulging, his face was red, he had blood on his shirt and his hands looked gigantic. 'Are you going to kill me, too?' " she now claimed she asked him. She said Chuck beat her, then forced her to help with the disposal of what she "assumed" must be the bodies of her parents, wrapped in bedclothes. In this version, she remained chastely in the car while Chuck burned the bodies of her parents, and was then virtually held prisoner by Chuck and his fellow drug dealers. Numbed by her prescription medications, and repeatedly beaten, she could only remember being in a "state of shock."[18]

The court was profoundly unmoved by this obviously self-serving story, and Judge Best ruled that "Marlene Olive did encourage, instigate, aide, abet and act as accomplice in the homicide of her parents." Although the crime was first-degree murder, California's obsolete law specified that as a juvenile, she could only be found guilty of violating a minor section of the state's welfare code, and would therefore be eligible for release before she turned twenty-one. Chuck, on the other hand, was slightly older and could therefore be tried as an adult: he would face the state's mandatory death penalty for multiple murder. Lovestruck Chuck, however, was concerned less with his sentence than with his enforced separation from Marlene: he was especially agitated because police had confiscated his "magic" bracelet, which Marlene had told him enabled them to communicate. "They took my bracelet away," Chuck complained. "Please help me get it back. I need to talk to Marlene so bad. If I had my bracelet I could talk to her. She sends me signals through it. She's a witch, you know. She can control people's minds."[19]

Chuck waited for months before he decided to rewrite his participation in the murders. In this revised edition, he raised the possibility that it may have been Marlene, not him, who killed Naomi Olive. As he wrote in his diary at that time, he intended "to clear my name with friends and family and to let the Law and Lord know I didn't do it. All other statements are false, for the protection of the one I love." Chuck now claimed that he had been confused about the events surrounding the killings until he had dreamt that he had found Naomi already dead when he opened her bedroom door. The reality of this intuition was confirmed for him when an inmate at juvenile hall claimed Marlene had told him that she had killed both her parents, and that "if things got too hot for Chuck," she would tell the court the truth. Upon hearing this, Chuck's second version emerged, essentially an embroidery of his dream in which he had discovered Naomi's body with the claw hammer stuck in her forehead.[20]

The contradictions in Chuck's and Marlene's stories led Chuck's lawyer to turn elsewhere for confirmation. Despite hypnosis's well-established capacity for memory-tainting, Chuck was hypnotized. He proved to be as astonishingly susceptible to hypnotism as he had been to Marlene: in his several trances, he reiterated his discovery of Naomi's body which, if accepted by the court, would allow him to evade the mandatory death penalty for multiple murder. In his trance, he said,

> I am terrified to walk in the house. . . . there is a door and it was closed. It was Marlene's bedroom. I opened it and there was Mrs. Olive on the bed and she was dead. There's a hammer in her head. Yeah, coming out of her forehead. I didn't know what to do. The more I stood there, the more I had to get that hammer out. Do you know what it is like to see a hammer in somebody? I didn't know—I think she was dead. I couldn't tell. I was hoping she was because I just couldn't see her living like that. I couldn't see it. It hurt so much to see that. . . . I had to touch her to take the hammer out. It was really hard. Blood. Blood. No. No.[21]

In a later session, he added more information to confirm his innocence. Now Marlene had told him that she had "sneaked back into the house while my dad was waiting for me in the car, and I went and killed my mother, hit her with the hammer and went back outside." Chuck explained that he had first lied to police in order to protect Marlene: "I loved her so much, and I was looking for the answers from her. I would do anything to save her, even give my life for her. I know she loves me. . . . Marlene killed her mother. She did it. She did it." The jury was not convinced by these claims and found him guilty of the first-degree murder of both Olives. He was sent to San Quentin to await execution, but after the U.S. Supreme Court overturned the state's capital punishment legislation, his death sentence was converted to life imprisonment.[22]

THE MENTAL HEALTH PROFESSIONALS

> She stood in the doorway of death,
> Closed her eyes and held her breath.
> And although she was alive,
> She knew she couldn't survive.
>
> —MARLENE OLIVE[23]

The family's first brush with psychiatry was a profoundly disturbing one, the cruelty of which reverberated through the generations. Naomi's natural mother had spent her adult life in an institution, and Naomi had come to share the destructive and unfounded folk belief—often promulgated by psychiatry itself—that mental illness is somehow inherited, like red hair or blue eyes.* Anthropology has long demonstrated that folk beliefs of this kind can act as self-fulfilling prophecies. Just as primitive tribesmen who believe they will be destroyed by spirit possession may in fact wither and die, so members of modern civilizations bearing the stigma of an institutionalized parent may act out the culture's dictate that they will inherit the insanity. Terrified that she might inherit her mother's illness, Naomi's anxiety pushed her into the state—a direction assured by the instability in her childhood (her mother in an institution, her father placing her in a foster home) and the unending social and economic failures of her husband. Similarly fearful that her own adopted daughter would inherit Marlene's natural mother's alleged promiscuity, Naomi in her anxious and punitive parenting deformed Marlene as she herself had been deformed.[24]

Paradoxically, after that first destabilizing message, the Olive family received only the highest quality of psychological and psychiatric counselling. Time and again with extraordinary prescience, psychiatrists, social workers, and psychologists predicted the direction in which the family might evolve. Although the professionals warned of impending disaster, the Olives took no action, since Naomi was fearful and contemptuous of psychology, and husband and wife both resisted what Jim called "airing the family's dirty linen." Thus their distrust of the authorities and their desire to appear to be a stable, middle-class family overwhelmed their judgment.

Naomi's morbid sensitivity and dependence on alcohol had prompted her sister-in-law as early as the summer of 1964, when Namoi was living in S. America, to persuade her to visit a psychiatric clinic, Levine discovered. The astute psychiatric social worker who interviewed Naomi noted that the "patient is isolated in Ecuador where she feels she cannot stay because of the difference of culture and lack of family life and freedom that American women have in the country. She has been depressed for the past two years and then she started to drink heavily. She gave up drinking a month ago and then she became more depressed. She could not sleep or eat properly. She cries and was hopeless and frightened that

---

* The level of this analysis is typically low, often lacking even a hypothetical explanatory mechanism, and relying on simpleminded correlations. Thus if I play tennis and both my sons play tennis, they have inherited my susceptibility to tennis—or even my tennis genes.

something would happen to her or her husband." Jim and Naomi attended four group-therapy sessions together, and the staff psychologist diagnosed her case as "schizoid personality with paranoid features." He urged continued therapy and prescribed antidepressant and tranquilizing pills, but Naomi could never again be induced to seek treatment. As she angrily told her sister-in-law, "you'd just love to see me locked up, wouldn't you? That way you could have your little brother all to yourself." In what was his accustomed response to conflict, Jim avoided the subject.[25]

Naomi was delighted to return to the United States after Jim's repeated business failures had driven them out of Ecuador, but rather than finding peace both she and Marlene experienced an increase in their problems. Marlene developed sleeplessness and stomachaches, which prompted her doctor to discover her duodenal ulcer. For her tension and mood shifts, asthma, ulcer, and allergies, he prescribed sleeping pills and sedatives, to which Marlene rapidly became addicted. Marlene thought the drugs "washed over your head like a wave" and buried all anxieties. Naomi descended further into mental illness. In California, locked alone in her bedroom, Naomi would speak the parts of four or five relatives in angry argument, changing her voice for each part.[26]

Typically, the optimistic salesman did his best to ignore these matters until events abruptly forced him to pay attention. When Marlene entered the ninth grade, she and a girlfriend were arrested in a drugstore for shoplifting. Juvenile Officer Scott Nelson's interview with the family led him to believe that Jim possessed the quality that would get a child out of trouble—"a parent who really cares about what happens to his kid"—but both parents' private reaction to the incident was in keeping with their personalities. Jim tried to gloss over the incident and the resulting tension in the family. Naomi screamed at Marlene in front of the house: "Why do you do things like this? Don't you know you can get arrested? Don't your father and mother take good enough care of you so you don't have to steal?"[27]

Marlene ran away from home on January 15, her sixteenth birthday. After juvenile authorities recaptured her, state regulations forced Naomi to attend family counselling. Juvenile Officer Nelson conducted the preliminary session, which was designed to see if the family needed more extensive care. Nelson was struck by the fact that Jim seemed more concerned about Marlene's "drug habit" than about her relationship with her mother. As always, he avoided conflict and failed to see what was significant. Nelson was taken aback by the intensity of anger between mother and daughter, and recommended further counselling. The Olives refused and Levine records that Naomi was furious, and vowed never to be "dragged through that cesspool again." Resolutely tending to the bright side, Jim led his family to their fate.[28]

Not long after the counselling session, Marlene considered an alternative method of coping with the familial tension: she approached Officer Nelson with a request that she be allowed to move into a foster home. As Nelson later recalled,

> Marlene told me that the mother hated her and was on her case for every little thing, sometimes getting physically abusive when she was drunk. She showed me a cut on her arm that she said she got when Mrs. Olive pushed her through a plate-glass window. She said that her mother slept in the spare room opposite her bedroom because her father couldn't stand sleeping next to a drunk and that she kept Marlene up at night talking to herself. She even made a point of saying the parents never had sex. She kept calling her mother "that bitch." The only complaint she seemed to have about her father was that he kowtowed to the mother to keep things peaceful.

Marlene's request was honored and she was placed in a foster home, but she was unable to live up to the home's regulations and she was returned to her parents within weeks.[29]

By then Marlene and Chuck had embarked on a massive shoplifting adventure for which they were apprehended on March 26 and booked under the California juvenile code. Her intake officer noted that Naomi Olive "was quite irate, loud and angry, stating that, 'Why hadn't she been notified of her daughter being in detention?'" The officer observed that Naomi was "a possible chronic alcoholic ... which has a profound effect on her daughter. I suspect there are many other problems in the home and that it is not feasible to release Marlene to her parents at this point in time." The explanation for this tension between Marlene and her parents was articulated with extraordinary insight by a juvenile hall probation officer, Nancy Boggs, who had transferred to affluent Marin County after nine years in Los Angeles' black ghetto. She found Marin's prosperous families "much more seriously disturbed" than the impoverished Watts families. *"The kids here are angry at their parents, not at society. And the parents are more concerned with what the neighbors will think than with improving the situation at home,"* Boggs concluded.[30]

When Boggs insisted that family therapy was necessary, Jim Olive admitted that there were serious problems at home, but "stated that his wife is 'scared to death' of psychiatrists and refuses to participate in any form of counseling," Boggs wrote. Like previous workers on the case, Boggs was surprised by the bellicosity of the relationship between mother and daughter, and her report on Marlene observed, "She states that the primary problem is her mother, who drinks to excess and talks to herself all the time, which 'drives me up the wall.'" Marlene complained to her that her father seemed incapable of positive action and could only say, "We have to learn to cope with mother's problem." Nonetheless, Marlene appeared to capitulate: she told Boggs "she wanted to go home and would try to go along with what her parents wanted." Marlene made a list for Boggs of changes she would make in her behaviour, including such items as "Go strictly by parents' rules," and "Feed and groom cats." However, Boggs thought Marlene should have remained in custody until matters improved, and warned Jim that "without therapy and some drastic changes at home you're going to be headed for serious trouble."[31]

When Marlene was released from custody on the following day over Boggs' objections, Boggs reported that "It is felt that although Marlene states she wants to go home and will abide by her parents' requests, she will be unable to do so because of the disturbed family situation." The court ignored her recommendation for "a complete psychological evaluation" of the family, and Boggs asked to be removed from the Olive case. As she explained her actions to the family biographer, Levine, "I felt that I was loaded up with crazy families and couldn't do the situation justice." To her colleague, she wrote with her customary acuity: "There's going to be more trouble with this one. Marlene is angry at her parents—legitimately so. She has a disturbed mother, an ineffective father unable to make decisions, a boyfriend her parents disapprove of strongly. She's acting out. It's a classic blowup situation." Similarly, a few weeks before the killings when Marlene's new probation officer, Mary Sigler, was preparing to go on vacation, she sent the Olive file to her supervisor with an attached note that read, "This one could blow up while I'm gone."[32]

After the killings when Marlene was charged with the murders, she was given a psychiatric examination. Dr. Stanley Upshaw found her legally sane but suffering from "an elongated diminished capacity that culminated in killing." The battery of psychological tests, administered by Dr. Lawrence Katz, revealed only a "highly affect-laden" response to the incomplete sentences test: "*A mother* ... ' should love her daughter.' *I can't* . . . 'live without the emptiness replaced.' " The Rorschach ink-blot card often seen as the "mother card" elicited from Marlene the comment, "Desolation, sorrow and emptiness." Katz concluded that Marlene

> is a very interesting young woman and one who is obviously very troubled. Miss Olive is functioning intellectually in the High Average range. She does not give evidence of overt thinking disturbance. On the other hand, she seems to be someone whose judgment could be poor in those areas where love is involved, even though in many respects her capacity to perceive reality clearly seems to be intact. She shows an unusual mixture of maturity in some areas and considerable immaturity in others, with a tendency to be quite hysterical and histrionic and very easily given to poetic flights of fancy and oversymbolic, vague and amorphous styles of relating to the world.[33]

Meanwhile, Chuck Riley is reported to have told a fellow inmate in prison, "I'm insa-a-a-a-ne. A couple of years on a green lawn and I'll be back out." In an apparent attempt to have Chuck declared insane, his attorney ordered a psychiatric examination. Dr. John Steinhelber's report to the court said Chuck "readily admitted killing Marlene's parents, describing the events as something that Marlene directed him to do and that he couldn't help doing. He couldn't explain what he meant by his conviction that he couldn't help it, and he was uncertain whether Marlene's powers as a witch were or were not involved." The psychiatrist concluded that Chuck had "a chronic psychotic thought disorder, and current extreme emotional distress." He thought that Chuck's "extreme subjective need for Marlene [was] a real and symbolic fulfillment of his inadequately met social and sexual needs," and that Chuck's "perception of her parents as symbolic sources of his frustrations" led to his participation in the killings.[34]

Dr. Charles Cress, a San Francisco psychiatrist, saw Chuck on several occasions and diagnosed him as a "border-line personality," capable of occasional psychotic lapses, but not legally insane. He thought the relationship between Marlene and Chuck was "symbiotic," "an attachment between two people in which at least one of them . . . feels that he or she cannot survive without the other." He thought Chuck was "enthralled" by Marlene: " 'Enthralled' sounds somewhat poetic but I think it fairly accurately describes the state of mind that this man had towards Marlene Olive. He felt in her power. . . . She was able to direct his activity, whether she was in the room or not. In a fairy tale he would be said to be 'under her magic spell.' " Both defence psychiatrists agreed that Chuck was "seriously impaired" by his servitude to Marlene, "extremely suggestible," and quite capable of killing the Olives.[35]

Unable to prove his client was insane, Chuck's attorney settled for a defence based on diminished capacity. During the trial, which opened on October 30, 1975, psychiatrist Dr. John Hess elaborated on Chuck's subservience to Marlene.

> What took place was a kind of psychological merging in which he, in exchange for the continued fulfillment of his needs and his fantasies, would trade in, as it were, his own capacity to think objectively, to act independently. He became essentially enslaved. His relationship with Marlene was a kind of grotesque caricature of love, filled with fantasies of dying for her, filled with fantasies of sacrificing anything in accord with her wishes.... Finally, his relationship with Marlene was so intense and her role in his life, psychologically speaking, became so great as to actually destroy— not totally, but to a large degree—his very sense of himself as an independent, separate individual. Yes. I think that the control was essentially total. Yes. I have a very firm opinion that had Marlene proposed in an appropriate way that, for example, Mr. Riley jump off the Golden Gate Bridge, that he would have done so.

If the professionals had delivered insightful advice from beginning to end, however, their understanding was necessarily quite ineffective without the cooperation of the Olives. At no time had they been granted such cooperation.[36]

SOCIAL HISTORY OF THE OLIVE FAMILY

[Dad] was holding everything together
While he slowly fell apart.

—MARLENE OLIVE[37]

The rise and fall of the Olive family began before the First World War, when Jim's Scots-Irish grandfather settled in western New York: an ambitious agricultural labourer, he worked himself into the ownership of a prosperous dairy farm. Jim's father, Chester, moved to Panama in 1925 to become business manager of a new English-language newspaper; Jim was then nine. The business soon floundered, and while Jim's elder sister Elsie was despatched to collect outstanding bills from their customers, Jim sold the newspaper on the streets. In what Levine correctly thought was "the key document" in Jim Olive's life—his job resume—Jim both documented and concealed the continuing failures in his life. "Jim Olive, Marketeer," described his modest beginnings in positive terms: "My experience in foreign sales began at the age of nine, hawking the new tabloid in company with a screeching horde of unwashed urchins. They taught me colloquial Spanish, the elements of street fighting, and the value of persistence in salesmanship." Eventually, the *Panama American* prospered, and Jim Olive grew up, he thought, a "thoroughly Latinized American"—but that may have been true only linguistically, since his mind could focus only on his career, and he felt uncomfortable when trying to express his inner feelings. As his biographer, Levine, sadly noted after interviewing many of Jim's friends: "If the conversation turned too personal, one would likely find him staring off into space, lost in thoughts of his future fame and fortune."[38]

When still a youth, Jim had demonstrated his remarkable propensity for harebrained schemes designed to bring him instant wealth, and his predilection for failure. His science career at Pennsylvania State College ended abruptly when he caused an explosion in the chemistry lab; he switched to business administration, graduating in 1937. He worked for a short time with a New York literary agency where, his resume reads, "I learned the value of personal contacts." Returning to Panama, he tried to develop beachfront building lots, oblivious to the fact that they were located far from any population center: none were sold. He worked as a mail censor during the Second World War, rising to the rank of major. On leave during the summer of 1944, he met and married Naomi, ten years his junior.[39]

Naomi, the daughter of a family occupying a much lower and unstable social and economic niche, used her considerable beauty in the approved manner to marry "up" in the social order. Her father was a local farm labourer, and her mother was committed to a hospital for the remainder of her life when Naomi was only two. Naomi was shuttled between the two sets of grandparents while her mother was alive, but after her mother's death Naomi was "adopted out" to a well-to-do local family, the DeKays. As an adolescent growing up with the DeKays, she is remembered as remarkable only for her beauty, her depressive moods, and her temper. She had little contact with her natural father and brother and did not invite them to her wedding.[40]

The Olives returned to Panama after Jim was discharged from the military and he briefly tried his hand at real estate. Naomi disliked the tropical heat and insects, the strange language and food, and the intense social activity into which she was unwillingly swept. Jim soon obtained what would be the first of many jobs in the oil industry when he was appointed Central American advertising manager for Standard Oil. His work kept him away from home for extended periods, and left Naomi ill-at-ease in her isolation: Jim's promotion four years later to be Esso's division manager in El Salvador did nothing to assuage Naomi's fearfulness, despite the large house and the many servants. Naomi recoiled from the lavish entertaining required by Jim's position and her anxieties surfaced in a growing list of compulsions and fears. Levine concluded that she felt socially inferior to Jim's family, and thought that they despised her. She thought people were stealing from her, and to forestall this she checked each piece of linen as it returned from the laundry. When Jim's mother died and left him a substantial inheritance, Naomi prevailed upon him to move back to the United States. They purchased an apartment block in Florida and Jim spun his money-making schemes, all of which failed, dissipating the inheritance.[41]

It was at this time, during the early 1950s, that Jim embarked on a new career as a writer. He longed to write a grand historical novel about William Walker, the freebooting American who for a brief period in the nineteeth century had declared himself ruler of Nicaragua. He failed in this as in all else, and for the same reason. When his agent criticized his work, rather than bending his energies to mastering the craft of writing, Levine observed, Jim invented new strategies for marketing it. The salesman reminded his agent of the imminent centenary of Walker's campaign, and that his book would therefore

mean plenty to the Nicaraguan Tourist Commission ... if a well-directed campaign of publicity were put on, built around the 6,000 ghosts of Walker's army of adventurers. ... I hate to miss a good bet. When a parade comes along it seems that everyone wants to jump on the bandwagon. I don't mind standing on the curb, but I don't want to miss the spectacle completely. This thing has dynamite in it. If it's sales ideas you need, I got 'em. If

it's maps or authentification you need, I got 'em. I've got a
library of books written by Walker and his men. . . . Nobody's
got what I've got. I've even been to Nicaragua! Let's get on this
thing, Mr. Meredith. There's a big parade a 'coming.[42]

The novel came to nothing, as had his entrepreneurial activities in
Florida, all of which exacerbated Naomi's insecurity and reliance on
alcohol. By 1955 Jim had taken a position in Virginia with Phillips
Petroleum, but it was a poor choice since fifteen major oil companies
were active in the area and Jim had to work day and night merely to
avert bankruptcy. It was at this point that they decided to adopt a child.
A family friend from that period recalled that "it wasn't really Jim's idea.
Naomi wanted a child desperately. She needed something of her own."
The child they found was Marlene, the daughter of a young woman from
a socially prominent Norfolk family and a Scandinavian sailor. Family
friends were surprised at Naomi's compulsive possessiveness of her new
daughter: "She was very clinical in her approach to motherhood," one
remembered. "I don't remember her being overly loving in a spontaneous
way. It was not a question of lying in bed and bouncing Marlene around
on her tummy." Another friend noted that Naomi "would never go out,
not even to the movies or a dinner party. 'Nomi,' I'd tell her, 'you'll
smother the child to death.' "[43]

It was at this point that Jim's business deals bankrupted him and he
lost all of his life savings. Naomi was devastated. She developed a nervous
tic in her eyebrows and a tendency to public tantrums and compulsive
talking. A friend from the period remembered inviting the Olives to
dinner, only to find Naomi and the baby closeted in a bedroom for the
evening. "I fixed a plate of food," she told Levine, "and Jim took it in to
her. Well, the next thing I knew the bedroom door opened and Naomi
hurled the plate of food at Jim and stomped around yelling, 'You threw
away a hundred and fifty thousand dollars. How could you do that?
You've thrown it all away.' Jim and my husband had to pack her home
and I spent the rest of the evening scraping food off the walls. The next
time I met Naomi she was perfectly sweet and never once mentioned the
incident."[44]

Soon Jim joined the Tennessee Gas Transmission Company as their
Ecuador sales manager. If he slipped easily into the Latin American social
scene, crisscrossing the country to build sales, Naomi withdrew still
further. She stayed at home while the maids did the shopping and Jim

THE SALESMAN'S SALESMAN: THE OLIVES

worked or attended the round of business social functions. As her social isolation and anxiety deepened, she began to imagine that the merchants were cheating her, that the American country club wives were conspiring to steal her husband, and that her maids were stealing her silverware. The only part of her life that she felt competent to control was Marlene, and her need to dominate seemed to intensify. Then Jim was fired once more. Ever the optimistic salesman, he wrote to his sister: "My morale is OK for a guy who just got shot out of the saddle while crossing the Mojave Desert. I know everything will turn out alright but the suspense is killing me." Naomi was distraught. Jim took a sales position with the Alexander Hamilton Institute, a business correspondence school, which, Levine wryly observed, "offered for $325, a 'lifetime subscription' to materials designed to lift readers 'from the crowded ranks of junior and middle-level executives,' where Jim himself had long languished, 'to the top 5% of management,' where he fervently wished to be."[45]

In 1966, he convinced Gulf Oil to make him their general manager in Ecuador. By now, husband and wife slept in separate bedrooms. Jim was demoted to head of sales when his limited abilities soon became apparent to Gulf, but he continued to hand out a business card that described him as general manager. Even here his performance was unremarkable and he presided over several major fiascos. Naomi's drinking grew worse, and since she would not accompany him to social functions he began to take Marlene as his escort. He was fired by Gulf a few months before he would have been eligible for retirement benefits. Once again his resume began to circulate, and he considered writing a book about Ecuador, tentatively titled *The Greatest Little Country in the World*. He tried to use his many Ecuadorian connections to get him a job in the country, then tried to persuade his friends to invest in a horsebreeding scheme—but political considerations made the former impossible, and his friends had previously lost money in Jim's schemes.[46]

An advertisement in *The Wall Street Journal* launched him on what would be his final career. "Become the businessman's businessman," General Business Services urged the public. "America's leading business management and tax service offers franchises to qualified counselors." Jim bought the franchise, selected Marin County as his sales base, and returned to the United States. Once settled in Marin, he rose at six A.M. and worked harder than he had ever worked before, Levine astutely concluded, "trying to convince owners of marginal businesses that they needed to increase their overhead further by hiring him as a consultant." Business was painfully slow, but his optimism perennially resurfaced. As he wrote to a friend in Ecuador,

I felt just as backward and uncomfortable as if I had never sold anything in my life. I had to force myself to walk into people's stores and offices and tell them my story. And I didn't sell anybody anything. I didn't know my line well enough. I had two outright rejections ("Leave me alone, I'm busy"), four bored *impaciencias,* and two people who were much interested in my ideas but I just didn't have the knowledge to put it across. Then I got one guy who was sure I was going to save his life! And I have a date with him tomorrow. If I can make one Christian every day, I'll get rich. That's the nicest thing about selling. When you finally get rich, pie in the sky![47]

Things were harder on his wife and daughter. Both experienced real culture shock after a decade in Latin America, and Naomi had also to adjust to what she continuously referred to as her "reduced circumstances" —the loss of her fine house and personal servants. For her part, Marlene exchanged the conservative life in a Latin American city for the hectic pace of a suburban California high school, and did so while her primary emotional support, Jim, was buried in his own work and unable to spare her time. A year later, Jim's letter to his Ecuadorian friend expressed his continued alienation. "We are completely rootless and have left all our friends behind. Sure we are making many new acquaintances here, but it is still too early to feel completely at home. Marlene still suffers from pangs of homesickness and nostalgia. Good reason. In Quito she was a privileged character. Here she is just another brat in blue jeans." An old friend told Levine that she thought Naomi's conversation had become incoherent: "It was like she had just gotten out of solitary confinement. After what I learned later about her life I realized that's just what had happened."[48]

Naomi's mounting status-anxiety expressed itself in an increasing snobbery. She was upset when their reduced income forced them to purchase a modest house; in company, she frequently alluded to her previously higher status. A client of Jim's who owned a clothing shop told Levine of one such broadcast: "Naomi explained that she didn't like to try on clothes in stores because she was used to having them sent to her house for approval. At that point I said to myself, 'Lady, this place ain't Yves St. Laurent's salon and you sure ain't Jackie Kennedy.'" Her fear of failure became a fear of starvation, and she began to stuff the house and garage with cases of canned food, and her "voices" were heard more frequently through the locked bedroom door, raised in ancient familial disputes. When Marlene was sent to what was virtually a state-financed reform school, Naomi referred to it as an expensive and exclusive private school. Perhaps her status hysteria was best expressed in her confrontation with Chuck's mother, when Naomi closed a conversation with the pompous comment, "I understand you're a nurse's aide and live in a lower-income area. I can't imagine why Marlene would want to see Chuck when she knows so many boys from influential families."[49]

Naomi's insecurities must have been aggravated still further by Jim's decision to spend their last $50,000—and take out a large bank loan—to buy General Business Services' regional franchise for all of northern California. As a final blow to Marlene, this business expansion forced him to abandon his office at home for a rental office in town, separating them still further. To further destabilize an already volatile situation, Naomi's foster mother died two weeks before the murders: Anna DeKay had been her only source of stability and now she was gone. Jim's last official act at General Business Services was to chair a meeting of his area directors. Filled with enthusiasm, he drove the ninety miles to the meeting, his partner later recalled. If few of the "disgruntled" area directors bothered to attend the meeting, Jim nevertheless managed what Royce called "a typical gung-ho Jim Olive pep talk." After years of failure, Jim joked, his business was about to lose its "nonprofit status."[50]

THE DECISION TO KILL

I wish you could have stayed here
Beside me father to keep
Things straight.
Who knows these days what might happen?
I just might break.

—MARLENE OLIVE[51]

The decision to kill did not come out of nowhere, and it was no sudden explosion of uncontrollable rage. Quite the contrary, it evolved naturally from a frustrated fantasy (imagined increasingly seriously), through specific sets of detailed alternative plans, to a fumbling and halfhearted series of failed rehearsals. Only after all that, did the decision assume its final articulate form. Under hypnosis after the killings, Chuck recalled the first time he heard Marlene raise the subject: "We were all bitching about things we didn't like—school, being hassled by the police, our parents laying down all these rules. Marlene began talking about how much she hated her parents. She said, 'I wish they were dead. I wish someone would kill them.' 'I know what you mean,' I said. 'My parents are a real drag too.'" She discussed the matter frequently thereafter, but Chuck claims he thought it was all "normal teenage talk about wishing your folks would drop dead." Her friend Sharon Dillon echoed this: "Sure, Marlene kept saying she wished her parents were dead. But no one took her seriously. We all sometimes wish our parents were dead."[52]

Within weeks her fantasy had progressed beyond a vague wish for their deaths to specifics of how she might kill them and how she might benefit financially from their deaths. She told another friend, "I could lace it [Naomi's soup] with fifty tabs of acid and watch her space to death." Leaving the house after an argument with her mother, she told one friend, "I hate those sons of bitches. Do you know anyone who'd get rid of them for me?" She said she would inherit a "bunch of money" after their deaths. In a letter to another friend, she considered hiring a killer: "I was thinking about what you said," Marlene wrote. "About that man who would take care of my mom. I think we should talk it over together, you and I." Marlene suggested her confidante shoot Naomi. He was surprised: "She had mentioned wanting to kill her mom before, but I never thought anything would come of it. One day she called me up and said, 'I've got to get rid of her or I'm gonna kill myself.' She had it all worked out."[53]

The nominated killer thought Marlene's obsession intensified each day. "She was a little more up to her eyeballs with everything," he told Levine. "She had a plan to poison her mother one night when her dad worked late and she had to cook dinner for the two of them. She said she'd leave an empty bottle of pills by the bed to make it look like suicide. She talked about hitting her mother over the head and making it look like she was drunk and fell in the driveway. She had a lot of crazy ideas. How many ways can you kill a person?" Then her plan altered to killing her father instead:

> She'd ask her dad to drive her to a friend's house. . . . When the car was going through China Camp she'd pretend that she was sick or just lose something out the window. Any distraction to

stop the car and have him get out of it. I'd be up on a hill and when he got out of the car I'd hit him. Then we'd stuff him back in and drive into the woods and bury him. Everyone knew how crazy her mother was. . . . People would think the old man just up and left. And with him gone Marlene figured there was ninety-nine out of a hundred percent chance her mom would really go overboard and have to be put away. Then she'd be home free.

Not surprisingly, her confidante soon tired of the fantasy and asked Marlene to stop discussing it.[54] With one avenue closed, Marlene turned to her obese and subservient new boyfriend, Chuck. " 'It's either me or that bitch,' " Chuck remembered her telling him in one of their telephone conversations. " 'Either I'm gonna do her in or myself. You *must* know someone who'd do it to help us out.' " The fantasy's first physical expression occurred after an argument over Naomi's insistence that Marlene cut the celery on the *bias* rather than straight across. It ended with shouts of "Bitch! Crazy lady! One day they're gonna cart you off in a straightjacket" from Marlene. This time, however, rather than biting her heavily scarred forearm in frustrated rage as was her usual practice, Marlene threw the vegetable knife at Naomi, and yelled "If they don't take you away, I'll kill you myself!"[55]

On first learning of this savage quarrel, Jim adopted his customary position, dismissing both mother and daughter as "fishermen's wives," Levine records. But this time he soon changed his mind and sided with Naomi against Marlene. Responding to this treason, Marlene's homicidal fantasy in the following weeks began to take the form of killing both parents. In May she made her first halfhearted attempt to kill, dumping Darvon and Dalmane into her mother's lunch, but her mother disliked the taste and refused to ingest much of the poisoned soup. "We have to take care of a disease," she wrote Chuck. "I told Mrs. Olive she wasn't considered my mother anymore and that I smoked dope and took pills and was just as bad as you, just as savage. I'm going to be soo [sic] good to you."[56]

The last straw for Marlene occurred at the end of the school year. Jim had discovered how badly she was performing in school; he made the decision to send her away to boarding school in the fall, and perhaps insist she spend the summer in custody in Juvenile Hall. When he told Marlene, she replied, "No way, Father dear. I'd rather die." To Chuck, she said, "They're sending me away. You better do something fast or we're finished. If you can't find someone else [to do the killings], you do it, Chuck. Do it yourself.... Please, Chuck. Pretty please. After we collect the insurance money we'll have enough to get married and move away. We can go down to South America.... We can get the best coke for practically nothing. We'll be rich, Chuck. And we'll be together. I just want to be with you. No one else matters." This was the first time Chuck had been asked personally to perform the executions, but he seems to have accepted the responsibility. When Sharon Dillon asked, "If it came down to it, would you do it yourself? Do you love her that much?" Sharon remembers Chuck's melodramatic reply: "If it has to be done, I'd do it. I'd die for Marlene."[57]

All that was needed now was one provocative incident. The morning of the killings, Levine noted, Marlene and Naomi fought bitterly. Naomi raised yet again the issue of Marlene's natural mother, the "Norfolk whore" who had been "knocked up" and "gave you away." Marlene kicked her mother, who shoved her against the wall in retaliation. Amid shouts of "bitch!" and "shut your damn foul mouth!", Marlene later said, "I opened my big mouth one time too many. Everything exploded. Everything that was building up inside of me for years. 'Get your gun,'" she yelled to Chuck over the telephone. "'We've got to kill that bitch today. They're gonna put me in the hall all summer.'"[58]

SOCIALIZATION OF A FAMILICIDE

When you mouth your obscenities and your eyes mirror
   your enjoyment
Of the orgy of hatred you carry on verbally with yourself
With me as your audience,
Shall I share in the cacophony of self-hatred?

—MARLENE OLIVE[59]

As each unhappy family is unhappy in its own way, so each troubled family finds its own way of swallowing, even unconsciously deforming, the identity of the child who may destroy it. Each of the families in this book created a hothouse atmosphere so cloying that it seemed to offer only one escape for the incipient killer. Yet the Olives were not quite like the other families. The mother did instruct the daughter in the use of violence, but the family had few unrealistic expectations as there had been among the Bensons—although Marlene's rush from a privileged Latin childhood to a suburban California high school milieu must have been deeply unsettling. There was less of an unreasonable demand that Marlene become someone she did not wish to be, as had poisoned the De La Roche family— although one consequence of Naomi's parenting style was to convince Marlene that her "blood" assured her whoredom.

The origins of the tensions we describe in this book lie in the special social and economic niche each family occupies. As Levine noted, the shock of downward social mobility that many middle-class Americans felt in the economically troubled mid-1970s was experienced with special intensity by the ambitious but untalented Jim Olive. His succession of jobs and failed projects left his fostered and alcoholic wife (isolated from those around her for much of her life by a social and linguistic barrier) able to cope with her mounting anxiety only with an expanding armamentarium of compulsive habits. This compulsiveness consumed her mothering, converting it into an unreasoning obsession with the most trivial matters— from ancient familial slights to slicing celery. It also took the form of an identity-crushing need to control her daughter's behaviour. These assumed such significance to the confused and unhappy mother that they provoked demeaning verbal and physical assaults on Marlene. In this manner, the family wrote the script—as had the DeFeos—in which their daughter became a criminal and a whore.[60]

First they stole her identity. Marlene discovered, at a time when she had not been prepared for such a revelation, that she had been adopted. Rummaging through her father's filing cabinet at the age of ten, she told Levine, she came across an official document entitled, "In the matter of the Adoption of an Unnamed Girl Child under the age of Fourteen Years." She showed the document to her parents, and asked them what adoption meant, before bursting into tears. As she later remembered the incident, "I was so confused because I didn't understand how that other woman was my mother and my mother was, too. I began to wonder if they loved me or were just taking care of me and didn't love me or what was happening. Then I started thinking about who my real mother was, but I didn't say anything about it for a long time." Her adoption, and the true identity of her natural mother, came to obsess her. In the sixth grade at the Colegio Americano in Ecuador, her teacher remembered: "One day we were discussing motherhood, what it's like to be a mother and how your life changes. Marlene raised her hand and said, out of the blue, 'I hate my mother.' Just that matter-of-fact. Well, the other kids were shocked into silence and I guess Marlene felt she had to do some more explaining. So after a while she added, 'She's not my real mother. I'm adopted. That's why she doesn't love me.' " In their deepening alienation, Marlene learned that the simplest way to anger her adopted mother was to enquire about her natural mother; this would provoke enraged shouts that her natural mother had been a "gutter tramp." Once, Naomi said in her fury that neither she nor Jim had really wanted to adopt Marlene. "There are words you never forget," Marlene later said of that remark. After these arguments, Marlene might run away to the home of a friend, but she would awaken in the morning in urine-soaked sheets.[61]

Then they stole her independence. Naomi's restless anxiety inevitably led her to restrict her child's freedom to a remarkable degree. Often Marlene was not allowed to leave the house. A family friend recalled that "Naomi kept Marlene under her wing, and when she withdrew, the little girl did too. She seemed to use the child as a crutch, a companion to talk to when she lost contact with others, almost like a pet. You never saw Marlene out screaming and running about with friends like kids should. There was great love and concern from Naomi, but it was often misguided." Even there, however, there was no consistency. As another family friend told Levine, "there was no in between with Naomi. She either smothered Marlene or ignored her. It wasn't that she didn't love her. She loved her desperately. It was more that nobody had taught Naomi how to be a mother." Marlene soon displayed more symptoms of inner turmoil than mere bed-wetting: now there was hay fever and a succession of allergies.[62]

Marlene's primary emotional relationships appeared to be with the family's maids—necessarily so when the father was frequently absent on business trips and the mother's fearfulness and alcoholism kept her imprisoned in her own bedroom. But the maids were fired in rapid succession for trivial or imagined offences, and none of these relationships endured. If the growing Marlene expressed a desire for some minimal freedom, her mother was too nervous to permit it. In their arguments over Marlene's modest demands, the daughter first developed her habit of closing an argument by pounding her head against the wall or biting her forearm. Typically, Naomi would wildly overreact to any childish rebellion: if Marlene lingered at a friend's house, Naomi would frantically begin calling friends and colleagues. Once she even brought in the militia. In what would become both symbol and precursor of all Marlene's foiled attempts to escape, the Ecuadorian cavalry found her and took her home.[63]

Typically, too, Jim was able to close his eyes to the terrible friction in his home. Even in California, when the tension had reached unbearable heights, Levine records, he was able to write his sister in the blandest way: "Marlene is being a fifteen-year-old successfully. Tonight she is out working behind the scenes at a high school production of *The Mikado*. (We will go see it tomorrow). Big doings. More independent every day," he thought, apparently unaware of the fact that all her attempts to declare independence had been throttled. Had Jim read Marlene's poetry, he might have been more concerned: "A broken sound/Cries out in pain. /People hear/But they don't listen," she wrote at that time.[64]

Then they taught her aggression and violence. The family quarrels tended to follow a simple script. Naomi would exaggerate some minor transgression of Marlene's—failing to tidy up her bedroom—and this would provoke an equal and opposite overreaction from Marlene, often beginning with a Nazi salute and a shout of "Heil Hitler." Naomi would then demean her daughter by suggesting that such behaviour was quite in character with the spawn of a "Norfolk whore," and Marlene would dismiss her mother as a "crazy lady" who was not even related to her. This would often escalate to physical violence, with one shoving or kicking, even throwing heavy objects or knives, until they locked themselves in a bedroom to await Jim's return. Rather than settle matters, Jim would dismiss them both as "fishermen's wives": a negotiated ceasefire was the highest state to which his diplomacy could aspire. The Olives were not the stereotypical abusive family, for Jim was a gentle soul and it was only Naomi's sense of anxiety and impotence that made her lash out. Nonetheless, the cultural message validating violence was clearly transmitted to their daughter.

Marlene was quite unprepared for suburban California life and her early attempts to make friends were ineffective, leaving her lonely in the television room. When she did find a social circle, Jim dismissed her new friends as her social inferiors. Moreover, her adolescent clothing and makeup were intolerable to Naomi. In a poem addressed to her mother, Marlene wrote: "I don't know what your world's about/I can only live in mine/It's funny about that imaginary line/That's no longer imaginary/It's scarlet/Don't call me harlot." Their arguments, Marlene told Levine, became increasingly abusive: "Don't you curse at your mother, you no-good swine," would precede a, "Who you callin' a swine, crazy lady?

You're the one who lays around like a pig drinking all day. Besides, you're not even my mother." "Thank God for that," Naomi would respond. "She's probably some gutter tramp who couldn't take care of you." "Even if she is, I'd like to find her. She'd be better than you." "Some two-bit whore who . . ." "Don't you go callin' my mom a whore, bitch!" Labelled a whore, Marlene began to think of becoming one: "I couldn't understand why my real mom would give me up unless maybe she was a hooker and was forced to. So maybe I'd become one too."[65]

Near the end, the violence in their relationship was explicit. Sharon Dillon watched one quarrel, which ended with Naomi throwing a hot iron at Marlene, leaving an angry scar. In what was one of their very last disputes, Marlene remembered Naomi yelling at her, "You look like a tramp." "Well," Marlene replied, "I guess if my mom was one, I'm one. . . . Crazy lady! One day they're gonna cart you off in a straitjacket!" Marlene responded to the tension with her customary habit of biting deeply into her forearm, but then threw the vegetable knife at her mother and shouted, "If they don't take you away, I'll kill you myself!"[66]

Having stolen her identity, crushed her fledgling attempts to stake her independence, and taught her aggression as the appropriate verbal and physical language for dispute resolution, both parents abdicated their parental roles. Long before they returned to the United States, Naomi had alternated between abdication (when she would withdraw alone into her bedroom to drink, stare at her aquarium, and create the voices raised in shrill argument) and occasional clumsy and violent attempts to control her daughter. Once they moved to California, however, Jim also abdicated. Desperately struggling to achieve his lifelong dreams and make his new business a success, he lacked the time and energy to deal with anything else. Once he had merely tried to negotiate uneasy truces: "Let's not rock the boat," he had told Marlene, "you know how sensitive your mother is." Now his tactics changed and he began to take Naomi's side in the family quarrels—a move that Marlene saw as betrayal and contempt. Now Marlene's friends noticed that her hatred for her father began to match what she expressed towards her mother.[67]

Her abandonment by her father wounded her so powerfully because it was such an abrupt change from their relationship in Ecuador. There Marlene had moved into the vacuum created by her mother's social withdrawal: "Here's my *other* girl friend," Jim would say to introduce his daughter/escort at parties, making explicit the seductive nuances in their relationship. Certainly Marlene frequently joined her father in his lonely bed at night, and a poem she addressed to him in Ecuador dwelt on these points. Entitled "Daddy's Sweetheart," the poem read: "Long brown hair could entice any man/And her green eyes could light the night/Daddy couldn't have chosen any better." Such passion and exclusivity die hard, and the contrast between their quasi-romantic relationship in Ecuador and what lay ahead in California provoked great anger. During the last year, she began to see her parents as "matching robots," mindlessly playing empty roles—or her mother was the "crazy lady" and her father a bogus "white knight." When she complained to her school guidance counsellor about her problems at home, Jim was furious, not responsive: He shouted at Marlene, warning her never to "wash our dirty linen in public" again. Their mutual alienation would soon be complete.[68]

THE PATH TO THE KILLINGS

Don't call me a harlot.

—MARLENE OLIVE[69]

We are still left without a full understanding of how such a massacre could erupt in such an unexceptional family. It is true that the Olive family was filled with conflict, but few modern families with adolescent children escape disharmony for long, and many are disfigured by passionate hatreds. Moreover, the tensions that beset the Olives (Jim's perpetual failures, Naomi's unstable childhood and her quite understandable hysterical response to her husband's profligacy) are by no means uncommon. Marlene was neither the first nor the last adolescent forced to deal with the frustrations of having one parent lost in his work and another lost in her broken dreams: yet she was one of a tiny proportion whose response is homicidal.

To understand the Olive killings it is necessary to see how the chain of social, economic, and historical events shaped the collisions of personalities. Without the entire sequence, the killings might never have occurred: Marlene might merely have become one more troubled adolescent who graduated to a life of drugs and prostitution, making only occasional attempts to contact her family—most often when she needed money. What were the elements in this sequence? First, we needed a parent whose social and economic aspirations were far loftier than his ability to achieve them. This problem is exacerbated in troubled economic times, when an individual's performance may be evaluated most harshly and the unimaginative is deemed expendable. Still, if Jim had always been so involved in his work that he had neither time nor energy for Marlene, if he had not been so close to her in Ecuador, introducing her at parties as Señora Olive, then Marlene would have developed an alienated disinterest, not the passionate dependence on her father that must have been so disturbing to her when it ended abruptly in California.

The killings might not have happened if the family had remained in Ecuador. Marlene would have remained a troubled but privileged child, reared in a soft social climate: in such a milieu, with so many supportive friends and servants, they might all have survived. But the realities of politics and business forced the family to return to the United States. In her early teens, and without any cultural preparation, Marlene was suddenly hurled into the heady California whirl; as she struggled to adjust to the culture shock, her father no longer had time for her. His "little mistress" (as one friend of Jim's had called her), writing him love poems and fantasizing about sleeping with him, was transformed into his spurned daughter/suitor, rejected by her peers in high school and watching television alone. Even then, they might all have survived if Jim, frustrated and utterly involved in building his new firm, had not decided radically to alter his tactics as husband and father. When he relinquished his customary role of peacemaker between the two women in his life, dismissing his daughter with an increasing level of contempt, Marlene felt totally betrayed.

If Naomi had come from a less unstable personal background, she would have been a more secure person and a better mother. Certainly she would not have needed such profound isolation from the social world or such absolute and finicky control of her child. Comprehending motherhood only as control and overprotectiveness, Naomi must have been both bewildered and hurt by Marlene's rejection of her: even in Ecuador, after all, in front of her unilingual mother, the bilingual Marlene would speak only Spanish to her father. The issue of Marlene's adoption served as the subject matter for much of their combat, but it was by no means the reality that divided mother and daughter. In fact, the familial vacuum created by Jim's ambiguous affection for his wife and his seductive relationship with his daughter left great space for rivalry between the two women.

Had Naomi responded to the growing tension between mother and daughter by retreating deeper into her bedroom, with its alcohol and fish tanks, there would have been no murders. But Naomi did quite the opposite, increasing her hysterical attempts to dominate Marlene and escalating the level of abuse and even assault. After a day locked in her bedroom consuming large quantities of alcohol, talking to her "fishies" and speaking in her "voices," Naomi would stumble forth to do battle with her daughter over the correct way to prepare a salad. If Jim's failures in business had not increased her lifelong personal and social insecurity, she might have been able to retreat into her snobbery, emerging from her bedroom only to address imperiously her social inferiors. Yet that crutch was removed just as the social bond between mother and daughter began to snap.

For Marlene's part, paradoxically, if she had not had a warm and pleasant early relationship with her father, she might have emerged as an adolescent too submissive and lacking in self-confidence to express overt anger. If her familial culture had not provided her with continuous messages that her "bad blood" preordained her to be a second-generation harlot, and that verbal and physical aggression was an appropriate response to tension, then the murders would not have taken place. Even then, it would not have happened if the parents had not foreclosed so harshly on her various attempts to run away; but whenever she tried to escape, she would be returned, by an escort of mounted cavalry in Ecuador or by a social worker in California, to a family whose primary concern appeared to be the impression all this gave the neighbours. If Marlene had not landed in a cultural milieu in which the airing of fantasies about killing one's parents was regarded as a normal means of coping with frustrations between the generations; or if either of her parents had read and responded to the adolescent anguish expressed in her poetry; even if they had had the wit to see in Marlene's shoplifting sprees a delinquent code,* in which the adolescent demands reinstatement in a family from which she feels excommunicated—then they might all have been spared. As in all our familicidal families, so many things were left undone.

An additional element remains unexamined—the identity of the actual killer. We will never know if Marlene played a physical role in the murder of her mother, although most commentators on the case do not

---

* For a detailed examination of this "code," this perceived familial rejection, see my *The Myth of Delinquency*, a study of the inmates of one Atlantic reform school and their families.

think it likely. We do know from her own testimony that she stood over her sleeping father with a claw hammer in her hand, only to discover that she lacked the resolution to do the killing. Clearly, without her enslaved boyfriend the murders might never have happened. Thus it was necessary for Marlene to meet someone, himself obese and inadequate, who would be so grateful for her sexual and emotional favors that he would utterly subordinate himself to her will. She found such a man in Chuck Riley. Chuck was soon transformed into the vehicle with which she indulged all her fantasies—whether masturbating with his hunting knife or his car's gearshift lever, having him bind and "rape" her in the masochistic mode, sharing him sexually with another girl, or exploring the limits of her own aggressive imagination in her many alternative plots to kill one or both parents. Without Chuck to do her bidding, the story would have ended differently.

Even then, with all the causal factors locked so firmly in place, the tragedy might not have occurred if Jim (sensing at long last that business success was just around the corner) had not demonstrated a new and complete indifference to Marlene by deciding to send her to boarding school in the fall (and perhaps to juvenile hall for the summer). It was that final contemptuous dismissal from his emotional life and his home that prodded Marlene to take her stand. She would now retreat no further. She had her rationalization; now all she needed was a provocation, a border incident, which Naomi supplied in their last argument. This time it was Marlene who initiated the physical assault. This time, "everything exploded. Everything that was building up inside of me for years."[70]

But why *kill* her parents? Why not simply steal their credit cards and run away with Chuck to build a life of shoplifting and drug-dealing; why not go with one of her pimp friends to become the harlot her mother "wished" her to be? In her frenzied adolescent imagination and memory, escape had always been impossible: the cavalry, social workers, juvenile hall counsellors, and police had always brought her back. Her dilemma seemed to offer only two alternatives: either she accepted the intolerable fate of a summer in juvenile hall and the remainder of the year in boarding school, or she washed her hands of the source of all her torment and, in annihilating them, free herself. All that it would take was a single command to her devoted sex slave, Chuck. After that she could indulge all her fantasies.

AN ADIEU

Marlene virtually escaped punishment because she was a juvenile at the time of the killings. As the absurd law stipulated, she was released from custody before her twenty-first birthday, in 1979, and her criminal record was destroyed. During her brief incarceration, she prepared for her career as a prostitute and fell in love with the daughter of a Beverly Hills medical doctor. Levine hears from her occasionally and notes sadly that she has been a heavy user of speed and heroin, and that her veins are blackened by the frequent insertion of needles. She visited Chuck in prison once, but could only offer to supply him with illegal drugs. According to her adult police record, she appears to have pursued a career in prostitution.[71]

Chuck's method of dealing with his life imprisonment, he recently wrote Levine, is "to take one day at a time, keep my hopes down and try to get the maximum freedom I can from the system." He exercises regularly and is apparently in fine physical condition. "Society punishes us with wasted years," he wrote. "One way to get even is to come out looking younger—or at least in better shape—than when you went in." Since Chuck has refused to admit that he participated in both murders, the parole board refuses to reduce his sentence. Chuck expects to be at least forty-five years old before he is released.[72]

CHAPTER SIX

Towards an Historical Sociology of Familicide

Love is not love
When it is mingled with regards that stand
Aloof from the entire point.

—KING LEAR

The cases in this volume have not been examined so microscopically simply because of a fascination for such exotic behavior. Rather, it has proven to be an economical way to discover many of the hidden stresses and cleavages within the modern family. This book thus falls naturally into the series I have been writing for decades on the diverse ways in which modern stratified bureaucratic societies—regardless of their political ideologies or their rival claims to moral superiority—deform the identities of their vulnerable citizens.*

My method† has been essentially an anthropological one, prowling with a hand lens through whatever low-level data are available, in a search for their social and symbolic meaning. For this apparently idiosyncratic approach to the problem, I take heart from the master historian Robert Darnton, who argued that it is precisely "when we run into something that seems unthinkable to us [that] we may have hit upon a valid point of entry into an alien mentality." Through an explication of the lives of those who flout all the laws of humanity, we have "puzzled through to the natives' point of view" and mounted an explanation of the inexplicable.[1]

The attitudes of our time, influenced so profoundly by progressive

* See References.
† See Appendix.

social activists, naturally lead us to assume that this ultimate manifestation of family violence must surely be the result of terrible child abuse. Yet only a minority of the killers we have studied came from homes that showed any evidence of serious physical abuse, and rarely in the data is their sexual exploitation even implied. Neither can the belief be sustained that it is only the insensitive and tyrannical father, constructing his paternalistic prison alone, who is solely responsible for the deformation of the child.* In the bulk of our cases, the abuse was mental, not physical; unconscious, not intended; and the result of acts, statements, and constraints imposed by both parents. We must search elsewhere for an explanation of Benson, who wished to become a millionaire, and Olive, who wished to become a drug-abusing prostitute. To enrich our understanding, we must turn to the historical and anthropological record: only then can we begin to integrate the life history of the individual into the flow of social evolution.

THE HISTORICAL METAMORPHOSES
OF FAMILY AND HOMICIDE

> The nearer and dearere any persons be,
> the more violent will be that hatred
> which is fastened on them.
>
> —WILLIAM GOUDE[2]

HOMICIDE IN THE PRIMITIVE FAMILY

We search the anthropological literature in vain for any reference to familicide. This should not be surprising given the enhanced significance of kinship in simpler societies: here, the family was the building block for all social relationships, and the wider kinship networks were the organizing principle of social life—providing the principle of recruitment to all social groups, and regulating virtually all social, economic, political, and religious activities. Family households were not isolated as they so often are in modern societies, but were submerged in an interlocking mesh of

* Throughout this volume, I use the notion of "paternalistic," rather than the currently fashionable (and structurally misleading) patriarchal, following Elizabeth Fox-Genovese, in her fine *Within the Plantation Household.*

genealogical ties, both real and mythical, which linked them to the larger groups of kindred, clan, and lineage. So flexible and powerful were these kinship bonds that they could with equal effectiveness mobilize a half-dozen individuals to harvest a few fields, or organize thousands of men to make war on neighbouring tribes.

It is plausible to assume that kin killings would be relatively infrequent, and familicide nonexistent, in a social context in which family is the only available protection against the dangerous world of strangers. This should not disguise the fact that there are costs as well as benefits to membership in these kinship groupings (most especially in the realm of conflict over the power and authority vested in senior kin), and that these social costs may often produce violence and even homicide. Among the African Gisu, one of the few people in the anthropological record with a relatively high incidence of parent murders, anthropologist Jean La Fontaine noted that the bulk of killings had their origin in the struggle for power between a man and his senior paternal kin over "property, land, and cattle." This authority clash often fed "personal rivalries and jealousies," for which the system offered no solution other than violence. Still, even among the Gisu, with their endemic conflict, there were no recorded instances of familicide.[3]

In his broader review of the African data, anthropologist Paul Bohannan commented on the strangeness to Western eyes of the prevalent African forms of homicide, and the relative rarity of parent killings. At the time he was writing (1960), accusations of sorcery and witchcraft were among the most common provocations to murder: "witches were or still are 'fair game' in many African societies, and killing a witch was sometimes considered not only nonculpable but justifiable." Similarly, there were few cultural compunctions about killing a foreigner. Bohannan describes the case of one Tiv who, released from prison after serving a three-year sentence for killing a non-Tiv, "thought his sentence grossly unjust because he had killed a mere stranger." Moreover, while an economic motive for murder is familiar enough in modern societies, it is less so in primitive contexts: such cultures normally dictate that all wealth be shared among members of the kin group, and therefore "it is not possible for an individual to enjoy the gains of his crimes any more than it is for him to enjoy any other sort of gains." Indeed, it may well be that in the majority of primitive societies, the most prevalent form of homicide is what anthropologist Patricia Draper found among the !Kung Bushmen—the "legal" execution of rogues, deviants, and outcasts who would not obey the unwritten rules of the society.[4]

HOMICIDE IN THE MEDIEVAL AND EARLY MODERN FAMILY

The much richer evidence offered us by historians makes it clear that European homicide rates have been consistently and precipitously declining since the Middle Ages. The quality and depth of this historical analysis is both outstanding and insufficiently appreciated by nonhistorians: a wider knowledge of it would go a long way towards quelling "moral panics" about nonexistent modern crime waves. Princeton historian Lawrence Stone concluded that "it looks as if the homicide rates in 13th century England were about twice as high as those in the 16th and 17th centuries and that those of the 16th and 17th centuries were some five to ten times higher than those today." This continuous decline was broken periodically by short-term crime waves (as occurred in much of the Western world in the late 1960s and early 1970s). These short-lived upsurges were caused by social stresses specific to the time: historian Ted Robert Gurr speculated that "the most devastating episodes of public disorder . . . seem to occur when social dislocation coincides with changes in values which legitimate violence."[5]

Curiously, however, although the general homicide rate has radically declined over the centuries, the rate of murders within the family has remained relatively unchanged and constant. Offence rates are usually calculated per 100,000 population, and because they are proportional to the population they are the most useful guide to the relative frequency of a crime. Readers fascinated by statistics will note the apparent anomaly that because total homicide rates have declined while familial homicide rates have remained unchanged, the proportion of all English homicides that take place within the family has risen from 8 percent in the fourteenth century to 15 percent in the seventeenth century, to close to 50 percent where they remain today. Still, if there are in fact many murders of individual kinsmen over this seven-hundred-year period, familicides by a son or daughter do not appear at all until the nineteenth century. This social fact is central to our analysis. What was there in the nature of the medieval and early modern family that would militate against familicide? Or, put another way, what is the quality of the modern family that facilitates familicide?[6]

In their review of the medieval family, historians Gies and Gies observe that the modern family has its origins in the "momentous social and economic transformations" that occurred at the beginning of the medieval era. Then, the great slave plantations of the late Roman Empire were swept aside and replaced by the smallholdings of the peasant proprietor. The factors contributing to the collapse of the old slave system are unclear, but it created a revolution in the nature of the peasant family, now clustered around an owned or controlled resource. "Gradually," Gies and Gies write, "the industrious peasant families acquired a moral, in medieval terms a 'customary,' right to their use of the land, a right they passed on to their children."[7]

The family's primary responsibilities at this time were control of the economic estate, however tiny it may have been, and the pursuit of justice through the "law" of the blood feud. In societies without police or public courts, blood vengeance was the only social mechanism that allowed families both to maintain their honour and to right wrongs by other unrelated kin groups. Thus one of the primary functions of family was to *commit* homicide, avenging the dishonour or death of their kin. Wherever the law of the blood feud reigns supreme, the cycle of retaliation and counterretaliation can result in the extinction of whole families. In sixth-century Tournai, one man's attempt to defend his sister against her husband's philandering led him to kill the husband "and some of his relations." Fulfilling their sacred obligations according to the law of blood vengeance, relatives of the murdered husband assassinated his killer, creating a homicidal cycle whose conclusion, Gregory of Tours recorded, was that "not a single member of either family remained alive, except one survivor for whom there was no opponent left."[8]

By the medieval era, the emerging bureaucracies of church and state had already begun the long process of expropriating the family's powers and responsibilities. "The single most important change in the European family between Roman times and the Reformation," Gies and Gies summarized, "was *the reduction in its functions*." The Christian Church had taken religion away from the family as the lay and ecclesiastical courts were beginning to monopolize justice. "Feudal custom, craft guilds, national governments and armed forces, schools and universities had further impinged on the family's economic, social, and educational roles." This necessarily entailed the eclipsing of the extended kinship networks— the kindreds, lineages, and clans—which had been of such critical importance to both primitive and ancient societies.[9]

Medieval society, Gurr wrote, was still a dangerous one "in which men (but rarely women) were easily provoked to violent anger and were unrestrained in the brutality with which they attacked their opponents." Despite these high levels of physical aggression, however, "scarcely any" murders took place within the family, and "at least one-third" of all killings were the result of disputes between strangers. Indeed, as historian James Buchanan Given makes clear, the major role kinsmen played in this domain was still as coconspirators in the commission of murder—obtaining vengeance through the blood feud. Only 6.5 percent of the 2,434 victims in the English murder records of the time were actually killed by relatives: of these, "almost as many homicides involved parents and children as involved siblings"; but "slightly more children were killed by parents" than vice versa. Given felt that the conflict between father and son over control of the family patrimony and the reluctance of many fathers to retire may have precipitated many of the parricides.[10]

Neither Given nor historian Carl Hammer, Jr., in the latter's study of the extraordinarily violent fourteenth-century town of Oxford (with its homicide rate of 110 per 100,000—many times the current Mexican rate!) uncovered any case of a son or daughter committing familicide. Despite the violent atmosphere of the time and the ready availability of weapons, intrafamilial homicide of any kind was relatively infrequent. Hammer attributed Oxford's high rate of stranger murders to the prevailing culture, in which "sharp tongues, quick tempers, and strong drink seem often to have been a fatal combination," but he does not speculate why these ingredients did not affect the family.[11]

Historian Barbara Hanawalt's research in the fifteenth-century English records revealed the same relative absence of family violence, and even "the small role intra-familial crime played in the total crime picture." In Hanawalt's examination of the coroners' archives, 8.4 percent of murders took place within the family, but many of these were spouses, not biological relatives. Parents were still more likely to kill children than vice versa, but those who did so were usually taken to be insane, even then—usually, a desperate or deluded mother killed her children. In one case described by Hanawalt, a destitute widow, Matilda le Waleys of Buthamwell, "killed her two sons, Thomas and Robert, and her daughter, Anastasia, on St. Valentines Day, 1329. Earlier that day she had tried to commit suicide by throwing herself into a ditch filled with water. After neighbors rescued her, she returned home and killed her children."[12]

This pattern of homicide remained unchanged throughout the early modern period, despite the continued reduction of the family's functions and the dimming of the extended kinship groups. Historian J. A. Sharpe's study of homicide in Essex between 1560 and 1709 recorded a continued low incidence of domestic homicide against a background of falling murder rates. The majority of domestic killings were parents killing children. Sharpe did note one change from the medieval period: in the Middle Ages, half of family homicides involved spouses and about a third were children, but in the early modern period, these proportions had reversed themselves. Another "striking feature" of the early modern statistics was "the comparative rareness with which siblings killed each other." In Sharpe's period, "only five cases involved brothers or sisters as victim and accused," and "only two fathers and one mother suffered death from their children."[13]

There were still no familicides by children, and Sharpe emphasized the essentially unchanging nature of domestic homicide over the centuries— viewing it as a useful index of the stability of familial relationships in any period. Yet it seems odd to talk of stability in an era characterized by such radical demographic change, in which the population of Europe, especially its cities, was rapidly increasing. Historian Michael Weisser observed that these new population concentrations created a "lower class for which petty crime directed at the upper classes became a way of life." But if these criminal classes now "threatened the social order," the social dislocations that created them did not appear to disfigure the family. Familicide by sons or daughters remained unborn.[14]

HOMICIDE IN THE EMERGING INDUSTRIAL FAMILY

Your children will rise up and kill you.

—CHARLES MANSON FOLLOWER

Familicide did not appear in the record until the early nineteenth century, and it did so as a response to specific social developments. By the late eighteenth century, the accelerating triumph of industrial production had toppled the old feudal and mercantile regimes, making room for a new species, the bourgeois—what historian Robert Darnton called "a certain variety of Economic man with his own way of life and his own ideology." This bourgeois "acquired class consciousness and revolted [against the old aristocracy], leading a popular front of peasants and artisans." The political culture necessary for the fusion of this "striking force," Darnton argues, was designed to allow the bourgeoisie "to saturate the common people with its own ideas of liberty (especially free trade) and equality (especially the destruction of aristocratic privilege)." The construction and maintenance of this new economic order required an enormous expansion of the bureaucracies of industry and the state; and with this came the creation of a host of new occupations and professions, an infinite social ladder, which the most worthy might climb.[15]

These new middle classes, these functionaries of the emerging modern nation-state, must have gazed with excitement at the breaking of the feudal order's shackles. Yet each great victory hides another defeat. If the bourgeois revolution (with its promise of social mobility) was the great liberating force of the age, it also served to heighten the insecurity of the common people. Anthropologist Eric Wolf described how both the conservative and the radical social critics of the time railed against this savage new economic order, which "cut through the integument of custom, severing people from their accustomed social matrix in order to transform them into economic actors, independent of prior social commitments to kin and neighbours." Now men and women had to look upon themselves as marketable commodities, and look upon their friends and neighbours as rivals. Men and women poured into the already gorged cities to seek work in the new factories and bureaucracies, abandoning the warm blanket of kin and community. Thus naked, the workers were exposed to the excesses of the new system. One of the more virulent of these was that the new bourgeois ideology penalized the losers (the unemployed and underemployed) as much as it rewarded the winners, since this cultural system transmuted "the distinction between the classes into distinctions of virtue and merit."[16]

Thus the new system demanded social ambition in a way that had hitherto been neither possible nor desirable. Regrettably, not all human beings are well equipped to bear the personal stresses imposed by such demands. As French sociologist Emile Durkheim observed many years ago, the contented human being is one who "vaguely realizes the extreme limit set to his ambitions and aspires to nothing beyond," who "feels that it is not well to ask more." In an important sense then, the new regime substituted a subtler discontent for the feudal order's brutal exploitation. Now men and women could aspire to much, however unrealistic the chances of success might be. In doing so, unfortunately, they violated the principle that it is "relative limitation and the moderation it involves [that] makes men contented with their lot while stimulating them moderately to improve it; and this average contentment causes the feeling of calm, active happiness, the pleasure in existing and living which characterizes health for societies as well as for individuals."[17]

The nineteenth-century family, its functions and powers steadily curtailed, was inevitably subjected to the tensions linked to the drive for social achievement. Still, the general homicide rate continued its centuries-old decline, and there was no change in the intrafamilial murder rate. As it had been in the primitive, medieval, and early modern families, the murder of an individual parent or sibling continued to be an occasional event in the nineteenth century. French philosopher Michel Foucault observed that "cases of parricide were fairly common in the assize courts in that period (ten to fifteen yearly, sometimes more)."[18] Still, it is in this period that the first documented case of familicide by a child appears.

Since that time, familicide by a son or daughter has remained an extremely rare event. Rarer still are those familicides who are willing to discuss their own acts. Most of them remain mute about their crimes, either denying them or admitting them only partly and haltingly. They usually wish to close the book on the matter, and deny themselves the opportunity to explain their actions. But the first documented young familicide, the son of a French peasant, struggled to explain himself, and even wrote his autobiography while sitting in prison. According to Foucault, who compiled the brilliant study of the killer, the public reacted with "some surprise" to the autobiography, but only because "someone who had been held to be a 'kind of idiot' in his village turned out to be able to write and reason." The case is an imperfect familicide, for he murdered his mother and two siblings while sparing his father and several remaining siblings. But in many other respects it has the texture and quality of modern familicides—not the least of which is reflected in the family's compulsive use of lawyers, deeds, contracts, and legal suits to underwrite their attempted social rise.[19]

THE CASE OF PIERRE RIVIÉRE*

In 1835, twenty-year-old Pierre Riviére was living in the Norman village of Aunay. A neighbour, seventy-four-year-old Marie Riviére, sped to the cantonal judge to say that she had witnessed a terrible crime:

*   See Michel Foucault (ed.), *I, Pierre Riviére, having slaughtered my mother, my sister, and my brother* ... for the complete autobiography, as well as the superb analysis by Foucault and his gifted colleagues.

I saw the girl Victoire Riviére at her door facing our yard being held by her brother by her hair. She seemed to be trying to run away. When I approached them Pierre Riviére was holding a pruning bill in his hand and was raising it against his sister. I cried out: "Oh wretched boy, what are you about to do," and tried to seize his arm, but at the same instant he gave his sister several blows on the head with the bill and stretched her dead at his feet. All this happened in less than a minute. He fled by the door giving on the local road toward the town of Aunay, at the same instant I put my head inside the house and saw the corpses of his mother and his little brother, I lost my senses and set to crying out my god what a terrible thing my god what a terrible thing.[20]

Shortly after, the judge, accompanied by the mayor of Aunay, the doctor, and the local health officer, arrived at the Riviére farm. As the judge reported,

we there found three bodies lying on the ground, viz. (1) a woman about forty years of age lying on her back opposite the fireplace at which she had seemingly been busied at the time she was murdered cooking a gruel which was still in a pot on the hearth. The woman was dressed in her ordinary clothes, her hair in disorder; the neck and the back of the skull were slashed and "cutlassed"; (2) a small boy aged seven or eight, dressed in a blue smock, trousers, stockings, and shoes, lying prone face to the ground, with his head split behind to a very great depth; (3) a girl dressed in a calico print, stockings, no shoes or clogs, lying on her back.

At her feet was "a large fistful of her hair which seems to have been torn out at the time of the murder; the right side of the face and the neck 'cutlassed' to a very great depth."[21]

The alarm was sounded for Pierre, but he had escaped into the forest and would not be captured for a full month. While the search for him continued, the district prosecutor royal moved to explain Riviére's act and life. He interviewed the surviving members of Pierre's family, and reported that "from his childhood Pierre Riviére was an affliction to his family, he was obstinate and taciturn; even being with his parents was a burden to him. Never did he show a son's affection for his father and mother. His mother especially was odious to him. At times he felt a wave of something like repulsion and frenzy when she approached him." The prosecutor thought Pierre's character was a sadistic one, and he concluded: "Solitary, wild, and cruel, that is Pierre Riviére as seen from the moral point of view; he is, so to speak, a being apart, a savage, not subject to the ordinary laws of sympathy and sociability, for society was as odious to him as his family."[22]

Once in captivity, Pierre struck a modern note by feigning insanity during his preliminary interrogation. He told the judge that he murdered his family: "Because God ordered me to justify his providence, they were united. All three of them were in league to persecute my father." Continuing his bogus delusion, he claimed, "I was in a field when God appeared to me in the company of angels and gave me the order to justify his providence." However, he soon admitted that he had been lying, and that he had never thought God had commanded him to kill: "I wish no longer to maintain the system of defense," he told the judge, "and the part which I have been acting. I shall tell the truth, I did it to help my father out of his difficulties. I wished to deliver him from an evil woman who had plagued him continually ever since she became his wife, who was ruining him, who was driving him to such despair that he was sometimes tempted to commit suicide. I killed my sister Victoire because she took my mother's part. I killed my brother by reason of his love for my mother and my sister." Riviére then gave what the judge described as "an orderly and methodical ... account of the innumerable afflictions which, according to him, his father suffered from his wife." Riviére promised to provide the court with a full explanation of the murders in writing, and he did so three weeks after his capture.[23]

In his memoir, Riviére described his father as a man who "was always of a mild and peaceable disposition and affable toward all, and was so esteemed by all who knew him." His father had entered into an arranged marriage with Victoire Brion, whose family were also small peasant proprietors, but the marriage seemed doomed from the start. "After the marriage," Riviére wrote, "my mother stayed on with her parents at Courvaudon [the family home], and my father went there to do what work there was to be done. In the early days of his union with my mother he often went to visit her, but she received him with a coldness which put him out of countenance ... [and] because of this coldness my mother showed him he ceased visiting her as often as he had."[24]

Evidently not one to keep her dissatisfaction to herself, Victoire began publicly to air her real and imagined grievances against her husband; and if she made occasional and brief attempts to live in her husband's home, she would soon return to her family's home and spread rumors of her husband's perfidy. "My mother showed a great dislike for my father," Pierre wrote, "she put it about in Courvaudon that she had returned only because they [her husband's family] were letting her starve, she lacked everything." Even when Riviére, Sr. went to her home to help her family with their work,

> she displayed all her dislike to my father; he tried to win her over, he said to her: since you were unwilling to stay with me would you like me to come and stay here with your parents? What would they do with you, she answered; he asked her what she wanted him to do, she wanted him to hire himself out as a servant and bring her the money from his wages every year for her to do as she pleased with. My father said that since he had work to do on his own land he would not hire out as a servant and then, seeing how she treated him he resolved not to go back to see her any more.[25]

According to Pierre, his father "did everything in his power to try to secure peace and quiet with my mother ... [but] of all the dealings he did for her she maintained that none of them was done properly; when he bought it was always too dear, when he sold it was always too cheap, she flared up in a rage at every trifle." If his father would not cooperate with Victoire's attempts to extort more money from him, Pierre claimed, she would become enraged:

> My mother said to him: oh dear you would like to rob me, when you have money on hand to keep it, you old villain, you clapped-out old beast, you old whoremaster you would rather support your [mistress], you starve your children to support hers (she meant a woman in my father's village, who was left a widow with three children, she is a very good woman, she owns a few roods of land and paid my father to work them), you sow her land and plow it. My mother told him, all you want is your fun, she is a forward bitch, she has a damn good arse, Sulpice told me so, you ought to be ashamed of yourself.[26]

In the final years of the marriage, vituperation had turned to physical assault. Once, when father and son were removing a chest from Victoire's house, "she set to scratching his face and bit him several places, my little

brother Jule coming up, she told him: bite him, bite that wretch, my
father told me he got his fingers in his mouth but did not dare clench his
teeth on them; but seeing that the child was worrying him, I caught hold
of him and carried him into a neighbouring house." When they returned
to the house again later that afternoon, and Riviére, Sr. climbed through a
window,

> she seized him by the legs and pulled him down, broke his
> watch-chain and tore his clothes, he did not strike her at all, but
> he said he would shut her up in a house to keep her quiet, he
> caught hold of her to carry her away, but her hands were free
> and she scratched him again even worse than the first time, then
> he seized her hands to take her into that house and she fell down
> purposely; he did not drag her, as she said, but he tried to get her
> on her feet to take her there, my sister joined in to stop my
> father, and seeing that she was hindering him, I pulled her away
> and slapped her several times while my father took my mother
> off, she was shouting and so was my sister; vengeance, he is
> murdering me, he is killing me, vengeance my god vengeance.[27]

Tormented beyond endurance by his parents' demeaning squabbles,
Pierre began to see himself as the savior of the family's tarnished honour.

> I regarded my father as being in the power of mad dogs or
> barbarians against whom I must take up arms, religion forbade
> me such things, but I disregarded its rules, it even seemed to me
> that God had destined me for this and that I would be executing
> his justice. I knew the rules of man and the rules of ordered
> society, but I deemed myself wiser than they, I regarded them as
> ignoble and shameful.... I wished to defy the laws, it seemed to
> me that it would be a glory to me, that I should immortalize
> myself by dying for my father. I conjured up the warriors who
> died for their king and country, the valor of the students of the
> Polytechnic college at the taking of Paris in 1814, and I said to
> myself: these people died to uphold the cause of a man whom
> they did not know and who did not know them either, who had
> never given them a thought; and I, I would be dying to deliver a
> man who loves and cherishes me.

He abandoned his heroics after the killings, and felt a form of self-
absorbed remorse: "little did I think I would one day be in this plight;

poor mother, poor sister, guilty maybe in some sort, but never did they have ideas so unworthy as mine, poor unhappy child." He hanged himself in Beaulieu prison on October 20, 1840.[28]

How do we explain the familicide of Pierre Riviére? Intellectuals often claim to be objective scientists, but in fact they customarily harness their data to the ideological blinkers they find most agreeable.* In this predictable spirit, the French doctors who examined Riviére found him to be insane. In their report to the minister of justice, they said that "Riviére has never been in possession of the full mental faculties which constitute a rational being; the convicted man is a taciturn and reserved madman, a prey to obsessions, wholly lacking in judgment, fearfully dangerous." Similarly, some radical modern feminists have interpreted the massacre as a male attempt to restore the patriarchal regime challenged by the rebellious Victoire and her daughter. On the other hand, Marxist analysis has painted Riviére as a kind of revolutionary hero: "If the peasants had a Plutarch," wrote Peter and Favret, "Pierre Riviére would have his chapter in *Illustrious Lives*. And not he alone. His whole family falls into a rank of exemplary victims, a challenge, so to speak, to the galleries of storied urns and animated busts in the lofty ancestral mansions." Thus for the Marxists, Riviére was a kind of impoverished working-class hero who through his killings was "able to speak the truth, and, as a monster, display in their monstrous light the rule of lies and the foul machine at whose whim his fellows, the disinherited of the earth, are and have always been crushed, each day, each life."[29]

But they do Pierre too much honour. His parents were not, by the standards of the day, the poorest peasants. On the contrary, they both owned land and several houses, and aspired to much more; and young Pierre would eventually have fallen heir to much of this modest estate. His credentials as a member of the dispossessed are as much in doubt as his mother's credentials as an early feminist. So are any claims that they were revolutionary, for the family's obsession with property, expressed in its endless quarrels with neighbours over a few centimeters of land—and recorded in crushing legalistic detail by Pierre—is much less a challenge than an embrace of the bourgeois social order. Riviére's murders were no revolution against king or mercantile power, still less any brutal assertion of patriarchy.

---

* For a splendid illustration of how objective scientists can find whatever they are looking for, even in the forensic domain, see the meticulous reconstruction of Australia's Chamberlain murder case in John Bryson's *Evil Angels*.

Rather, they were the acts of a troubled and compulsive young man —unhinged by the unending greed and pugnacity of his parents and their extraordinary drive to share their marital woes with their children—who resolved to bring himself a form of peace by ending the matter in favor of the parent he loved. If in forming his plan he wrapped himself in a tissue of romantic nonsense, comparing himself to the culture heroes of the time, intending thus to "immortalize" himself "by dying for my father," he was by no means the first or last rebel to do so. Neither was he the last to regret his deed, for as soon as it was done; "I asked myself, monster that I am! Hapless victims! can I possibly have done that, oh it is but a dream! ah but it is all too true! chasms gape beneath my feet, earth swallow me; I wept. I fell to the ground." How exquisitely modern is young Riviére: indeed, the only old-fashioned note he ever struck was his melodramatic suicide.[30]

The forces that inexorably drove him towards his murders echo many of the qualities in our modern cases. The father, wishing to avoid conscription by Napoleon's armies, made an offer of marriage; the mother, more ambitious than either her own family or her preferred husband, prevaricated until, for reasons that we cannot now know, she finally accepted the marriage proposal. Once married, the mother was able to repent at leisure her social error, for through the marriage she had joined her life to a simple peasant who could not begin to provide her with the social and economic benefits she clearly desired. She appears to have resolved the matter for herself (but not for her husband) with a kind of manipulative compromise: she would not live with him, but she would exploit his sexual labour to give her children, his manual labour on her farm, and his loans and gifts to enrich her own estate.

Only status-hysteria can explain the ferocity with which she began to confront her husband; her mounting fear of failure must have grossly exacerbated the situation. Such hysteria, the origin of which lies in the individual's frustrated desire for social improvement, is a modern, not a primitive or ancient, corrosion. Indeed, this aspect of the case is reminiscent of no one as much as the university-administrator mother of California matricide and serial killer Edmund Kemper,* terrorizing her highway-flagman son and her succession of working-class husbands for their social and economic inadequacies. Considered from this perspective, Victoire's incessant and bitter quarrels with her husband, and her fraudulent habit of unloading her personal debts on him, take on a quite different meaning.

---

*   See *Hunting Humans,* Chapter Two.

In this society, which allowed no divorce, her vehement public and private humiliation of her husband was the only method available to her which could put social distance between herself and her low-status husband. Viewed in this light, her frequent outbursts are not simply an expression of her confusion and frustration, but part of a half-conscious stratagem. This explosive distancing could be provoked by any trivial issue. Pierre describes the purchase of a bed for his mother:

> ... since she needed a bed and there was one for sale in a village not far away, she told my father she wanted it. He asked her whether she would not rather have a new one, but she said no, and kept at him telling him that he would be too late getting there. My father then thought he would buy it no matter what the price, and he bought it for about what it was worth, but during the sale other women told my mother that they would not want secondhand rubbish, and she told my father that she did not want it and it was too dear; he answered her: but it is bought now, someone must use it. She said she did not want it, my father said: it is not worth so much fuss and took the bed away and had to resell it.[31]

Her antagonistic insecurity revealed itself in quarrels with everyone in her life, including her own mother. According to Pierre, "every day she quarrelled with her mother, not a word she said to her that was not by way of mortifying her, they blamed each other constantly for fifty thousand things." Similarly, she fought with her neighbours over her property: "One day when one of her neighbours had planted some stakes perhaps an inch or two inside her land, she told my father about it; unfortunately enough he said that no great harm was done, she set to abusing him and got into such a fury that she foamed at the mouth." She had "nothing but mortifying words" for her husband and brother-in-law, even when they slavishly journeyed to her farm to help her with the plowing or the wood-chopping. Pierre remembered that his uncle, less amiable than his father, "could not bear all my mother said to him; when I hear her nagging like that, he said, she drives me too far, if she goes on I shall end by knocking her teeth in." In the meantime, she continued to run up debts and charge them to her husband without his knowledge.[32]

Significantly, the only period when the marriage was harmonious was when Victoire's lack of business acumen had resulted in a lawsuit that threatened to confiscate much of her property. Riviére, Sr. had stepped in to pay the damages, even though it put him in debt for many years. "During the whole of this suit," Pierre remembered, "my mother was very kind to my father, and from that time until two years ago there were no serious quarrels between them." Once the legal matter was finally settled, however, relations returned to their previous state. Even when one young son, Jean, lay dying from some malady of the brain, his body wracked by convulsions "which made him writhe horribly," Victoire presented her husband with more unpaid bills and demands from the tax collector. Jean died the following day, and "my mother went back to her house and did not fail to put it about everywhere that my father had starved her child to death, and she continued to run up debts."[33]

Pierre took his father's side, painting his mother as evil incarnate and his father as its opposite, so we shall never know the role Riviére, Sr. played in creating this marital nightmare. In any case, as the martyr father and the shrew mother played out their antagonistic roles, they did so according to a cultural script that had its origins in the liberating mentality of the time. As the rising industrialists used their new economic and legal powers to challenge and defeat the old aristocratic order, the more ambitious of the peasantry could use those same bourgeois instruments of deeds, contracts, lawsuits, and acquisitions (that so fascinated the Riviére family) to expand their own modest enterprises. Yet carried out so compulsively and pugnaciously by at least one of Riviére's parents against a foreground of their own marital warfare, it left the son disordered, dehumanized, confused, and enraged, grasping for an identity that might give him meaning and fulfilment. In choosing to embrace the identity but not the mentality of a revolutionary hero, Pierre nudged familicide towards its modern form.

HOMICIDE IN THE
TWENTIETH-CENTURY FAMILY

The murder of biological kin is rare and it appears to have been so in all epochs and in all civilizations. This stands in stark contrast to overall homicide rates, which vary enormously over both time and distance. Our evidence for this claim comes from a variety of sources, not the least of which is Stone's historical overview of the rich English data, which prompted him to conclude that "over the centuries, the rate per 100,000 [of family murders] has remained relatively unchanged." Similarly, in their provocative review of national differences, psychologists Daly and Wilson dwell on the unusual crosscultural consistency of family murders, observing that "intrafamilial homicides are [much] less variable in their incidence from one country to another" than any other form of homicide. Indeed, in their international survey, the murder of biological kin ranged narrowly from 2 percent to 8 percent of all murders. As a familiar example, Daly and Wilson offered Detroit in 1972, in which of a total of 508 homicides, 47.8 percent were unrelated acquaintances, 27.2 percent were strangers, and only 6.3 percent were blood relatives.[34]

The multiple murder of biological kin is rarer still, and of that handful of killings the majority are committed by parents, not by children. The stunning inadequacy of the international agencies charged with the responsibility for the collection of criminal statistics makes it impossible for us to make any solid statistical statements on the national and international frequencies of our form of familicide.* Except for Canada, we have only rough approximations from scattered research reports. In England, for example, for the six-year period ending in 1962, criminologists Morris and Blom-Cooper reported only three cases in which a son or daughter had murdered both parents, but eight mothers and seven fathers who had killed their children. In psychiatrist Christopher Green's more recent study of fifty-eight male patients in Britain's Broadmoor mental hospital, there were only nine cases of familicide by a child.[35]

Canada is the only nation for which we have detailed and reliable long-term evidence. Table 1 shows the incidence and character of familicide in Canada between 1962 and 1987; and demonstrates clearly that familicide has remained relatively constant over time, especially when increasing population is taken into account. Here, a slight rise in the early 1980s was countered by a decline in the late 1980s and a total of thirty-eight

---

*   This inability of the world's fact-gathering agencies to deliver anything other than the crudest statistics on homicide is both well-known and lamentable. With the publication of Archer and Gartner's monumental *Violence and Crime in Cross-National Perspective,* we now have a rich and good-humored account of the chicanery that is necessary to extort information. Yet Archer and Gartner's stupefying task was relatively easy, since they were dealing in the same commodities—crude, overall, undifferentiated homicide rates—as the bureaucracies with which they negotiated. They were thus able eventually to assemble important and useful data. However, scholars seeking data on specific (and especially previously unstudied) forms of homicide soon encounter an impenetrable official wall. Soviet-bloc nations do not, of course, release criminological information of any kind to their apparently impressionable citizens (cf. Chalidze 1977; Connor 1972). Within the Western bloc, I must single out the famed Interpol, which in response to my query on international familicide rates sent me xeroxed copies (in both Swedish and Chinese) of those nations' overall homicide rates. The only country that appears to take this knowledge vacuum seriously is Canada, whose Centre for Justice Statistics in Ottawa is the most sophisticated in the world.

incidents occurred over twenty-six years, claiming ninety-three victims—an annual average of but 1.5 incidents, claiming perhaps 3.5 victims each year. This demonstrates the unremarkable, even unsensational character of familicide. We have no comparable data for other nations, but the Canadian incidence differs little from that described by Foucault for France in the mid-nineteenth century—a few cases each year. Familicides are a regularly occurring but statistically insignificant feature of modern social life. What then do they say about the nature of the modern family?

TABLE 1.

INCIDENTS OF MULTIPLE MURDER WITHIN THE FAMILY

BY A SON OR DAUGHTER,

CANADA 1962–1987[a]

YEAR	NATURE OF INCIDENT	NUMBER OF INCIDENTS	NUMBER OF VICTIMS
1962	Son killed his wife & 1 parent	1	2
1963	Son killed 2 parents & 1 sibling		
	Son killed 2 parents	2	5
1964	None	0	0
1965	Son killed 2 parents		
	Son killed 2 parents & 4 siblings	2	8
1966	Son killed 2 parents		
	Son killed 2 parents		
	Son killed 1 parent & 1 relative	3	6
1967	Son killed 1 parent & 1 relative	1	2
1968	None	0	0
1969	None	0	0
1970	Son killed 2 parents		
	Son killed 2 parents, 1 sibling, & 1 relative		
	Son killed 1 parent & 1 sibling	3	8
1971	Son killed 2 parents & 1 sibling	1	3
1972	Son killed 2 parents	1	2
1973	Son killed wife & 1 parent	1	2
1974	Son killed 2 parents & 1 sibling	1	3
1975	Son killed 1 parent & 1 sibling	1	2
1976	Son killed 1 parent & 1 sibling	1	2
1977	None	0	0
1978	None	0	0
1979	Son killed 1 parent & 1 step-parent	1	2
1980	None	0	0

YEAR	NATURE OF INCIDENT	NUMBER OF INCIDENTS	NUMBER OF VICTIMS
1981	Son killed 2 parents		
	Son killed 2 parents		
	Son killed 2 parents	3	6
1982	Son killed 2 parents		
	Son killed 2 parents		
	Son killed 2 parents & 1 sibling		
	Daughter killed her husband,		
	1 parent, 1 child	4	10
1983	Son killed 2 parents		
	Son killed 1 parent & 1 relative		
	Son killed 2 parents, 3 siblings,		
	& 1 relative		
	Son killed 2 parents	4	12
1984	Son killed 2 parents		
	Son killed 2 parents	2	4
1985	Son killed 1 parent & 1 sibling		
	Son killed 2 parents, 1 sibling		
	& 1 relative		
	Son killed 2 parents & 1 sibling		
	Son killed 2 parents	4	11
1986	None	0	0
1987	Son killed 2 parents & 1 sibling		
	Daughter killed 1 parent & 1 sibling	2	5
	TOTALS	38	95

[a] Source: Canadian Centre for Justice Statistics. Canadian overall homicide rates rose in the late 1960s, as they did in most of the western world, and began to decline once more in the late 1970s. (cf. Boyd 1988)

THE EVOLUTION OF FAMILY AND SOCIETY

The essence of this book is the claim that if familicide is of little statistical significance, it is nonetheless a matter of considerable social moment, for it is the ultimate revelation of hidden tensions in the modern family. Yet what is special about the modern family? Has the family itself changed? Are there additions to the responsibilities of the family? What follows is an attempt to show how a rare homicidal event can sometimes tell us more about a widespread dilemma (and one that causes untold anguish) than ten thousand common events.

The archaeological and anthropological data make it reasonable to assert that most of human prehistoric experience took place in relatively egalitarian societies. Such societies were devoid of social caste and class, and any role specialization was based primarily upon age and gender. In such a primitive milieu, the coveted social commodities of power, prestige, and wealth are distributed with a measure of real equality throughout the society. Indeed, many of the customs of primitive cultures make no sense until it is understood that they are social mechanisms for ensuring the widest possible sharing of these commodities.

Thus the ubiquitous primitive practice in which food is distributed according to formal kinship criteria (one piece, for example, to a mother's brother, another to a father's sister);* thus the widespread custom of demeaning the successful hunter to ensure that his swollen head does not insist upon loftier prestige;† and thus the almost universal taboo against any individual trying to impose his will on others (that is, to exercise power). These are all *social levelling mechanisms,* and are found throughout primitive societies. Their function is to use the power of custom to resist the enhancement of any individual's power, prestige, or wealth—for such aggrandizement can only come at the expense of others, an imposition that is foreign to the mentality of most simple and egalitarian societies. In this social context, the family's only demands on the individual are for participation in communal social, religious, economic, and political activities; in return, it offers them all the benefits such a society can provide.

The history of human civilization can be viewed most profitably as the chronology of subversion of these levelling mechanisms by the more ambitious and aggressive individuals and families. Their attempt to expropriate the lion's share of these social commodities could not be successful until the agricultural revolution created an economy that could produce a surplus and a social structure that could be based on coercion. When eight could produce sufficient food to feed ten, the stage was set for the emergence of elite classes of warriors, nobles, and clergy. In this manner, the form and structure of human society was undoubtedly rewritten; now rank, hierarchy, and force—not mutual obligation—became the organizing principle. This development is the basis for the growth of caste and class—clusters of individuals with shared interests and privileges who oppose and dominate those of different rank.[36]

These new rigidly stratified social systems persisted for millennia without any fundamental change. Moreover, they functioned with a

---

*   See Georg Henriksen's *Hunters in the Barrens* for one of the many anthropological discussions of this practice.
†   See Draper, 1978.

limited number of social classes. French historian Fernand Braudel emphasized that as late as the eighteenth century, the world still "consisted of one vast peasantry, where between 80% and 90% of people lived from the land and from nothing else." The overwhelming majority of the people were peasants, and there were only a limited number of positions as artisans, merchants, soldiers, and functionaries of the royal regime. This is not to suggest that there was no social mobility, since the sons of peasants could rise to become artisans just as the merchant bourgeoisie could assimilate into the ranks of the gentry or nobility. Yet most were frozen in subservience and immobility.[37]

Indeed, no radical change comparable to the agricultural revolution was possible until an equally powerful force once more transformed the division of labour. The industrial revolution, and the social dislocation it entailed, was that force. The taming of mass production expanded services, transport, commerce, and the state; each domain developed its own occupations, ranks, and bureaucracies to feed the new system. Braudel writes that while "the state, with its thousands of administrative responsibilities was acquiring its own bureaucracy," commerce created "factors, accountants, inspectors, actuaries, [and] commissioners." Moreover, a growing host of "professionals" were incorporated to legalize the financial transactions of the new system, to heal its sick, and to teach its young people the rudimentary skills required by the new industrial order. "By the end of the eighteenth century," Braudel notes, "all the professions were expanding steadily and tending to change their structures and traditional forms of organization." This process accelerated still further during the twentieth century when the state, in refining its mandate as a total war-making machine, continuously provided new occupations to shepherd the new technologies and services. This in turn would have a major impact on the social function of the family.[38]

THE ASPIRING MODERN FAMILY

The modern era is more than just the triumph of the bourgeois, the commissar, and the ayatollah: it is also the dizzying expansion of newly created and hierarchically ranked occupations. It has always been possible for a wealthy merchant family like the Bensons to aspire to admission to the nobility, but now it was feasible for the illegitimate administrator in the export department of the Ford Motor Company to desire for his son a career as a military officer, as did Harry De la Roche, Sr. Now it was realistic for a Buick dealer's service manager to grope for the status and lifestyle of the upper-middle classes, converting his dubious income into the appropriate possessions, as did DeFeo. Now too those failing in the system might feel a special deprivation and insecurity, as did Jim and Naomi Olive when they insisted their lonely and culture-shocked daughter conform to their social goals and neurotic fantasies.

Conventional scholarship has acknowledged this radical change in modern society but has focussed too narrowly on the functions the family has thereby lost to the institutional sector. Thus Mintz and Kellogg conclude that "as many of [the family's] traditional economic, educational, and welfare functions were transferred outside the home, the family ceased to be a largely autonomous, independent, self-contained, and self-sufficient unit." All that remains to this castrated modern family are a few surviving roles: "the socialization of children and the provision of emotional support and affection." But this otherwise reasonable assessment conceals one of the primary functions of the family. The modern family's prime mandate is much more than socialization and affection, and its stability rests on far more than "affection, compatibility, and mutual interest."[39]

Curiously, what has always been one of the fundamental social roles of the family—the maintenance and enhancement of kin-group *status*—is relatively neglected in the modern literature. Through the millennia, the family has been the institution that assigns and protects the *status* of its members, as when the medieval family acted together to avenge its dishonor, and as when the spouse and children of a psychiatrist share her prestige as they share her income and her home. It is the family that regulates the social rise or fall of its members, and this task structures much of the thought and behaviour of an aspiring family. In such a milieu, children can become the vehicles for the social expectations of the parents: sometimes, that is *all* they are. In the insecure aspiring family, a corollary to this is often an atmosphere of diminished affection and inattentiveness to the child's true needs and abilities. The children may thus be ordered to curtail their social lives, surround themselves with the appropriate friends and possessions, obtain the "correct" occupations, and otherwise submerge their identities merely to fulfil their parents' ambitions. Many of the fundamental tensions within the modern family can be accounted for by this depersonalizing prime mandate.

If this phenomenon has been neglected in recent literature, it has nevertheless been well understood. Years ago, the great American sociologist, Robert Merton, described the overwhelming demands that can be encountered by those whose parents' social expectations have been foiled. As Merton expressed it, "many parents confronted with personal 'failure' or limited 'success' may mute their original goal-emphasis and may defer further efforts to reach the goal, attempting to reach it vicariously through their children." Ironically, however, these "failures" and "frustrates," who have the least to teach their children about the avenues to achievement, put the greatest "pressure upon their children for high achievement. And this syndrome of lofty aspirations and limited realistic opportunities . . . is precisely the pattern which invites deviant behavior."[40]

All of the families we have examined in detail in this book have been failures and frustrates—not of course in any real or human sense, but in terms of their own ambitions. Margaret Benson failed to penetrate the social elites because her social performance was too flamboyant and inept. DeFeo was unable to mute the violent behaviour that had given him his wealth, but the extinction of which was vital if he was to purchase entrance to the upper-middle-class world whose house High Hopes he had acquired. The insecure and dominating De La Roche, with his aristocratic-sounding name and his higher-status wife, made no progress other than to secure a middle-class possession by evicting his mother-in-law from her own home. The Olives, struggling to pay for their regrettably outré home in fashionable Marin County, could not banish their fears of imminent social collapse. As if in recompense, all of the families surrounded themselves with material possessions—most especially their homes, the ultimate emblem of status—that were at the upper reaches of their economic capacity. Whether it was Benson constructing her garish Florida mansion, DeFeo purchasing the spacious waterfront home, the Olives in their non-Eichler, De La Roche stealing his mother-in-law's family home, or the Burtons reeling from the mortgage rates, the same excruciating fear of social failure was being expressed.

These forces are felt most intensely in families that cling to the margins of the social class in which they covet membership. This unbridgeable chasm generates that profound and demoralizing insecurity felt by those who do not quite belong, however good their marriages and however appropriate their social activities may be. Such families are deeply stressed in societies that place "a high premium on economic affluence and social ascent," and that humiliate those who fail. All modern societies share these pressures, but Merton thought they were especially intense in America. "Diverse sources," he argued, maintained this deforming pressure on the family, relentlessly urging it to ever-higher aspirations and attributing failure to personal inadequacy. Merton found the text for this process in America's "exhortational literature," in which "the symbolism of a commoner rising to the estate of economic royalty is woven deep in the" American culture, "finding what is perhaps its ultimate expression in the words of one who knew whereof he spoke, Andrew Carnegie: 'Be a king in your dreams.' Say to yourself, 'My place is at the top.' "[41]

This is precisely the character of the families we have examined in this volume. The parents' social aspirations may well stem from altruistic motives, such as the enrichment of the lives of their children, or the satisfactions of a more fulfilling profession. Yet everywhere in the human experience we find those who take their goals to extremes, who cannot accommodate their desire for achievement to their abilities, and who will sustain their ambitions regardless of the price. In their sometimes frenzied efforts to succeed, they may grow deaf to the suffering of those they wish to help. It is this untrammelled and frustrated desire that lies behind many of the behaviours of both the nouveau riche and the nouveau pauvre that strike the outsider as inexplicably flamboyant, disordered, cruel, irrational, or hysterical.

The scientific literature is studded with insights into the social patholo-gies that may be generated in this manner. In their splendid review of the subject, psychologists Kleiner and Dalgard concluded that "social mobility is significantly related to functional psychiatric disorders," and that the "rates of [mental] illness have been higher for the upwardly and down-wardly mobile populations relative to the socially stable." Moreover, as the social distance covered in either direction increases so do the rates of mental illness. As the consequences of these ambitions, foiled or success-ful, reverberate through the family, they can create far more than insecur-ity and mental illness; they can fashion anything from the acquisition of racially or sexually bigoted attitudes, or extreme social snobbery, to the seeds of a familicide. They can also create personalities that are too detached from the emotional and moral order—deviant persons for whom, Merton wrote, "calculations of personal advantage and fear of punishment are the only regulating agencies."[42] *

---

* It may be at precisely this point that the long-postponed marriage between psychology and sociology will one day be consummated, since it is the social and cultural forces analyzed in this volume (and in *Hunting Humans*) that produce the type of personality capable of annihilating his or her family. Indeed, this socially mobile or

If all our families aspire to higher social rank, the nature of their involvement in the system handicaps them most grievously. Notions such as taste and style are not of course real phenomena: rather, they are the stratagems the social classes deploy to maintain their rigid borders, create scarcity, and restrict entry. In any stratified society, it is the family that has the prime responsibility for instructing its members in the taste and behavior that is appropriate to its class. Aspiring families, however, are reared in one class and expected to perform in another. They therefore frequently fail to grasp the often-unwritten rules for membership.[43]

On the other hand, established families—whatever their class—offer their kin a kind of curriculum from which outsiders are barred. As auto-anthropologist Nelson Aldrich, Jr. observed in his remarkable study of his own class, "for a beneficiary of Old Money, the educational function of the estate he was born to seems the most striking feature of the landscape." For old money, the lessons are the country club and the yacht club, the Grand Tour and the proper private schools, and the right clubs, summer places, and jobs. In fact, Aldrich writes, "all these stations of Old Money life appear not only as constitutive of the class but instructive of it—as so many courses that have to be taken, so many credentials tested, so many qualifications proclaimed." For the failing, aspiring, *un*established families in this volume, the system offered no curriculum and operated to preordain failure. Small wonder then that, cut off from all reliable instructors, the Bensons, Dresbachs, De La Roches, DeFeos, and Olives so misconstrued the appropriate behaviours and courted class rejections.[44]

The failure to rise produces an anxiety in many parents that leads them to try to control every dimension of their children's lives—for how else can they be assured their children will do the "right thing," and not compromise their status? Thus the tendency to monitor and govern in incredible detail the social performances of their children, choosing their friends, clothing, automobiles, houses, occupations, and spouses. These decisions are based entirely on their potential for status enhancement, not the personal preference of the children. Thus the desire becomes intense to

---

aspiring family may prove to be one of the primary social contexts that incubate what psychologists call psychopathy—that remorseless personality that cannot respond to the humanity in other people. Although a number of terms are used to describe the syndrome (including psychopathy, sociopathy, antisocial personality, and antisocial personality disorder), psychologist Robert Hare notes that they all refer "to a common core of attributes," which encompass "unreliability, insincerity, pathological lying, egocentricity, impulsivity and poor judgment; a lack of remorse, guilt and shame; [and] inability to experience empathy or concern for others, or to maintain warm, affectional attachments."[43]

mold their children, children-in-law, and grandchildren (often, ironically, to inappropriate styles), as when the Bensons dyed their daughter-in-law's hair "Benson blonde"; the Dresbachs unilaterally selected their sons' sports, school, and friends; the DeFeos bound their son to them in both work and residence; and the Olives force-fed an essentially Latin schoolgirl into becoming the daughter of a California business executive. Moreover, their social failure is accompanied by an increasing isolation from the life that whirls around them; this in turn intensifies the anxious concern with which they scrutinize one another's behaviour. All this takes place in a modern cultural milieu in which even adolescent children expect enormous personal freedom. Often, the contradiction between the familial and cultural forces leaves the child feeling deprived of all autonomy, personality, and identity.

Yet it is not just the children whose identities are crushed in such families. All of these families are structured along rigid, traditional, paternalistic lines, in which all authority (often brutal, as with Dresbach, De La Roche and DeFeo) resides in the paternal figure. The mothers were expected to put aside any thoughts they may have had of independent careers and abandon themselves to the purely status concerns of the fathers. In variations on this theme, the Benson women were ordered to scuttle their careers; the prime function of the De La Roche, Dresbach, and DeFeo women was to elevate the family through their own headier social origins; and Mrs. Olive was socially legitimized through her artificially constructed snobberies and her foster-child status to the aristocratic DeKays. In declaring their women nonpersons, and relegating them to purely status-enhancing roles, such families ensure the intensification of the characteristic atmosphere of status-hysteria.

Moreover, all of the families create a kind of trap, and the children may come to feel there is no escape from this snare other than its total annihilation. Sometimes the trap is a literal one, as when one downwardly mobile son of a famous politician locked his children, when they misbehaved, in cages he had constructed in his basement.* More typically, the cage is social and economic: DeFeo stole his son's car and threatened his income when the boy moved to his own apartment; the Bensons used a combination of emotional blackmail and expensive bribery to tie their children to them; Dresbach's physical (and the Olives' mental) assaults

---

*   In this case, the grandson, when twenty-one, armed with a knife, was interrupted before he could do more than slice through the cheeks and cut out the tongue of his sleeping father.

intensified until there seemed no end; and De La Roche chained his son to a school and a career. Thus the parental regime uses a variety of means to create a spirit of utter dependence among its children, and then closes all escape through physical, verbal, or economic force.

All of the families also transmitted a familial culture that was heavily laden with violence and duplicity, signalling aggression and manipulation as appropriate and effective means for the resolution of any dilemma. In some families the violence was brutal and direct, as in the regime of fear maintained by Dresbach, DeFeo, and De La Roche. In other families it was more subtle, as among the Bensons and the Olives, substituting squabbling and committal to mental institutions for heavy blows. In either case, the lesson was freely dispensed that problems within the family could be resolved not through the rational arbitration of opposing interests, but by the collision of physical and emotional forces.

All of these parents, but especially the fathers, treated their children with varieties of contempt. This was frequently expressed in behaviour less obvious than physical and verbal assault. The Benson and Olive men, tending compulsively to their financial empires and spending their lives in sales meetings in Manila and Marin, showed a real indifference for their children when they abandoned them utterly to whatever the mother might provide. Both Benson and DeFeo placed their sons in untitled positions and then overpaid them for work of no value. De La Roche dismissed any right his son might have had to construct an independent life.

The origin of this contempt felt by some aspiring parents for their children appears to lie in what seems to them to be bland and slothful behaviour, willfully directed against the family's status aspirations. Thus the parents first crush the children's independence and then despise them for their dependence. Moreover, the parent often creates a double-bind for his children, oscillating between a non-negotiable demand that the child do everything he commands (a subservience that earns his contempt); and the contradictory desire that the child be an independent person, one worthy of respect (but if he becomes one he is challenging their prior demand for subservience and therefore earns the parent's anger).

Stumbling blindly towards their fate, the parents of familicides continue to humiliate their children with a flurry of emotional tactics designed purely to manipulate and dominate. Sometimes these are less subtle than the commonplace obliteration of identity, as when one self-made American multimillionaire shouted at his middle-aged and dependent daughters, apropos of nothing, "You're all worthless garbage. Without me, you're nothing!" Small wonder then, that imprisoned within this histrionic playhouse a minority of children begin to incubate a plan to terminate for all time these intolerable and incompatible demands. As they inch towards this decision, they do so with intense anxiety and confusion. Apparently unloved, beset on all sides by contradictory demands (to none of which they can sufficiently acquiesce to win their parents' approval), they begin to dwell on the idea that is at once an existential blow and a liberating act. Thus the prospect of familicide takes on the colours of a creative and progressive rebellion, where once it may have been, as it was in an early school essay by Marlene Olive, an inconceivable breach of the social contract. Now it allows them, perhaps for the first time, to glimpse the possibility of an independent identity.[45]

But why kill the entire family? In so many of these cases, the killer's hatred seems to focus on only one or two members of the family (Sawanoi's parents, Olive's mother, DeFeo's father and sister, De La Roche's father), not all of them. Yet the innocent are massacred along with the guilty, and they even kill any kin they may enthusiastically love, as Sawanoi killed his beloved grandmother. This seems most puzzling of all, but it is in fact determined by the structure of these paternalistic families. In such families, ruled by traditional fathers (or, as with the Bensons, the inheriting matriarch) all the other members of the family are seen as allies of the dominant enemy parent. Thus they too are players in the oppressive game, whether their role-playing is quite passive (as with Mrs. De La Roche, Mrs. DeFeo, and the siblings), or fully active (as with Mr. Olive, the Benson siblings, and Dawn DeFeo).

Pierre Riviére explained it fully when he said that, "I killed my sister Victoire because she took my mother's part. I killed my brother by reason of his love for my mother and my sister." To the killers, whose perception is warped by the morbid anxiety generated by the assaults upon their identities, the "innocence" of some is more apparent than real. Each subordinate family member is understood to play a significant role in the creation and maintenance of the oppressive regime. By failing to oppose the system, the innocent have endorsed it—as much as the more active members had done so by energetically allying themselves with the dominant parent. Thus the entire family seems to become a monster bent on the social extinction of the incipient killer, and the entire family participates in closing all avenues of escape. It makes a certain twisted sense, then, that only the annihilating mechanism, the knife, can "shut down" the system, as young Sawanoi explained it in Tokyo.

Yet millions of families are exposed to these same pressures without provoking a killing, let alone a familicide. How do they avoid such explosions? Enquiries of this nature are usually handicapped by the absence of any control group. Fortunately, we have one for our thesis: the thirty-year Ostroff Project, which studied a rising merchant family with almost all of the qualities of the Bensons, provides us with some of the answers. The founding fathers, the Ostroff tycoons, are now all elderly, and their offspring are well into middle age. Those offspring who labour in the family empire have accepted their cowed and dependent status. The searing familial tension surfaces in them as psychosomatic disorders, compulsive eating, or hysterical personalities with powerful phobias, sei-zures, and tantrums. The tension, continuously maintained by the elderly tycoons, centres around the inevitable failure of the offspring to live up to the contradictory expectations of their parents. In addition, each of the offspring is consumed with fear that his siblings may be secretly better treated, more generously rewarded, than himself.

The diffusion of this potential for violence is accomplished among the Ostroffs by a bogus but effective family mythology. Thus the ceremonial family gatherings for landmark anniversaries and birthdays are ideologi-cally charged: warm and public expressions of love are mixed with plausible claims that all previous outrages were accidental misunderstand-ings, or motivated by surpassing love, not contempt. More often, these transgressions remain unmentioned, but their memory is temporarily eased by the earnest professions of the sacred quality of the family and its eternal love. Our familicides have no such believable mythologies. In such maudlin encounters, orchestrated from time to time by the tycoons, the Ostroff offspring are befuddled afresh into accepting the family values and power structure, as well as in recapturing their hope that they will soon be rewarded for this subservience. Thus the anger is typically diffused in the wave of positive emotions (and guilt for prior hatred and frustration) generated by the sentimental ideology, only to return later when the intoxicating effects of the occasion—or the accompanying lavish gift—have begun to dissipate. A second and fundamental characteristic of our control group is that unlike the DeFeos and the Bensons, the Olives and the De La Roches, the Ostroffs permit the trap to be sprung by the most rebellious of their children. Those who escape either embrace radical politics and lifestyles, putting themselves beyond the pale and even severing all contact; or they simply move far away, and allow geography to blunt the familial assaults.[46]

Foucault and his colleagues were mistaken to conclude that the origins of familicide lie in the child striking a blow against the social order on behalf of all the dispossessed. Like all multiple murderers, our killers act only on their own behalf, and their blows are aimed at the family, not the social system. Driven beyond endurance by the emotional fireworks that can characterize the aspiring family, trapped in the obliterating maze of relationships from which they can see no exit, they begin to foment an uprising. Its purpose is to reclaim their identities, not spark a revolution.

The tragedy and irony of all this is that the cause of these occasional massacres is also one of the great achievements of modern civilization— the offer of social mobility to many, and the crushing of the enslaving shackles of family, race, religion, and gender. If such social fluidity is one of mankind's headier victories, it also exacts a heavy price from families thrust into unaccustomed roles and on those struggling for social elevation. One of these costs is the occasional, frenzied, family annihilation by a child for whom the parents thought they had laboured so mightily. Human history is studded with such ironies.

A Note on Method

Sole Survivor was originally planned to be part of *Hunting Humans*, but the latter book grew too large—and the explanations too diverse—for them to be contained within one volume. Still, this new book is written in a very similar style, and it collects and deploys data in much the same way. Despite, or perhaps because of, the extraordinary international success of *Hunting Humans*, my colleagues have raised a number of methodological and procedural points which deserve a response.

DATA

In writing *Hunting Humans*, I assembled the hundreds of books and articles on multiple murderers in order to generate a social explanation for such massacres. With careful winnowing, it was possible to obtain reliable social histories for twenty-four killers, and detailed data for a half-dozen of these. Such rich data were not available to me for *Sole Survivor*. The annihilation of family is not a subject that attracts a large number of writers and I was thus gravely handicapped in my search. In fact reliable books were available on only a handful of cases, and we cannot pretend to state in what way they are representative of the entire universe of familicides. Thus even more than *Hunting Humans*, this book must be regarded as speculative and provocative in nature, not definitive. Its aim, like its predecessor's, is twofold: first, to emphasize that this behaviour is a social phenomenon worthy of study; and second, to mount a tentative and general social explanation of what has hitherto been dismissed as isolated, idiosyncratic, and bizarre psychopathology.

But why select one killer over another? Why was a chapter of *Hunting Humans* devoted to Edmund Kemper, but not to Juan Corona? The answer is entirely pragmatic: the source material for Kemper consisted of three books, two of which were of the highest quality, while only one unreliable book had been written on Corona. This task was more complicated for *Sole Survivor*. Since there are far fewer books on familicides, I was forced to use virtually all the competent material in existence and to lean more heavily on journalistic accounts in the finest newspapers for confirmation and enrichment.

What is the value of such sources? As sociologist Jack Katz has written in his fascinating new book, *Seductions of Crime,* the time has come for criminologists to take seriously these "nonfiction novels," these carefully crafted accounts of crimes that have been published during the last thirty years. To do otherwise, Katz insists, is to abandon the material (much of it superb), to "journalists, politicians and literary critics." Katz notes quite correctly that "we can get the necessary methodological angle by examining comparatively different books and different parts of the same book.

> For starters, we can apply some of the evidentiary criteria developed for evaluating ethnographic research, such as assigning higher evidentiary value to (1) conduct reported versus thoughts imputed (by the author) to the killer (2) individual acts by the killer that are recounted by many observers versus those recounted by one observer, and (3) a pattern of conduct reported by multiple observers, each observing a different time and situation versus an act reported once.[1]

They thus constitute a useful alternative source for data, and to neglect them is a tactical misjudgment, especially since they contain so many of the words and rationalizations of the killers themselves.

But why not interview the killers ourselves, as so many journalists have done before us? The first difficulty here is purely practical: for a scholar who is neither a psychiatrist nor a police officer (with their special access to the system), it takes a web of contacts and a great deal of personal influence to be admitted to any of the prisons or mental hospitals that house one killer. Many journalists have accomplished this with one killer, but should a scholar wish to write about the general phenomenon and require not one case but dozens of cases, the task becomes impossible.

However, even if such access were granted by the various municipal, state, provincial, national, psychiatric, and prison authorities, and even if the killers agreed to be interviewed, the interview method itself yields much less useful information than is widely believed. Many scholars and journalists naively feel that they cannot know a person unless they have met and interviewed him or her. I have published more interview-based books and articles in the scholarly journals than most, and I understand full well that a few interviews, conducted long after the burst of honesty that can characterize early confessions, can lead to more superficial results than no interviews at all. As Katz observed, "any interviews or observations of the killer that authors may obtain are almost inevitably subject to the distortions of retrospective, self-interested memory," which increases with the time elapsed since the crimes. Indeed, the interview must be seen as a theatrical exercise in which the killer most often writes the script: he presents the interviewer with the face he wishes the world to see, and reveals precious little behind his mask. I personally left the interview method behind me with the publication of my 1979 book, *The Myth of Delinquency;* and since then I have elicited far richer data from the police interrogations, psychiatric interviews, confessions in court, personal diaries, and journalists' corroborative interviews of friends and families than I could ever have hoped to obtain singlehandedly.[2]

Finally, what is the value of a book that presents so little fresh material and confines itself primarily to the revision of classic texts? Although *Sole Survivor* contains much more unpublished data than *Hunting Humans,* that was never my intent: the aim of both books has been to struggle to enrich our understanding of a phenomenon, not contribute to the proliferation of case studies of individual killers. We do so not only because too few aim at the former, but also because the production of more and more unanalyzed case studies encourages the civilization to see such killings as bizarre, random, and unrelated events instead of what they truly are— full expressions of deforming aspects of modern industrial societies and cultures.

METHOD

An obsession with methodology can be one of the hallmarks of an intellectually bankrupt discipline. In striving to ape science there is sometimes (especially in modern criminology) an inverse relationship between the quality of a discipline's insights and the rigidity of its notions about sound procedures. That said, the careful consideration of data is central to the legitimacy of any explanatory enterprise, and there are a number of important issues that remain unexamined.

First, of what scientific use are nine cases? How can we have any idea if this tiny sample represents in any way the total universe of familicides? In fact we do not. Some scholars feel that if there are no solid, international, government statistics available on a subject, then it should simply not be studied. Yet this stance abandons social science to the whims of the anonymous bureaucrats in Washington, London, New York, and Paris who manufacture crime statistics—a concession few scholars should surely make willingly. The fact of the matter is that there are no worldwide statistics on familicide because the statisticians have not yet recognized it as a phenomenon. This paucity of data is less disturbing than it might seem, especially for a book that is a first and exploratory look at the subject.

Anthropologists are accustomed to taking their data where and when they find it; they must cultivate an indifference to having their data acquisition irrevocably curtailed by such entirely unscientific matters as sudden monsoons, clashes of personality, or unfriendly government officials. Were the truth known, much of the genius of anthropology is based on the intimate study of a small number of cases, which mere circumstance enabled the anthropologist to study. If the weaknesses of such a method are obvious—we cannot state with confidence the generality of our findings—the strengths yield rich and detailed human data. The fact is that in the rough-and-tumble of field research, the opportunities for data collection appear most unpredictably and for quite idiosyncratic reasons, such as mutual affection, an unrelated bureaucratic decision, or self-interest of the informant. What the method provides is an extraordinary amount of personal information that is essential to any attempt to comprehend the motivation of individuals. I have tried to extend this method to the writings and statements of killers, and to the material offered by crime writers in books, magazines, and newspapers. After a decade's immersion in their work, I see little difference in quality between the best journalism and academic scholarship (except that the former is likely to be better written). In any case, official statistics present their own problems and are equally unreliable.

Second, what are we to make of the anthropological biographer, whose competence certainly concerns social movements and the mass of humanity, not individuals and their meandering life histories? The historical sociologist Philip Abrams examined this problem in great depth, and concluded that "accounting sociologically for the individual in particular is really only a more precise version of the problem of accounting for individuals in general." Analyzed thus in historical terms, "Lenin and Luther, the Sun King and Shakespeare no more elude or defy explanation than do Russian proletarians in 1900." Embracing criminality is "a negotiated passage to a possible identity," and an individual must be seen as "creatively seizing opportunities for personal self-definition."

> Individuals *are* their biographies. And insofar as a biography is fully and honestly recorded what it reveals is some historically located history of self-construction—a moral career in fact. The setting of the biography is this or that historically given system of probabilities or life chances. The biography realizes some life chances within that system and perforce abandons others.

Thus to understand a Benson or a Sawanoi, a De La Roche or a Burton, we must observe "the meshing of life-history and social history in a singular fate." Only then can we begin to understand how an individual calculates his or her future before assuming the identity of familicide.[3]

Yet the ultimate embarrassment of the social sciences remains unresolved. We are still unable to explain fully why one person responds in one way to social pressures while a second reacts quite differently—why some members of the poor and oppressed, for example, turn to crime, while others study medicine or Sanskrit. Abrams has insisted that if we know enough about the life of any individual, we can with hindsight demonstrate how his or her career moved logically and inexorably in one direction or another, being diverted only by some event or relationship. But the fact is that humans are fully sentient beings, capable of assessing their personal lives and their alternative responses in complicated and individual ways. They are not mere reactive organisms programmed by some computer or genetic code to do what they do. They also have available to them a variety of cultural options through which they may protest their condition: an identical conundrum may be responded to with alcohol and drugs, political activity, religious fundamentalism, sharing sorrows with lovers or friends, or in incubating a homicidal mission. The infinitely varying interaction between human consciousness and our complex social and cultural environments limits the possibility of precise prediction, possibly for all time. Certainly it cannot happen before the insights of psychology, sociology, biology, and history are integrated in a new and meaningful way.

ALTERNATIVE EXPLANATIONS

Feminist scholars have complained that I ignored their case in *Hunting Humans*. I do not do so in this volume. This is a consequence of the different foci of the two books. The feminist argument is that all multiple murder constitutes a misogynistic war on women, leading one radical feminist to overstate her case with the remark that "there is a worldwide conspiracy for the mass extermination of women."[4] Women are indeed grievously abused in most societies and men are overwhelmingly the primary abusers—but men are also the primary victim of homicide, since more men than women are murdered in virtually every civilization.

Additionally, I have never been persuaded by the suggestion that sexism is somehow different from, or any more reprehensible than, racism—that other great provocateur of simplistic subordination and hatred among humanity. Nor can I grasp any fundamental difference between the racist massacre of Asian children in a schoolyard in Stockton, California, and the sexist massacre of university women in Montreal. In any case, my interpretation of our civilization tentatively concludes that men are reared not just to misogyny, the hatred of women, but to misanthropy, the hatred of people. Men are socialized to strive to dominate and humiliate all others, and to abuse any social group that, in refusing to remain subservient, poses a threat to their position—be it Asian immigrants, black sharecroppers, or university women. Multiple murderers, drawing their virulent ideas from the dominant culture, may assault any of these social groups.

Moreover, the misogyny argument does not perfectly fit the data. Both mass and serial killers typically murder representatives of the social group (a race, class, community, ethnic group, religion, or gender) that they imagine has threatened, rejected, or excluded them. But mass killers (those who murder in one brief explosion and expect to die within minutes of their assault, as in the McDonald's massacre in San Ysidro) are typically indifferent to gender in the selection of their victims.* Serial killers (such as the Yorkshire Ripper or Ted Bundy, who kill over an extended period of time and who wish to tell their stories and bask in their newfound infamy) typically select the gender they find sexually

---

* The tragic murder of fourteen women in December of 1989 at the University of Montreal constitutes an ominous exception to this rule.

desirable from among the social group they are assaulting. Thus homosexual serial killers (who appear to constitute a minority of both the homicidal and nonhomicidal populations) prey on vulnerable men and boys, while heterosexual serial killers prey on women. Moreover, while there are no recorded cases of female serial killers, there are a number of women who have with varying degrees of enthusiasm assisted their husbands and lovers in such murders. There are of course a number of female mass killers, as in the recent case of Lorie Dann, who opened fire in a school in Winnetka, Illinois. Thus I remain unconvinced by the feminist case on multiple murder.

On the other hand, the feminist critique of the modern paternalistic family is supremely plausible and essential to any understanding of the families in this volume. If misogyny tells us relatively little about multiple killers, paternalistic family structure tells us a great deal about the creation of oppressive familial regimes, the obliteration of female identities, and the factors underlying the construction of the familicidal web. Thus I draw heavily on feminist interpretations in *Sole Survivor*.

Practitioners of psychiatry will also note that this book is more tolerant of their perspective. Once again this should not be taken as a capitulation. *Hunting Humans* was a sustained and justified critique of the abuse of psychiatry in the courts, and a more general criticism of the limitations of the psychiatric interpretation of criminality. Regrettably, some have chosen to interpret my criticism as a wholesale assault on the very foundations of their enterprise. This is emphatically not the case. Still, the fact that the psychiatric sciences are among the most creative intellectual forces of this century—and that their ministrations have given comfort to many anguished people—does not justify their stranglehold on the judicial system, nor the pseudoscientific courtroom diagnoses routinely offered to their employers. Nor does its special expertise, developed to heal educated and thoughtful people who wish to examine their own psyches, apply so readily to the forensic domain, where those on trial manipulate the truth for their own immediate and self-serving legal ends.

Perhaps the most tragic mutual alienation in the forensic field is that between those espousing the biological and social traditions. Despite the potential for a full and balanced understanding of human deviance, practitioners of each discipline typically make their case in a fundamentally political, not scientific, fashion. So many sociologists are deaf even to the possibility that there may be a biological or hormonal element in the construction of criminality, just as those who retail the biological perspective seem blind to the overwhelming mass of social evidence. Moreover, the structure of intellectual empires makes it virtually impossible for a member of one domain to gain access to or understanding of the other. Distressingly, nothing even hints at a future detente to this meaningless and mutually destructive war.

STYLE

Many years ago, my first teacher in anthropology, Professor Harry Hawthorn, warned me that I wrote too clearly. If I continued to do so, he said, I would be easily understood and therefore subject to serious criticism. Better to hide behind a wall of jargon, he said. He was being droll at the time but a serious point remains: The scholar who is able to control his enthusiasm for the traditional style of sociological exposition runs the risk of being branded a mere popularizer, for people will be able to read him or her. Indeed, the modern academic who struggles to engage in a dialogue with his civilization—rather than with a handful of other academics scattered around the world—courts the status of renegade. This is a profound cultural tragedy and it is a symptom of the alienation of the university from the society that feeds it. For my part, I have always shared the views of McGill University archaeologist Bruce Trigger, who insists that to write in a language that is inaccessible to the informed general reader is both to emasculate social science and to betray the democratic spirit. The universities neglect at their peril their mandate to sustain a critical dialogue with their civilization.

Sensitive readers of both volumes will be relieved to see how much I have been able to reduce the level of homicidal gore in *Sole Survivor*. In *Hunting Humans*, the nature of my argument required me to force the reader through the same arduous process the writer had to endure (though with much less detail), examining the repellent physical acts of the killers. I did so because the meaning and symbolic significance of the murders was starkly revealed in the physical evidence. Yet if this applied to serial and mass killers, it did not do so with familicides. Their task is quite different: they usually go about their business as quickly and efficiently as they can, since their aim is less to humiliate and subjugate than simply to annihilate the source of their oppression. It has therefore been quite unnecessary to dwell upon the odious acts—beyond giving the reader a clear indication of methods, results, and further ramifications.

SOME ETHICAL QUESTIONS

Some colleagues have privately expressed the opinion that in turning from the subjects that had previously been my domain (industrial disease, workers' compensation, and delinquency), I have ceased to write social criticism. My belief is that they are quite mistaken, that these two murder volumes are indeed social criticism. Both concern themselves with the manner in which the social order deforms character and perception and creates terrible human suffering; both struggle to find some basis for the ultimate rectification of these matters. These statistically rare forms of homicide are all acted out by individuals—however disturbed and disordered they may be—who are profoundly influenced by their civilization's cleavages, mythologies, and prejudices. Whatever the causes of such unspeakable acts may be, any murderer kills more than one person: he kills the parents of the victim, the grandparents, siblings, lovers, and friends. And they do still more damage: they erode the social fabric; inculcate suspicion and hatred in the collective consciousness; transform public life from the joyous communal experience it might be to a savage zero-sum encounter; and demean the humanity of all.

Some colleagues have also been troubled by my consistent failure to excoriate the much-despised police. I share any thinking person's concern that a profession given so much discretionary power and so little social education must be closely monitored if democratic society is to survive. Moreover, I am aware of the many atrocities perpetrated by members of police forces in the name of law and order. However, I reserve the right to observe that experienced police can be more adept than mental health professionals or progressive social activists in dealing with, understanding, and assessing persons who may be programmed by the system to lie, finagle, and manipulate regarding their criminal acts. And I have met as many humane police officers as scholars, journalists, politicians, or civil servants.

Finally, what are we to make of those who deem murder an unacceptable subject for academic study? A corollary of this is the concern that in struggling to understand the killers we might also come to validate them. Such objections are often couched in fashionable radical rhetoric, but still mask profoundly unprogressive attitudes. Their logic would make us refrain from studying any behavior that was unhealthy or antisocial, and to do so would both deny intellectual enquiry and ensure our sustained lack of comprehension. In any case, far from validating such killers or reinforcing the culture of violence, these books struggle to emasculate them. If in a fundamental sense we are all victims of the civilization that produces us, those who refuse to kill deserve more respect than those who do not; and our deepest sympathies must always be rigidly fastened on those innocents whose lives have been wasted, and on their bereaved survivors who must fashion new and diminished lives.

N.B. In the interests of readability, one numeral has been assigned to each paragraph in the text requiring attribution. The sources under each numeral are listed in their order of appearance in the text.

CHAPTER ONE: INTRODUCTION

1 MacDowell (1963), p. 116. For a discussion of industrial disease, see Rosner and Markowitz (1987); Leyton (1975); or Stellman and Daum (1973). For government murders, see Kuper (1981) or Amnesty International (1983, 1984).
2 Peter McGill, in *The Globe & Mail*, Aug. 8, 1988; Sawanoi, in *ibid.*
3 *Ibid.*
4 M. Moya, *The Vancouver Sun*, Nov. 15, 1983; Ed Starkins, in *Vancouver*, March 1985; Bruce Blackman, in *ibid.*
5 *The Vancouver Sun*, Jan. 19, 1983; *The Province*, Nov. 4, 1983; Blackman, in *ibid.*
6 In Lunde (1979), p. 100.
7 See Keegan (1987), p. 1, for an uncharacteristically silly argument that "the methods of social scientists ... condemn those who practice them to the agony of making universal and general what is stubbornly local and particular."
8 *The Times* (London), Aug. 8, 1985, p. 3.
9 *Ibid.*, Aug. 9, 1985, p. 3; Oct. 4, 1986, p. 3.
10 *Ibid.*, Oct. 21, 1986, p. 3; Oct. 9, 1986, p. 3.
11 *Ibid.*, Oct. 8, 1986, p. 3; Oct. 10, 1986, p. 3.
12 *Ibid.*, Oct. 17, 1986, p. 3; Oct. 11, 1986, p. 3; Larsen (1980), p. 182; *The Times*, Oct. 18, 1986, p. 3.
13 *Ibid.*, Oct. 3, 1986, p. 3; Oct. 9, 1986, p. 1; Oct. 3, 1986, p. 3.
14 *Ibid.*, Oct. 13, 1986, p. 3; Oct. 14, 1986, p. 3.
15 *Ibid.*, Oct. 14, 1986, p. 3; Oct. 13, 1986, p. 3.
16 *Ibid.*, Oct. 3, 1986, p. 3.
17 *Ibid.*, Oct. 3, 1986, p. 3; Oct. 16, 1986, p. 3; Oct. 17, 1986, p. 3; Oct. 9, 1986, p. 3; Oct. 16, 1986, p. 3; Oct. 17, 1986, p. 3.
18 *Ibid.*, Oct. 3, 1986, p. 3; Oct. 9, 1986, p. 3.
19 *Ibid.*, Oct. 28, 1986, p. 3; Oct. 25, 1986, p. 3.

20 *Ibid.,* Oct. 29, 1986, p. 1.
21 Smith (1989), pp. 197–200.
22 Capote (1965), p. 351.
23 *Ibid.,* pp. 351–352.
24 *Ibid.,* p. 353.
25 Andrews, in *ibid.,* p. 353.
26 *Ibid.,* pp. 354, 356.
27 *Ibid.,* pp. 357, 373.
28 *Ibid.,* p. 372.
29 Mewshaw (1980), pp. 12, 23.
30 Dresbach, in *ibid.,* pp. 20–22.
31 In *ibid.,* p. 26.
32 *Ibid.,* pp. 28, 50.
33 *Ibid.,* p. 28.
34 *Ibid.,* pp. 59–60, 67, 71, 70.
35 *Ibid.,* pp. 76, 98, 87, 107.
36 *Ibid.,* p. 144; Guttmacher in *ibid.,* p. 172.
37 Porter (1982), pp. 6, 1–2, 3.
38 *Ibid.,* pp. 6, 9, 10.
39 Supreme Court of Newfoundland, Trial Division Archive, Tape 1051A.
40 *Ibid.,* Tape 1051A.
41 *Ibid.,* Tape 1051A.
42 *Ibid.,* Tape 1050B.
43 *Ibid.,* Tapes 1052A, 1053A, 1052B, 1055B.
44 *Ibid.,* Tape 1054B.
45 *Ibid.,* Tape 1057B.
46 *Ibid.,* Tapes 1059A, 1057B.
47 *Ibid.,* Tapes 1058B, 1057B.
48 *Ibid.,* Tapes 1062A, 1063A.
49 *Ibid.,* Tapes 1062A, 1063A.
50 See Lunde (1979).
51 For an amazingly unscientific illustration of this, see the apparently ghostwritten Norris (1988).
52 For a police version of this, see Ressler, Burgess and Douglas (1988); Morris (1985), p. 293.

CHAPTER TWO: THE BENSONS

1 Steven Benson, in Walton (1987), p. 33.
2 *New York Times,* Aug. 23, 1985, p. B18; Harry Hitchcock, in Walton (1987), p. 187.
3 Greenya (1987), p. 32; in Walton (1987), p. 168; Greenya (1987), p. 32; in Walton (1987), p. 163.
4 In Greenya (1987), p. 158.
5 Walton (1987), pp. 117–119.
6 *Ibid.,* pp. 120–121; Greenya (1987), p. 171.
7 In Walton (1987), p. 122.

8 *Ibid.,* p. 123; Greenya (1987), p. 220; *New York Times,* July 18, 1986, p. A7.

9 Carol Lynn Kendall, in Greenya (1987), pp. xii–xiii; Walton (1987), p. 5; Carol Lynn in Walton, p. 123; *Ibid.,* p. 7.

10 Steven Benson, in *ibid.,* pp. 128–129; *Ibid.,* pp. 7–9.

11 Harry Hitchcock, in Andersen (1987), p. 7.

12 Walton (1987), pp. 11–12.

13 Harry Hitchcock, in Greenya (1987), pp. 5–6.

14 Walton (1987), p. 13; Harry Hitchcock, in Greenya (1987), p. 6.

15 Harry Hitchcock, in Walton (1987), pp. 14–16.

16 Harry Hitchcock, in Greenya (1987), p. 6.

17 Harry Hitchcock, in *ibid.,* p. 3.

18 Margaret Benson, in Walton (1987), p. 45.

19 Greenya (1987), pp. 9–11; Walton (1987), pp. 13–14.

20 Greenya (1987); p. 18; Walton (1987), pp. 16–17; Andersen (1987), pp. 29–30.

21 Walton (1987), p. 19.

22 *Ibid.,* p. 45; Greenya (1987), p. 104 (my italics).

23 Walton (1987), pp. 43, 45, 72.

24 *Ibid.,* pp. 80, 92, 84; Greenya (1987), p. 69.

25 *Ibid.,* pp. 100, 103; Greenya (1987), p. 113; Margaret Benson, in Walton (1987), p. 110; Andersen (1987), p. 75; Walton (1987), pp. 81–82, 83.

26 *Ibid.,* p. 92.

27 Edward (Benny) Benson, in *ibid.,* p. 24.

28 *Ibid.,* pp. 21, 18–19.

29 *Ibid.,* pp. 23–24.

30 Carol Lynn Kendall, in Greenya (1987), pp. 28–29.

31 *Ibid.,* p. 75.

32 Walton (1987), pp. 24–26.

33 Carol Lynn Kendall, in Greenya, (1987), p. 43.

34 *Ibid.,* p. 88; Carol Lynn Kendall, in *ibid.,* p. 88.

35 Margaret Benson, in Walton (1987), p. 47.

36 *Ibid.,* pp. 34, 37.

37 Tracy Mullins, in *ibid.,* pp. 61–62; Scott Benson, in Andersen (1987), p. 82.

38 Kim Beegle, in Walton (1987), p. 74.

39 *Ibid.,* pp. 47, 97.

40 Scott and Margaret Benson, in Andersen (1987), pp. 88–89, and Walton (1987), pp. 75–76; *New York Times,* July 30, 1986, p. A12.

41 Michael Minney, in Andersen (1987), p. 40.

42 Walton (1987), p. 30; Nancy Ferguson, in Andersen (1987), p. 39; Walton (1987), p. 31; Margaret Benson, in Andersen (1987), p. 48.

43 Benny Benson, in Walton (1987), p. 32; Andersen (1987), p. 46; Walton (1987), pp. 31, 33.

44 Andersen (1987), p. 79.

45 Steven Benson, in *ibid.,* p. 49.

46 In Greenya (1987), p. 31.

47 Andersen (1987), pp. 26–27, 30; Walton (1987), pp. 20– 21.

48 Steven Benson, in *ibid.,* p. 25; Lynne Beyer, in *ibid.,* p. 27; Andersen (1987); p. 35.

49 Nancy Ferguson, in Greenya (1987), p. 33; Harry Hitchcock in *ibid.*, p. 31.

50 Andersen (1987), p. 38; Nancy Ferguson, in Greenya (1987), p. 34; Carol Lynn Kendall, in *ibid.*, p. 34; Nancy Ferguson, in Andersen (1987), p. 49.

51 Greenya (1987), p. 36.

52 Carol Lynn Kendall, in *ibid.*, pp. 34–35.

53 Andersen (1987), p. 48; Nancy Ferguson, in Greenya, p. 48; Kenneth Olson, in *ibid.*, p. 77.

54 Willem van Huystee, in *ibid.*, p. 50; Nancy Ferguson, in *ibid.*, p. 77.

55 Greenya (1987), p. 48; Andersen (1987), pp. 58–59; Greenya (1987), p. 78.

56 Carol Lynn Kendall, in *ibid.*, p. 49; Andersen (1987), pp. 64–65; Carol Lynn Kendall, in Greenya (1987), p. 38.

57 *Ibid.*, p. 83; Carol Lynn Kendall, in *ibid.*, pp. 85–86.

58 Andersen (1987), pp. 83–84; Carol Lynn Kendall, in Greenya (1987), p. 116; Andersen (1987), p. 84.

59 *Ibid.*, p. 85; Jerry Hester, in Greenya (1987), p. 117.

60 Walton (1987), p. 178; Andersen (1987), p. 159; Walton (1987), p. 108; Andersen (1987), p. 159; Walton (1987), p. 86.

61 Greenya (1987), pp. 121, 125; Wayne Kerr, in *ibid.*, p. 127; Andersen (1987), p. 124.

62 Greenya (1987), pp. 129–130.

63 Steven Benson, in Andersen (1987), p. 174.

64 Steven Benson, in Greenya (1987), p 153.

65 *New York Times,* July 19, 1986, p. 8; Andersen (1987), pp. 205, 209, 211.

66 Greenya (1987), pp. 146, 157, 153.

67 *New York Times,* Aug. 23, 1985, p. B18; in Greenya (1987), pp. 176, 170–171.

68 In *ibid.,* 176–177 (my italics).

69 Travis Kendall, in *ibid.*, p. 186.

70 In *ibid.*, p. 165; Andersen (1987), p. 171; Greenya (1987), p. 181; Steven Benson, in Andersen (1987), p. 174.

71 Laurance Spelman, in Collier and Horowitz (1976), p. 503.

72 Kim Beegle, in Walton (1987), pp. 151–152.

73 See Scheper-Hughes (1979).

74 *New York Times,* Aug. 8, 1986, p. A6; *Ibid.,* Sept. 3, 1986, p. A14; Carol Lynn Kendall, in Greenya (1987), p. 246.

75 Walton (1987), pp. 210–211.

CHAPTER THREE: THE DE LA ROCHES

1 Harry De La Roche, Jr., in Roesch (1979), p. 30.

2 *New York Times,* Nov. 29, 1976, p. 1; Harry, Jr., in Roesch (1979), p. 142.

3 Harry, Jr., in *ibid.,* pp. 144, 142, 144, 142, 146.

4 Harry, Jr., in *ibid.,* pp. 145, 142, 241.

5 Harry, Jr., in *ibid.,* pp. 142–143.

6 Harry, Jr., in *ibid.,* p. 143.

7 Patrolman Olsen, in *ibid.,* p. 8.

8 *Ibid.,* pp. 9, 131.

9 Harry, Jr., in *ibid.,* pp. 9, 114; *New York Times,* Nov. 29, 1976, p. 1.

10 Harry, Jr., in Roesch (1979), pp. 120–121.

11 *New York Times,* Nov. 29, 1976, p. 1; Harry, Jr., in Roesch (1979), pp. 125–126.

12 Harry, Jr., in *ibid.,* p. 127; *New York Times,* Oct. 25, 1976, p. 84.

13 Harry, Jr., in Roesch (1979), pp. 136, 137, 140; *ibid.,* p. 150.

14 Harry, Jr., in *ibid.,* pp. 147, 151, 156, 158.

15 Harry, Jr., in *ibid.,* pp. 159–160, 160–161.

16 Harry, Jr., in *ibid.,* pp. 163, 182.

17 Harry, Jr., in *ibid.,* pp. 182–183.

18 Harry, Jr., in *ibid.,* p. 183.

19 Harry, Jr., in *ibid.,* p. 184.

20 Harry, Jr., in *ibid.,* pp. 184–185.

21 Harry, Jr., in *ibid.,* p. 185.

22 Harry, Jr., in *ibid.,* pp. 185–186.

23 Harry, Jr., in *ibid.,* p. 186.

24 Harry, Jr., in *ibid.,* pp. 186–187.

25 Harry, Jr., in *ibid.,* p. 187.

26 Harry, Jr., in *ibid.,* pp. 187–188.

27 Harry, Jr., in *ibid.,* p. 188.

28 Harry, Jr., in *ibid.,* p. 255.

29 Gaylin (1983).

30 Dr. Zigarelli, in Roesch (1979), p. 191.

31 *New York Times,* Nov. 20, 1976, p. 1.

32 Dr. Zigarelli, in Roesch (1979), pp. 191–192 (my italics).

33 Dr. Zigarelli, in *ibid.,* p. 192.

34 *Ibid.,* pp. 196–197.

35 *Ibid.,* pp. 197–198.

36 Dr. Zigarelli, in *ibid.,* p. 196.

37 Dr. Gallina, in *ibid.,* p. 198.

38 Dr. Gallina, in *ibid.,* pp. 198–199 (my italics).

39 Dr. Gallina, in *ibid.,* p. 199.

40 Harry, Jr., in *ibid.,* p. 214.

41 *Ibid.,* pp. 228, 254; Dr. Gallina, in *ibid.,* p. 252.

42 Harry, Jr., in *ibid.,* pp. 252–253.

43 Harry, Jr., in *ibid.,* pp. 255–256.

44 Dr. Gallina, in *ibid.,* p. 256; Harry, Jr., in *ibid.,* p. 257.

45 Harry, Jr., in *ibid.,* p. 259; John Taylor, in *ibid.,* p. 260.

46 Harry, Jr., in *ibid.,* p. 258.

47 Richard Salkin, in *ibid.,* p. 260.

48 Dr. Gallina, in *ibid.,* p. 278; Dr. Tuckman, in *ibid.,* pp. 278–279.

49 Harry, Jr., in *ibid.,* p. 27.

50 *Ibid.,* pp. 17–18.

51 *Ibid.,* pp. 19–21.

52 *Ibid.,* p. 21.

53 *Ibid.,* pp. 22–23.

54 Harry, Jr., in *ibid.,* p. 27.

55 Harry, Jr., in *ibid.,* pp. 28–29.

56 *New York Times,* Nov. 29, 1976. p. 1; Harry, Jr., in Roesch (1979), p. 29.
57 Harry, Jr., in *ibid.,* pp. 29–30.
58 Margaret Greer, in *ibid.,* p. 26.
59 Ellen Notarangelo, in *New York Times,* Nov. 30, 1976, p. 81; Harry, Jr., in Roesch (1979), pp. 32, 33.
60 Harry, Jr., in *ibid.,* pp. 35–36.
61 Harry, Jr., in *ibid.,* pp. 36, 37, 38, 39.
62 Harry, Jr., in *ibid.,* p. 40.
63 Harry, Jr., in *ibid.,* p. 40.
64 Harry, Jr., in *ibid.,* pp. 44–45.
65 Harry, Jr., in *ibid.,* p. 50; Notarangelo, in *New York Times,* Nov. 30, 1976, p. 81; Roesch (1979), pp. 53, 62; Harry, Jr., in *ibid.,* p. 53.
66 Irene Bickerton, in *ibid.,* p. 67; *ibid.,* p. 74ff; Harry, Jr., in *ibid.,* pp. 76–77.
67 Harry, Jr., in *ibid.,* pp. 77, 79.
68 Notarangelo, in *New York Times,* Nov., 30, 1976, p. 81; Harry, Jr., in Roesch (1979), pp. 80–81.
69 Harry, Jr., in *ibid.,* p. 82.
70 Mr. and Mrs. De La Roche, in *ibid.,* pp. 87–89, 98–99.
71 Harry, Jr., in *ibid.,* p. 108.
72 Harry, Jr., in *ibid.,* p. 111.
73 *Ibid.,* p. 124.
74 Jeff De Causemaker, in *ibid.,* p. 168; *ibid.,* pp. 168–169; Mark Coker, in *ibid.,* p. 174.
75 Harry, Jr., in *ibid.,* p. 217; Ida Libby Dengrove, in *ibid.,* p. 276; Harry, Jr., in *ibid.,* p. 247.
76 Steve Madreperla, in *ibid.,* p. 170; *ibid.,* pp. 274–275.
77 Harry, Jr., in *ibid.,* p. 287.
78 *Ibid.,* p. 5; Notarangelo, in *New York Times,* Nov. 30, 1976, p. 81; Madreperla, in Roesch (1979), p. 274.
79 *Ibid.,* p. 57; Peter and Favret, in Foucault (1975), p. 186.
80 Harry, Jr., personal communications.

CHAPTER FOUR: THE DEFEOS

1 Ronald DeFeo, Jr., in Sullivan and Aronson (1981), p. 224.
2 Ronald DeFeo, Sr., in *New York Times,* Nov. 15, 1974, p. 49.
3 Sullivan and Aronson (1981), pp. 176–177; autopsy report, in *ibid.,* pp. 31–32; *New York Times,* Nov. 14, 1974, p. 97.
4 Autopsy report, in Sullivan and Aronson (1981), p. 32; *ibid.,* p. 178.
5 *Ibid.,* p. 179.
6 *New York Times,* Nov. 14, 1974, p. 97; in Sullivan and Aronson (1981), p. 35.
7 Ronald, Jr., in *ibid.,* p. 193.
8 *Ibid.,* p. 24.
9 *Ibid.,* pp. 24–25; *New York Times,* Nov. 14, 1974, p. 97.
10 Ronald, Jr., in Sullivan and Aronson (1981), pp. 41–42.
11 Ronald, Jr., in *ibid.,* pp. 43–45.

12 Ronald, Jr., in *ibid.*, pp. 45–46.
13 *Ibid.*, pp. 46–47, 49.
14 *Ibid.*, p. 87.
15 *Ibid.*, p. 92.
16 Ronald, Jr., in *ibid.*, pp. 122–123, 124.
17 Ronald, Jr., in *ibid.*, p. 131.
18 Ronald, Jr., in *ibid.*, pp. 131–132.
19 Ronald, Jr., in *ibid.*, pp. 132–134.
20 Mrs. Procita, in *ibid.*, pp. 199–200.
21 Mrs. Procita, in *ibid.*, p. 200.
22 Mrs. Procita, in *ibid.*, p. 200.
23 *New York Times*, Sept. 27, 1975, p. 15; Sullivan and Aronson (1981), pp. 159–160.
24 Ronald, Jr., in *ibid.*, pp. 221–222.
25 Ronald, Jr., in *ibid.*, p. 83.
26 John Kramer, in *ibid.*, pp. 93–94.
27 *Ibid.*, p. 95.
28 Dr. Schwartz, in *ibid.*, p. 234.
29 Dr. Schwartz, in *ibid.*, p. 235.
30 Dr. Schwartz, in *ibid.*, pp. 235–236.
31 Dr. Schwartz, in *ibid.*, p. 236.
32 Dr. Schwartz, in *ibid.*, p. 236.
33 Dr. Schwartz, in *ibid.*, p. 241.
34 Dr. Zolan, in *ibid.*, pp. 245–246.
35 Dr. Zolan, in *ibid.*, p. 247.
36 Dr. Zolan, in *ibid.*, p. 249.
37 Dr. Zolan, in *ibid.*, p. 250.
38 Dr. Zolan, in *ibid.*, pp. 250–251.
39 Dr. Zolan, in *ibid.*, pp. 252–253 (my italics).
40 *Ibid.*, pp. 272–273; *New York Times*, Nov. 22, 1974, p. 33.
41 Ronald, Sr., in Sullivan and Aronson (1981), p. 189.
42 *Ibid.*, pp. 5, 8.
43 Ronald, Sr., in *ibid.*, p. 9.
44 Steve Hicks, in *ibid.*, pp. 207–208; Michael Brigante, Jr., in *ibid.*, p. 212; *New York Times*, Nov. 15, 1974, p. 49.
45 Frank Davidge, in Sullivan and Aronson (1981), pp. 217–218; John Donahue, in *ibid.*, p. 257; *ibid.*, p. 60.
46 Ronald, Jr., in *ibid.*, pp. 126–127.
47 Ronald, Jr., in *ibid.*, p. 224.
48 *New York Times*, Nov. 17, 1974, p. 72; Ronald, Jr., in Sullivan and Aronson (1981), p. 27; *ibid.*, pp. 92–93.
49 Brigante, in *ibid.*, pp. 101–102.
50 *Ibid.*, pp. 51–52; Phyllis Procita, in *ibid.*, pp. 88–89.
51 Ronald, Jr., in *New York Times*, Nov. 22, 1974, p. 33.
52 Ronald, Jr., in Sullivan and Aronson (1981), pp. 220–221.
53 Ronald, Jr., in *ibid.*, pp. 220–221.
54 *Ibid.*, p. 251 (my italics).

55 Dr. Zolan, in *ibid.*, p. 252.
56 *Ibid.*, p. 114; Dr. Zolan, in *ibid.*, p. 250.
57 Ronald, Jr., in *ibid.*, pp. 125–126.
58 Ronald, Jr., in *ibid.*, pp. 10, 120; *ibid.*, p. 11.
59 Ronald, Jr., in *ibid.*, p. 37.
60 Ronald, Jr., in *ibid.*, pp. 96–97.
61 *Ibid.*, p. 112; Ronald, Jr., in *ibid.*, pp. 122, 126.
62 Ronald, Jr., in *ibid.*, pp. 127–128.
63 Ronald, Jr., in *ibid.*, pp. 127–128.
64 Ronald, Jr., in *ibid.*, p. 129.
65 Ronald, Jr., in *ibid.*, pp. 129–130 (my italics).
66 Ronald, Jr., in *ibid.*, p. 130.
67 Ronald, Jr., in *ibid.*, pp. 131, 134.
68 Ronald, Jr., in *ibid.*, pp. 135–136, 138.
69 Ronald, Jr., in *ibid.*, p. 223.
70 *New York Times,* Nov. 22, 1975, p. 33.
71 Det. Gozaloff, in *ibid.*, p. 50; Ronald Jr., in *ibid.*, p. 134.
72 Ronald, Jr., in *ibid.*, p. 27.
73 Michael Brigante, Jr., in *ibid.*, p. 213.
74 Belmonte (1979), p. 52.

CHAPTER FIVE: THE OLIVES

1 Marlene Olive, in Levine, (1982), p. 134.
2 *San Francisco Examiner,* July 8, 1975, p. 4; *ibid.*, Oct. 15, 1978, p. 5. The *New York Times* (July 6, 1975, p. 27) inaccurately described the Olives as "a wealthy suburban couple."
3 Marlene, in Levine (1982), p. 197.
4 *San Francisco Chronicle,* Nov. 10, 1975, p. 2; Marlene, in Levine (1982), pp. 208–209.
5 Chuck Riley, in *ibid.*, pp. 209–210.
6 See also the court testimony of Deanna Krieger, in *San Francisco Chronicle,* Nov. 13, 1975, p. 4; Nancy Dillon in Levine (1982), p. 211; Marlene, in *ibid.*, p. 212.
7 *San Francisco Chronicle,* July 2, 1975, p. 1; *ibid.*, Nov. 10, 1975, p. 2; Chuck, in Levine (1982), pp. 214–215.
8 Chuck, in *ibid.*, p. 215.
9 *San Francisco Chronicle,* Nov. 21, 1975, p. 3; Marlene, in Levine (1982), p. 216; Chuck, in *ibid.*, p. 216.
10 *San Francisco Chronicle,* Nov. 21, 1975, p. 3; Levine (1982), pp. 4, 5–6; Marlene, in *ibid.*, pp. 8, 10; Levine (1982), pp. 14–15.
11 *San Francisco Chronicle,* July 3, 1975, p. 1; Levine (1982), pp. 23, 25, 27.
12 *San Francisco Chronicle,* July 3, 1975, p. 1; Marlene, in Levine (1982), p. 243.
13 Leslie Slote, in *ibid.*, p. 219; Sharon Dillon, in *ibid.*, p. 220.
14 *San Francisco Chronicle,* July 3, 1975, p. 1; *New York Times,* July 6, 1975, p. 27; Marlene, in Levine (1982), p. 222; Col. Royce, in *ibid.*, p. 229; Officers Hool and Stinson, in *ibid.*, pp. 231–233.
15 Marlene, in *ibid.*, p. 234; in *ibid.*, pp. 234–235.

16 *San Francisco Chronicle,* July 3, 1975, p. 1; Marlene, in Levine (1982), pp. 236–237, 242–243.

17 Chuck, in *ibid.,* pp. 245–246.

18 *San Francisco Chronicle,* Feb. 13, 1976, p. 47; Marlene, in Levine (1982), pp. 261–263.

19 *San Francisco Chronicle,* March 2, 1976, p. 3; Judge Best, in Levine (1982), pp. 263–264; Chuck, in *ibid.,* pp. 266–267.

20 *San Francisco Chronicle,* Nov. 21, 1975, p. 3; Chuck, in Levine (1982), pp. 273–274.

21 *Ibid.,* pp. 276–277; Chuck, in *ibid.,* pp. 280–281.

22 *San Francisco Chronicle,* Dec. 23, 1975, p. 2; Chuck, in Levine (1982), pp. 284–285; *ibid.,* pp. 302, 311.

23 Marlene, in *ibid.,* p. 188.

24 *Ibid.,* p. 37.

25 *Ibid.,* p. 47; Naomi Olive, in *ibid.,* p. 48.

26 *Ibid.,* p. 91, Marlene, in *ibid.,* p. 103; in *ibid.,* p. 99.

27 Scott Nelson, in *ibid.,* pp. 101–102; *San Francisco Chronicle,* July 2, 1975, p. 1; Naomi, in Levine (1982), pp. 101–102.

28 Nelson, in *ibid.,* p. 153; Naomi, in *ibid.,* p. 155.

29 Nelson, in *ibid.,* pp. 161–162.

30 Clarence Underwood and Nancy Boggs, in *ibid.,* pp. 174–175.

31 Boggs, in *ibid.,* pp. 176–177.

32 Boggs, in *ibid.,* pp. 178–179; Mary Sigler, in *ibid.,* p. 198.

33 Drs. Upshaw and Katz, in *ibid.,* pp. 252–253.

34 Chuck, in *ibid.,* p. 256; Dr. John Steinhelber, in *ibid.,* pp 268–269.

35 Dr. Charles Cress, in *ibid.,* pp. 269–270, 275.

36 *San Francisco Chronicle,* Nov. 21, 1975, p. 3; Dr. John Hess, in Levine (1982), pp. 289–290.

37 Marlene, in *ibid.,* p. 187.

38 Jim Olive, in *ibid.,* pp. 34–35; Levine (1982), p. 35.

39 Jim, in *ibid.,* pp. 35–36; in *ibid.,* p. 36.

40 In *ibid.,* pp. 36–37.

41 In *ibid.,* pp. 37–38, 38–39.

42 Levine (1982), p. 39; Jim, in *ibid.,* pp. 39–40.

43 *Ibid.,* pp. 40–43; Ann Ellis and Russell Sommer, in *ibid.,* pp. 41–42.

44 Ellis, in *ibid.,* p. 43.

45 *Ibid.,* pp. 43–44, 46–47; Jim, in *ibid.,* p. 48; Levine (1982), pp. 48–49.

46 *Ibid.,* pp. 49–50, 55, 61–62.

47 Levine (1982), p. 87; Jim, in *ibid.,* p. 87.

48 *Ibid.,* p. 87; Jim, in *ibid.,* p. 88; Diana Koth, in *ibid.,* p. 92.

49 Alene Shilder, in *ibid.,* pp. 97–98; in *ibid.,* pp. 96–99; Mrs. Riley, in *ibid.,* p. 182.

50 According to the *San Francisco Chronicle* (March 2, 1976, p. 3), the Olive estate was worth only a few thousand dollars at the time of their deaths. Marlene was, of course, precluded from receiving their modest life insurance; in Levine (1982), pp. 186, 194; Col. Royce, in *ibid.,* p. 204.

51 Marlene, in *ibid.,* p. 184.

52 *San Francisco Chronicle,* Nov. 13, 1975, p. 4; Chuck, in Levine (1982), p. 139; Dillon, in *ibid.,* p. 139.
53 *San Francisco Chronicle,* Nov. 13, 1975, p. 4; Patti Metzger, in Levine (1982), p. 139; Travis Wheeler, in *ibid.,* pp. 139–140; *San Francisco Chronicle,* Nov. 15, 1975, p. 2.
54 Maddox, in Levine (1982), pp. 147–148.
55 Marlene, in *ibid.,* pp. 158–159, 183.
56 *Ibid.,* pp. 183, 190; Marlene, in *ibid.,* p. 195.
57 Marlene and Dillon, in *ibid.,* pp. 201–202.
58 Marlene, in *ibid.,* pp. 208–209.
59 Marlene, in *ibid.,* p. 177.
60 Levine (1982), p. vii.
61 *Ibid.,* p. 52; Marlene, in *ibid.,* p. 53; Mary Lou Pasquel, in *ibid.,* p. 56; *ibid.,* p. 58.
62 Marissa Moss, in *ibid.,* pp. 46–47; Ellis in *ibid.,* p. 50.
63 *Ibid.,* pp. 53–54, 57.
64 Jim and Marlene, in *ibid.,* p. 105.
65 Marlene, in *ibid.,* pp. 112–114, 136.
66 Levine (1982), p. 142; Marlene, in *ibid.,* pp. 182–183.
67 Jim, in *ibid.,* p. 58; in *ibid.,* pp. 182–183.
68 Marlene, in *ibid.,* pp. 114–115, 141.
69 Marlene, in *ibid.,* p. 112.
70 *San Francisco Chronicle,* March 2, 1976, p. 3; Levine (1982), p. 325.
71 *San Francisco Chronicle,* March 24, 1976, p. 35; *San Francisco Examiner,* Oct. 15, 1978, p. 1; Levine (1982), p. 325.
72 *San Francisco Chronicle,* Dec. 23, 1975, p. 2; in Levine (1982), p. 313.

CHAPTER SIX: TOWARDS AN HISTORICAL SOCIOLOGY

1 Darnton (1984), p. 262.
2 Gouge (1626), p. 203.
3 Leyton (1966); La Fontaine (1960), p. 107. Cross-cultural comparisons of this kind can be problematic, since European and African kinship categories—and the social behaviors they entail—can be so different as to be untranslatable. Such comparisons should therefore be approached with caution.
4 Bohannan (1960), pp. 254, 233, 234, 256; Draper (1978), p. 49.
5 Stone (1983), p. 25; Gurr (1981), p. 346.
6 Stone (1983), p. 27.
7 Gies and Gies (1987), pp. 45–46.
8 Cf. Hasluck (1967); Gregory of Tours, in Gies and Gies (1987), p. 48.
9 Gies and Gies (1987), pp. 295–296 (my italics).
10 Gurr (1981), pp. 307, 306; Given (1977); p. 44, 56, 60.
11 Hammer (1978), pp. 14, 20.
12 Hanawalt (1974), pp. 3, 11. See also Hanawalt (1976, 1986).
13 Sharpe (1981), pp. 37–38. See also Ruggiero (1980) and Slater (1984).
14 Weisser (1979), p. 89.
15 Darnton (1984), pp. 109–110.
16 Wolf (1973), pp. 279–280; Wolf (1982), pp. 389–390.

17 Durkheim (1961), p. 919.
18 Foucault (1975), p. viii.
19 Foucault (1975), p. 199.
20 *Ibid.,* pp. 7–8.
21 *Ibid.,* pp. 3–4.
22 *Ibid.,* p. 9, 10, 11.
23 Pierre Riviére, in *ibid.,* pp. 19–20, 21, 23–24.
24 Pierre Riviére, in *ibid.,* pp. 55, 58.
25 Pierre Riviére, in *ibid.,* pp. 60–61.
26 Pierre Riviére, in *ibid.,* pp. 66–67, 68.
27 Pierre Riviére, in *ibid.,* p. 74.
28 Pierre Riviére, in *ibid.,* pp. 105, 113.
29 *Ibid.,* p. 167; personal communication; Peter and Favret (1975), pp. 175, 177.
30 Pierre Riviére, in Foucault (1975), p. 113.
31 Pierre Riviére, in *ibid.,* p. 58.
32 Pierre Riviére, in *ibid.,* pp. 62, 67, 62.
33 Pierre Riviére, in *ibid.,* pp 65–66, 82, 83.
34 Stone (1983), p. 27; Daly and Wilson (1988), p. 27, 20.
35 Morris and Blom-Cooper (1962); Green (1981), pp. 209–210.
36 See, for example, Trigger (1985); Childe (1942, 1958); and Clark (1959).
37 Braudel (1981), p. 49, Braudel (1982), pp. 483, 479.
38 Braudel (1984), p. 599; Dyer (1985).
39 Mintz and Kellogg (1988), pp. xv, xx.
40 Merton (1957), p. 159.
41 *Ibid.,* pp. 146, 138.
42 Kleiner and Dalgard (1984), p. 271; Merton (1957), p. 157.
43 Hare, n.d., pp. 95–96.
44 Aldrich (1988), pp. 38–39.
45 The Ostroff Project (author's files).
46 The Ostroff Project; cf. Leyton (1965).

APPENDIX

1 Katz (1988), pp. 280–281.
2 *Ibid.,* p. 281; Leyton (1979).
3 Abrams (1982), pp. 267, 273–274, 280–297.
4 Rex Clark, personal communication.

R E F E R E N C E S

ABRAMS, PHILIP. *Historical Sociology*. Cornell University Press, 1982.
ALDRICH, NELSON W., JR. *Old Money: The Mythology of America's Upper Class*. Knopf, 1988.
AMNESTY INTERNATIONAL. *Political Killings by Governments*. A.I. Publications, 1983.
———. *Torture in the Eighties*. A.I. Publications, 1984.
ANDERSEN, CHRISTOPHER P. *The Serpent's Tooth*. St. Martin's Press, 1987.
ARCHER, DANE, AND ROSEMARY GARTNER. *Violence and Crime in Cross-National Perspective*. Yale University Press, 1984.
ARIES, PHILIPPE AND GEORGES DUBY, eds. *A History of Private Life: Revelations of the Medieval World*. Harvard University Press, 1988.
BELMONTE, THOMAS. *The Broken Fountain*. Columbia University Press, 1979.
BOHANNAN, PAUL, ed. *African Homicide and Suicide*. Princeton University Press, 1960.
———. *Law and Warfare: Studies in the Anthropology of Conflict*. Natural History Press, 1967.
BOYD, NEIL. *The Last Dance: Murder in Canada*. Prentice-Hall, 1988.
BRAUDEL, FERNAND. *The Perspective of the World*. Harper & Row, 1984.
———. *The Structures of Everyday Life: The Limits of the Possible*. Harper & Row, 1981.
———. *The Wheels of Commerce*. Harper & Row, 1982.
BRYSON, JOHN. *Evil Angels*. Penguin, 1986.
CAPOTE, TRUMAN. *In Cold Blood: A True Account of a Multiple Murder and its Consequences*. New American Library, 1965.
CHALIDZE, VALERY. *Criminal Russia: Essays on Crime in the Soviet Union*. Random House, 1977.
CHILDE, V GORDON. *The Prehistory of European Society*. Penguin, 1958.
———. *What Happened in History*. Penguin, 1942.
CLARK, J. DESMOND. *The Prehistory of Southern Africa*. Penguin, 1959.
CLEAVER, ELDRIDGE. *Soul on Ice*. Dell, 1968.
COLLIER, PETER, AND DAVID HOROWITZ. *The Rockefellers: An American Dynasty*. Holt, Rinehart & Winston, 1976.
CONNOR, WALTER D. *Deviance in Soviet Society: Crime, Delinquency, and Alcoholism*. Columbia University Press, 1972.
DALY, MARTIN, AND MARGO WILSON. *Homicide*. Aldine de Gruyter, 1988.

DARNTON, ROBERT. *The Great Cat Massacre: And Other Episodes in French Cultural History*. Basic Books, 1984.

DRAPER, PATRICIA. "The Learning Environment for Aggression and Anti-Social Behavior Among the !Kung." In A. Montagu, ed., 1978.

DURKHEIM, EMILE. "Anomic Suicide." *Theories of Society: Foundations of Modern Sociological Theory*, ed. Talcott Parsons, Edward Shils, Kasper D. Naegele, and Jesse R. Pitts. Free Press, 1961.

DYER, GWYNNE. *War*. Crown, 1985.

FOUCAULT, MICHEL, ed. *I, Pierre Rivière, Having Slaughtered My Mother, My Sister, and My Brother . . . A Case of Parricide in the 19th Century*. Pantheon, 1975.

FOX-GENOVESE, ELIZABETH. *Within the Plantation Household: Black and White Women of the Old South*. University of N. Carolina Press, 1988.

FRANK, GEROLD *The Boston Strangler*. New American Library, 1967.

GADDIS, THOMAS E., AND JAMES O. LONG. *Killer: A Journal of Murder*. Macmillan, 1970.

GAYLIN, WILLARD. *The Killing of Bonnie Garland: A Question of Justice*. Penguin, 1983.

GIES, FRANCES, AND JOSEPH GIES. *Marriage and the Family in the Middle Ages*. Harper & Row, 1987.

GIVEN, JAMES BUCHANAN. *Society and Homicide in Thirteenth-Century England*. Stanford University Press, 1977.

GOUDE, WILLIAM. "Of domestical duties, eight treatises." in *Workes*. London, 1626.

GREEN, CHRISTOPHER M. "Matricide by Sons." *Medicine, Science, and the Law*, Vol. 21, No. 3 (1981) 207–214.

GREENYA, JOHN. *Blood Relations*. Harcourt Brace Jovanovich, 1987.

GURR, TED ROBERT. "Historical Trends in Violent Crime: a Critical Review of the Evidence." *Crime and Justice: An Annual Review of Research*, Vol. 3 (1981) 295–353.

HAMMER, CARL I., JR. "Patterns of Homicide in a Medieval University Town: Fourteenth-Century Oxford." *Past and Present*, No. 78 (1978) 3–23.

HANAWALT, BARBARA A. "The Peasant Family and Crime in Fourteenth-Century England." *Journal of British Studies*, Vol. 13, No. 2 (1974) 1–18.

———. *The Ties That Bound: Peasant Families in Medieval England*. Oxford University Press, 1986.

———. "Violent Death in Fourteenth- and Early Fifteenth-Century England." *Comparative Studies in Society and History*, Vol. 18, No. 3 (1976) 297–320.

HARE, ROBERT D. "Psychopathy and Crime." *Colloquium on the Correlates of Crime and the Determinants of Criminal Behavior*, ed. Laura Otten. Mitre, n.d.

HASLUCK, MARGARET. "The Albanian Blood Feud." *Law and Warfare*, ed. P. Bohannan. Natural History Press, 1967.

HENRIKSEN, GEORG. *Hunters in the Barrens: The Naskapi on the Edge of the White Man's World*. Institute of Social & Economic Research Press, Memorial University, 1973.

KATZ, JACK. *Seductions of Crime: Moral and Sensual Attractions in Doing Evil*. Basic Books, 1988.

KEEGAN, JOHN. *The Mask of Command*. Viking, 1987.

KLAUSNER, LAWRENCE D. *Son of Sam*. McGraw-Hill, 1981.

KLEINER, ROBERT J. AND O.S. DALGARD. "Social Mobility and Psychiatric Disorder: a Reevaluation and Interpretation." *Culture and Psychopathology*, eds. Juan E. Mezzich and Carlos E. Berganza. Columbia University Press, 1984.

KUPER, LEO. *Genocide: Its Political Use in the Twentieth Century.* Penguin, 1981.

LA FONTAINE, JEAN. "Homicide and Suicide Among the Gisu." *African Homicide and Suicide,* ed. P. Bohannan. Princeton University Press, 1960.

LARSEN, RICHARD. *Bundy: The Deliberate Stranger.* Prentice-Hall, 1980.

LEVIN, JACK, AND JAMES FOX. *Mass Murder: America's Growing Menace.* Plenum, 1985.

LEVINE, RICHARD M. *Bad Blood: A Family Murder in Marin County.* Random House, 1982.

LEYTON, ELLIOTT. "Composite Descent Groups in Canada." *Man* LXV (1965) (98).

———. "Conscious Models and Dispute Regulation in an Ulster Village." *Man (N.S.)* 1 (1966) 534–542.

———. *Dying Hard: The Ravages of Industrial Carnage.* McClelland and Stewart, 1975.

———. *Hunting Humans: The Rise of the Modern Multiple Murderer.* McClelland and Stewart, and Bantam Seal Books (Canada), New York University Press, and Pocket Books (U.S.A.), Penguin (U.K.), Garzanti Editore (Italy), 1986.

———. *The Myth of Delinquency: An Anatomy of Juvenile Nihilism.* McClelland and Stewart, 1979.

———, and Don Handelman. *Bureaucracy and World View: Studies in the Logic of Official Interpretation.* ISER Press, Memorial University, 1978.

LUNDE, DONALD T. *Murder and Madness.* W. W. Norton, 1979.

———, and JEFFERSON MORGAN. *The Die Song: A Journey Into the Mind of a Mass Murderer.* W. W. Norton, 1980.

MACDOWELL, DOUGLAS M. *Athenian Homicide Law In the Age of the Orators.* Manchester University Press, 1963.

MERTON, ROBERT. *Social Theory and Social Structure.* Free Press, 1957.

MEWSHAW, MICHAEL. *Life For Death.* Doubleday, 1980.

MICHAUD, STEPHEN C., AND HUGH AYNESWORTH. *The Only Living Witness.* Simon & Schuster, 1983.

MINTZ, STEVEN, AND SUSAN KELLOGG. *Domestic Revolutions: A Social History of American Family Life.* Free Press, 1988.

MONTAGU, ASHLEY, ed. *Learning Non-Aggression: The Experience of Non-Literate Societies.* Oxford University Press, 1978.

MORRIS, GREGGORY W. *The Kids Next Door: Sons and Daughters Who Kill Their Parents.* William Morrow, 1985.

MORRIS, TERENCE, AND LOUIS BLOM-COOPER. *A Calendar of Murder: Criminal Homicide in England Since 1957.* Michael Joseph, 1964.

NORRIS, JOEL, with William Birnes. *Serial Killers: The Growing Menace.* Doubleday, 1988.

PALMER, STUART. *The Violent Society.* College & University Press, 1972.

PETER, JEAN-PIERRE, AND JEANNE FAVRET. "The Animal, the Madman, and Death." *I, Pierre Riviére,* ed. M. Foucault. Pantheon, 1975.

PORTER, GERALD. "Everybody Had Something to Say About Gary." Unpublished manuscript, 1982.

RESSLER, ROBERT K., ANN W. BURGESS, AND JOHN E. DOUGLAS. *Sexual Homicide: Patterns and Motives.* Lexington Books, 1988.

ROBINS, NATALIE, AND STEVEN M.L. ARONSON. *Savage Grace.* Gollancz, 1985.

ROESCH, ROBERTA, and Harry De La Roche, Jr. *Anyone's Son.* Andrews & McMeel, 1979.

ROSNER, DAVID, AND GERALD MARKOWITZ, eds. *Dying for Work: Workers' Safety and Health in Twentieth-Century America.* Indiana University Press, 1987.

RUGGIERO, GUIDO. *Violence in Early Renaissance Venice.* Rutgers University Press, 1980.

SCHEPER-HUGHES, NANCY. *Saints, Scholars, and Schizophrenics: Mental Illness in Rural Ireland.* University of California Press, 1979.

SHARPE, J. A. "Domestic Homicide in Early Modern England." *The Historical Journal* Vol. 24, No. 1 (1981), 29–48.

SLATER, MARIAM. *Family Life in the Seventeenth Century: The Verneys of Claydon House.* Routledge & Kegan Paul, 1984.

SMITH, KEN. *Inside Time.* Harrap, 1989.

STELLMAN, JEANNE M., and Susan M. Daum. *Work Is Dangerous to Your Health: A Handbook of Health Hazards in the Workplace.* Viking, 1973.

STONE, LAWRENCE. "Interpersonal Violence in English Society 1300-1980." *Past and Present* 101 (1983) 22–33.

SULLIVAN, GERARD, and Harvey Aronson. *High Hopes: The Amityville Murders.* Coward, McCann & Geoghegan, 1981.

TATARYN, LLOYD. *Dying for a Living: The Politics of Industrial Death.* Deneau & Greenberg, 1979.

TRIGGER, BRUCE G. *Archaeology as Historical Science.* Banaras Hindu University Press, 1985.

WALTON, MARY. *For Love of Money.* Pocket Books, 1987.

WEISSER, MICHAEL R. *Crime and Punishment in Early Modern Europe.* Humanities Press, 1979.

WOLF, ERIC R. *Europe and the People Without History.* University of California Press, 1982.

———. *Peasant Wars of the Twentieth Century.* Harper Torchbooks, 1973.

WOLFGANG, MARVIN E. *Patterns in Criminal Homicide.* Patterson Smith, 1975.

A C K N O W L E D G M E N T S

This book was meant to be a study of yet another form of multiple murder, but it rapidly evolved into an explication of the middle-class family. It thus closes an intellectual circle I first hesitantly scratched a quarter of a century ago with the publication (in the journal of the Royal Anthropological Institute) of an essay on the nouveau riche corporate family. Circles are best left closed, but the many armchair psychiatrists who have searched *Hunting Humans* in vain for my psyche would be better advised to examine the present volume in some detail.

When I was a very young man, one of the great English anthropologists took me aside. "Publishers are all gangsters," he warned, "and must be treated accordingly." Perhaps I have been uncommonly lucky but my life has been immeasurably enriched and my spirit fulfilled by the late and much lamented Marta Kurc, and by Patrick Crean and Jack McClelland, all once of McClelland and Stewart; by Sue Rutledge and Anna Porter of Bantam Seal Books; by Kitty Moore of New York University Press; Paul McCarthy of Pocket Books; the anonymous Italian translator at Garzanti Editore; by Anders Richter of the Johns Hopkins University Press; and by Jon Riley of Penguin Books in London.

Protecting me from gangsters, both real and imagined, has been my literary agent and friend, psychologist and financial advisor, Beverley Slopen. I must also repay special debts to the several hundred thoughtful and warmhearted members of my magical university class on aggression in the winter of 1988; to Professors Michael Staveley and Raoul Andersen of my own university for easing my writing life; to Professors James Stolzman and Judith Adler for critical encouragement; to Susan Longchamps of the Canadian Centre for Justice Statistics for her painstaking efforts to gather hard data, and then explain them to a statistical moron; and to

Elizabeth Stanford of my university's library, for her deft orchestration of interlibrary loans.

I wish also to acknowledge the many kindnesses of my cousins (consanguineal, affinal, and putative), Roy Faibish, Barbara Calvert, June and Morris Claman, and Delano and Jakie Ericson; and with great sadness, record the passing of my childhood hero and beloved uncle, Sam Feinstein. In what now seems to have become his custom, my one-time research assistant and long-time friend, David Bartlett, gave me the title for this volume—as so many other things.

ELLIOTT LEYTON

INDEX

Benson, Margaret Hitchcock (*cont.*)
  early life and marriage and, 39–40,
    51
  finances of, 41–42, 57–58
  nouveau riche style of, 40, 41
  social ambitions of, 40, 42, 65
Benson, Nancy (first wife), 49–50, 53,
    56
Benson, Scott (brother), 35, 41, 43, 44,
    51, 60, 66
  addiction to nitrous oxide, 47–48, 49
  commitment to mental institution,
    48–49
  indulgence of, 46–47
Benson, Steven Wayne, 32
  arrest of, 62
  financial mismanagement by, 53–59,
    67–68
  killing of family, 33–35
  position in family, 51–52
  posthomicidal indifference of, 60–62
  in prison, 68–69
  relationship with parents, 49–50, 53,
    66
  social ineptness of, 52
  submerged rebellion of, 50, 53, 59, 66
Biological explanation, 28–29, 213–214
Blackman, Bruce, 3–4
Blackman familicide, 3–4
Blood feud, 181
Boggs, Nancy, 154–155
Bohannan, Paul, 178
Braudel, Fernand, 197
Brigante, Michael, Jr., 138
Brigante, Michael, Sr., 124, 126, 140
Bundy, Ted, 7
Burton familicide, 19–26, 28
Burton, Gary, 19–26

C

Canada, incidence of familicide in,
    193–195
Capote, Truman, 11–12, 14

Carnegie, Andrew, 200
Castle Keep, 117–118
Child abuse, motive for familicide,
    16–18, 29, 177
Citadel, The, 83, 87–88, 89, 91, 97–100,
    104
Confessions, 12–13, 15, 22–23
  DeFeo familicide, 108–115
  De La Roche familicide, 73–82
  Olive familicide, 147–151
Corona, Juan, 207–208
Corporate family, familicide within,
    62–68
Cress, Charles, 156–157

D

Daly and Wilson, 193
Dameron, Virto, 12–13
Dann, Lorie, 213
Daridge, Frank, 124
Darnton, Robert, 176, 182–183
DeFeo, Allison (sister), 107, 110
DeFeo, Dawn (sister), 107, 110, 111,
    113, 125, 127, 131
DeFeo familicide, 106–141, 202, 203,
    204
  evolution of, 127–135
  and family violence, 122–127, 132–133,
    138
  killings, 107–115
  motivation for, 136–141
  psychiatric explanation, 116–122
DeFeo, John (brother), 107, 110
DeFeo, Louise (mother), 107, 123,
    124–125, 127, 128, 140
DeFeo, Mark (brother), 107, 110, 127
DeFeo, Peter (granduncle), 109
DeFeo, Ronald Joseph "Butch,"
    Jr., addictions of, 127, 132, 139,
    140
  confession of, 108–115, 137
  dependence on father, 120–121, 129,
    130, 133–134, 139